Social Life during COVID-19 in France, Germany, Italy and the UK

Elias Naumann
Ferruccio Biolcati Rinaldi
Alita Nandi
Ettore Recchi
Editors

Social Life during COVID-19 in France, Germany, Italy and the UK

palgrave
macmillan

Editors
Elias Naumann
GESIS Leibniz Institute for the Social Sciences
Mannheim, Germany

Alita Nandi
Institute for Social and Economic Research
University of Essex
Colchester, UK

Ferruccio Biolcati Rinaldi
Department of Social and Political Sciences
University of Milan
Milano, Italy

Ettore Recchi
Centre for Research on Social Inequalities (CRIS)
CNRS, Sciences Po
Paris, France

ISBN 978-3-031-99348-0 ISBN 978-3-031-99349-7 (eBook)
https://doi.org/10.1007/978-3-031-99349-7

This Palgrave Macmillan imprint is published by the registered company Springer Nature Switzerland AG.
The registered company address is: Gewerbestrasse 11, 6330 Cham, Switzerland

Acknowledgements

This book collects the research outcome of a collaborative project bringing together researchers from four countries to analyse how COVID-19 has affected societies. The group, which was initiated by Ettore Recchi, met first on December 9, 2021, in Paris. An intensive two-day workshop followed in May 2024 at Villa Vigoni where the final chapters were discussed. We also thank Dominic Abrams (University of Kent) for active contribution to the Paris workshop and the data harmonisation process. We thank Sophie Hill from Palgrave Macmillan for supporting this book project.

Funding acknowledgements

The Paris workshop was hosted by Sciences Po, which co-funded it with the French Agence Nationale de la Recherche (ANR, project "Faire face au Covid-19: Distanciation sociale, cohésion, et inégalité dans la France de 2020"; CoCo/ANR-20-COVI-000). We gratefully acknowledge funding of the workshop at Villa Vigoni from the German Research Foundation (Deutsche Forschungsgemeinschaft) through the German-Italian Center for the European Dialogue, Villa Vigoni. We would like to thank Annalisa Grazian and her team at Villa Vigoni for their hospitality and support in organising the workshop.

We gratefully acknowledge financial support for language editing from the Università degli Studi di Milano, the Centre de Recherche sur les Inégalités Sociales (CNRS), Sciences Po and GESIS—Leibniz Institut für Sozialwissenschaften.

Alita Nandi and Piotr Marzec are funded by the ESRC Understanding Society grant (ES/T002611/1).

Data acknowledgements

Understanding Society is an initiative funded by the Economic and Social Research Council and various Government Departments, with scientific leadership by the Institute for Social and Economic Research, University of Essex, and survey delivery by the National Centre for Social Research (NatCen) and Verian (formerly Kantar Public). The research data are distributed by the UK Data Service. The COVID-19 study (2020–2021) was funded by the Economic and Social Research Council and the Health Foundation. Serology testing was funded by the COVID-19 Longitudinal Health and Wealth—National Core Study. Fieldwork for the web survey was carried out by Ipsos MORI and for the telephone survey by Kantar.

"Faire face au Covid-19: Distanciation sociale, cohésion, et inégalité dans la France de 2020" (CoCo/ANR-20-COVI-000) was funded by Agence Nationale de la Recherche - "Winners and losers of the Covid-19 pandemic in Israël and France: Evaluating the long-term effects of the crisis on well-being" was funded by the Programme Hubert Curien Maïmonide 2022 (Campus France, MESR, MEAE).

The German Internet Panel (GIP) was funded by the German Research Foundation (DFG) as part of the Collaborative Research Center 884 (SFB 884; project number 139943784; project Z1). Data collection of the Mannheim Corona Study (MCS; DOI: 10.4232/1.13700; Blom et al. 2021) was funded as part of the German Internet Panel (GIP) by the German Research Foundation (DFG) as part of the Collaborative Research Center 884 "Political Economy of Reforms" (SFB 884; project number 139943784). Additional funding for the MCS was provided by the Federal Ministry of Labor and Social Affairs (BAMS).

The ResPOnsE Covid-19 project was developed within the framework of the 'Departments of Excellence 2018–2022' programme, promoted by the Italian Ministry of University and Research, and is supported by funding from the Cariplo Foundation.

Contents

Notes on Contributors

Marija Bashevska is a research fellow at the University of Turin, Department of Cultures, Politics and Society. Her research explores socio-economic and gender inequalities in the labour market, unpaid work, and work-life dynamics from a comparative and life course perspective. She focuses particularly on the effects of crises and the role of welfare states and cultural norms in shaping these inequalities.

Ferruccio Biolcati Rinaldi is Professor of Sociology at the Department of Social and Political Sciences of the University of Milan, where he is a member of the spsTREND research lab. His main research interests deal with religiosity and value change. He is Italian PI for the European Values Study (EVS) and the World Values Survey (WVS); he serves as chair of the Scientific Committee of EVS.

Giulia Dotti Sani is Associate Professor of Sociology in the Department of Social and Political Sciences at the University of Milan. She holds a PhD in Sociology and Social Research. Her research focuses on the sociology of the family, female employment, and social stratification. She has expertise in time budget analysis, multilevel and panel modelling, and specialises in managing and analysing large-scale longitudinal and cross-sectional household datasets (e.g., EU-SILC, ESS, ISTAT Household Survey).

Emanuele Ferragina is Professor of Sociology at Sciences Po. His fields of interest include international political economy, comparative social policy, labour market and family policy, the political economy of care and social reproduction, and the political economy of Italy. He is co-editor in chief of the *Journal of European Social Policy* and Board member of the European Social Policy Network (ESPAnet).

Marta Dominguez Folgueras is Associate Professor of Sociology at the Centre for Research on Social Inequalities (CRIS) at Sciences Po. Her research focuses on the sociology of the family, with a focus on gender inequalities as well as on the interplay between the public and the private sphere. Her research has investigated the division of work within the family and the relationship between unpaid work, paid work, and public policies.

Thierry Gagné is Research and Statistics Analyst at Indigenous Services Canada. He is leading research on Indigenous Peoples' economic wellbeing and developing data tools to support program and policy development. He previously worked as a research fellow at University College London. His research there focused on the social drivers of changes in health behaviours and mental health among young adults in Canada, the US, and the UK.

Simona Guglielmi is Associate Professor of Sociology in the Department of Social and Political Sciences at the University of Milan, where she is a member of the spsTREND research lab. She serves as the local representative for the International Social Survey Program (ISSP-Italy) alongside Andrea Pedrazzani. Her research focuses on public opinion, youth and value change, national identities, and political support.

Bartholomew Konechni is a doctoral candidate at Sciences Po Paris, Centre for Research on Social Inequalities (CRIS). He is also involved part-time on the SWECOV project at the University of Stockholm. His work focuses on the intersection of politics, policy, and public health: thinking both about how epidemiological crisis shapes decision making amongst policy makers and how in turn those decisions affect individual behaviours and outcomes across the population.

Riccardo Ladini is a postdoctoral researcher in Sociology at the University of Milan, where he is a member of the spsTREND research lab. His research focuses on political attitudes and behaviour, climate change attitudes, and religiosity. He is a member of the Italian team of the European Values Study (EVS) and the Italian National Election Study (ITANES).

Nicola Maggini is Tenured Assistant Professor of Political Science at the Department of Political and Social Sciences of the University of Bologna, where he is a member of the research centre CONNECT–Transnational Connections and Global Governance. He is also a member of the spsTREND research lab, CISE (Italian Centre for Electoral Studies), and the scientific council of ITANES (Italian National Election Study). His research focuses on socio-political attitudes, electoral systems, voting behaviour, and party competition from a comparative perspective.

Marco Maraffi is Professor of Sociology in the Department of Social and Political Sciences at the University of Milan. His research interests include elections, public opinion and voting behaviour, value change, and attitudes towards state/market relationships.

Piotr Marzec is a Senior Data Analyst and Training Officer at the Institute for Social and Economic Research (ISER) at the University of Essex. His research interests include class and social stratification, particularly in relation to lifestyle patterns, political attitudes, and voting behaviour.

Anne McMunn is Professor of Social Epidemiology and Co-Director of Equalise: ESRC Centre for Lifecourse Health Equity based at University College London in the UK. Her research is concentrated on the social determinants of health within a life course epidemiological framework. More specifically, she investigates the influence on health and wellbeing of family care and unpaid care work, employment and social relationship characteristics, and she is also interested in how gender and socioeconomic position structure these associations.

Francesco Molteni is a Tenure-Track Assistant Professor (RTT) in the Department of Social and Political Sciences at the University of Milan. He holds a PhD in Sociology and Methodology of Social Research. His main research interests include religion and religious change, values and attitudes' transmission and socialisation, migration, and acculturation processes. He mainly works with large-scale comparative and national surveys and has also worked on three original datasets: CARPE, ResPOnsE COVID-19, and COValues. He is the P.I. of the project "Between Origin and Destination (BOnD)", funded by the CARIPLO foundation.

Marta Moroni is a postdoctoral researcher at the Institute for Political Science and Social Policy at the Johannes Kepler University of Linz. Her research interests include public opinion, survey methods, and attitudes towards climate change and pro-environmental behaviours.

Alita Nandi is a professor at the Institute for Social and Economic Research, the University of Essex, and the Associate Director (Outreach) for Understanding Society. She is a quantitative social scientist conducting research in the areas of ethnicity and gender, primarily examining differences in economic and subjective wellbeing and mental health.

Elias Naumann is a postdoctoral researcher at GESIS-Leibniz Institute for the Social Sciences and external fellow at the Mannheim Center for European Social Research. His research interests are related to political sociology, comparative political economy, welfare state preferences, and survey methodology.

Olof Mpumwire Östergren is a sociologist and Associate Professor of Public Health at the Department of Public Health Sciences at Stockholm University. He has extensive experiences in transdisciplinary research on social inequalities in health and mortality. During 2020–2022 he served as an inquiry secretary for the Corona commission at the Ministry of Health and Social Affairs at the Swedish Government Offices. He is a coordinator and researcher within the SWECOV project, a national register-based research project for interdisciplinary research on the coronavirus pandemic in Sweden.

Marta Pasqualini holds a PhD in social statistics and demography. She explored the issues of social inequalities by working as a researcher at UPF (Barcelona), Sciences Po (Paris), and Sapienza (Rome). She is also a member of the Research Center for Internal Areas and the Apennines. Since February 2023 she has been General Director of the Fondazione Progetto Valtiberina, a third-sector organisation that promotes the sustainable development of the interregional inner area of Valtiberina in a logic of qualitative growth.

Ettore Recchi is Professor of Sociology at Sciences Po Paris, Centre for Research on Social Inequalities (CRIS). He is also part-time professor of the Migration Policy Centre (MPC) of the European University Institute (EUI) in Florence and Fellow of the Institut Convergences Migrations (Paris). He directs the Global Mobilities Project at EUI, a research programme that aims to collect and analyse global data on transnational population movements, and is a partner of Migmobs, an ERC Advanced Grant studying the relationships between human mobility and inequality.

Simone Sarti is Associate Professor in Sociology and Lecturer in Social Research Methodology at the Department of Social and Political Sciences, University of Milan. His research concentrates on social inequalities, in particular, with regard to health, quantitative methods, and socio-cultural evolution.

Andrea Turković is a postdoctoral researcher at the University of Milan, where she is a member of the spsTREND research lab. She specialises in migration, inter-ethnic relations, and religion, with a particular focus on how socio-cultural contexts shape these dynamics. Her research investigates how socio-cultural environments influence inter-ethnic relations and explores cross-cultural variations in the determinants and interactions of these dynamics across different societies.

Andrew Zola is a PhD candidate in Sociology at Sciences Po. He holds a BA in Economics-Political Science from Columbia University and a master's degree in Sociology from Sciences Po. His research examines popular support for social protection in a context of political economy and welfare state change.

List of Figures

List of Tables

CHAPTER 1

Introduction: Social Life During COVID-19 in France, Germany, Italy, and the UK

Ettore Recchi, Ferruccio Biolcati Rinaldi, Alita Nandi, and Elias Naumann

A string of major economic and political upheavals have demanded global attention across the first two decades of the twenty-first century. In addition to local conflicts and disasters, the 2008 financial crisis, deepening political divisions resulting from Donald Trump's first presidency, the departure of the UK from the European Union, the increasingly tangible effects of climate change, an ageing population, endless pressures of global

E. Recchi
Centre for Research on Social Inequalities (CRIS), CNRS, Sciences Po, Paris, France
e-mail: ettore.recchi@sciencespo.fr

F. Biolcati Rinaldi
Department of Social and Political Sciences, University of Milan, Milano, Italy
e-mail: ferruccio.biolcati@unimi.it

A. Nandi
Institute for Social and Economic Research, University of Essex, Colchester, UK
e-mail: anandi@essex.ac.uk

E. Naumann et al. (eds.), *Social Life during COVID-19 in France, Germany, Italy and the UK*,
https://doi.org/10.1007/978-3-031-99349-7_1

migration, and ever-increasing levels of inequality have all altered national landscapes and individual prospects. Within this context, at the start of 2020, as it became apparent to scientists that a newfound virus would soon spread across the globe, the influential journal *Foreign Policy* published a special issue in which numerous specialists and commentators claimed that 'the pandemic will change the world forever'.

In retrospect, it appears that this crisis did not prompt any sort of revolution within society. Accordingly, a cumulative study of the societal consequences of COVID-19 needs to provide a balanced account of both stability and change. Which aspects of social life have been altered and which aspects have remained (perhaps surprisingly) resilient to change? Are there groups within society who have been unfairly affected? Moreover, we might ask, as with the climate crisis, whether the pandemic triggered any social change, albeit in forms and with a latency that evade detection against the noise of other factors. Answering these questions requires thorough empirical analyses of high-quality data that document a wide range of diverse aspects of social life (Liebe, 2022).

Existing Research on the Societal Impact of COVID-19: A Bird's Eye View

Over the past five years, there has been a surge of research into the social impact of the COVID-19 pandemic. In this brief literature review, we focus our discussion on books and edited volumes that present empirical evidence regarding the intense societal impacts of the COVID-19 pandemic, drawing attention to the social, economic, and governance challenges that the crisis presented. Books and edited volumes tend to provide broader analyses than journal articles, which hone their investigations to specific aspects. The later chapters of this book will also review journal articles.

A special issue in *European Societies* (Grasso et al., 2021) comprises 58 studies examining the multidimensional effects of the COVID-19 pandemic across Europe. These studies show that (1) the pandemic has exacerbated existing disparities relating to gender, ethnicity, education, and employment; (2) there have been significant increases in cases of anxiety

E. Naumann (✉)
GESIS Leibniz Institute for the Social Sciences, Mannheim, Germany
e-mail: elias.naumann@gesis.org

and depression; (3) the crisis has influenced welfare states, social policies, and approaches to crisis governance; (4) COVID-19 has affected levels of social solidarity and cohesion within communities; (5) there have been notable changes to cultural practices and everyday lifestyles. Bambra et al. (2021) similarly stress that COVID-19 operated not merely as a health crisis but also as a 'syndemic', which disproportionately affected already vulnerable groups. They argue that the pandemic's unequal impacts were largely the result of political choices, which reflected broader societal disparities in resource distribution and policy priorities. Analysing SHARE survey data representative of the population 50 years and older from 28 countries and covering a period until summer 2021, Börsch-Supan et al. (2023) underscore how the pandemic's impacts varied across European countries, highlighting the disproportionate impact on older populations. They highlight increased economic hardships among economically active older adults and intensified social isolation among the elderly, exacerbating health, economic, and social inequalities. This observation is particularly evident in the UK, where COVID-19 resulted in high death rates and severe economic situations that disproportionally affected vulnerable groups. Cooper and Szreter (2021) correlate this with the longstanding adherence to neoliberal policies, characterised by sustained underinvestment in public welfare and social infrastructure. From a mainland European perspective, Börner and Seeleib-Kaiser (2023) contend that the COVID-19 pandemic tested the resilience of the welfare state, ultimately reinforcing its role. They emphasise the importance of social policies in stabilising societies during severe health and economic crises and view the EU's move towards enhanced social policy cooperation as a potential turning point in post-pandemic welfare state dynamics and policymaking. Meanwhile, from a US perspective, Parolin (2023) illustrates how robust governmental policy responses mitigated some of the pandemic's harshest economic impacts, particularly through poverty reduction, which was achieved via unprecedented legislative measures. These findings suggest the potential of targeted policy interventions in addressing social inequalities during future crises.

These studies offer comprehensive evidence on the ways in which COVID-19 has influenced various areas of society. However, they primarily focus on the immediate impacts observed during the first two years of the pandemic. What remains missing is a comparative analysis across countries that extends beyond these short-term effects, while simultaneously analysing diverse societal dimension, including work and employment, health, family and social life, and the political landscape.

Such an analysis could serve as the first empirical test of predictions regarding the permanent societal changes brought about by COVID-19. Social theorists widely agree that the pandemic significantly reshaped social interactions, institutions, and collective identities, promoting digitalisation, remote working, and new forms of social solidarity or exclusion (Lupton, 2022; Bordoni, 2022; Aarts et al., 2021). Moreover, Lange and Shullenberger (2024) examine how a new form of emergency capitalism during the pandemic, alongside the political left's retreat from its traditional role as a critical force against capital accumulation, social discrimination, and state power, has altered the political landscape of Western countries. Furthermore, ethical dilemmas related to public health measures—such as resource allocation and the balance between individual rights and collective safety—also gained increased visibility during the crisis (Searight, 2023; Burns, 2023).

In conclusion, these studies collectively demonstrate that the COVID-19 pandemic not only exposed systemic vulnerabilities but also created crucial opportunities for societal reflection. They highlight the potential for transformative change aimed at building a more equitable and resilient future.

This Book's Contribution

This book explores the behaviours and attitudes of the general population in France, Germany, Italy, and the UK, through engagement with high-quality, representative, and longitudinal datasets. Our analysis stands apart from existing studies on the societal implications of the COVID-19 pandemic by offering four distinct and novel contributions.

First, an interdisciplinary team of authors, including sociologists, political scientists, and public health experts, investigates various aspects of social life in parallel. These include personal health, family life, work, and political attitudes. This approach complements existing studies that have predominantly concentrated on just one of these areas of social life.

Second, our empirical analyses draw on high-quality individual-level panel data from the four largest European countries (France, Germany, Italy, and the UK) spanning a period of two years between 2020 and 2022, with comparisons to pre-COVID times. This enables us to investigate how individual behaviours and attitudes evolved over time, both in the short term during the initial shock of lockdowns and over the longer duration of nearly two years into the pandemic. Crucially, the panel data allow us to assess whether aggregate stability may also conceal underlying rifts or divergences based on individual characteristics. This approach adds depth to existing studies, which have mainly focused on the earlier periods of the pandemic, particularly within its first year.

Third, the chapters in this book emphasise the use of clear and consistent definitions of inequality dimensions. They explore possible divergences based on gender, age, socioeconomic position, and family situation (e.g. parents vs. non-parents), providing a nuanced understanding of these disparities.

Finally, by analysing the four largest Western European countries—France, Germany, Italy, and the UK—we are confident that our findings can be broadly generalised to Western Europe as a whole. Despite institutional differences between the four countries, their political responses and societal changes were largely similar. This comparative perspective addresses a notable gap in existing social science research on the impact of COVID-19, which has predominantly relied on single-country studies. However, a limitation of our case selection lies in the similarities among these four countries, in particular with regard to the policy choices adopted to cope with the crisis. To address this, we include an analysis of Sweden to contextualise our key findings against a more distinct case, particularly considering Sweden's unique policy approach to managing the pandemic.

Methodological Approach

The empirical investigation into the social impact of the COVID-19 pandemic requires robust longitudinal data. Given the pandemic's simultaneous effects across multiple countries and its influence on various aspects of social life, comparisons with pre-pandemic data and existing findings are essential. Ensuring the validity of longitudinal comparisons demands that the collected data remain consistent and comparable, avoiding the risk that observed changes result merely from methodological artefacts. Key considerations include preserving the comparability of measurement instruments across time and countries. Furthermore, the pandemic led to significant changes in survey methodologies, with many shifting from face-to-face interviews to self-administered formats, such as paper-based or online questionnaires. These shifts in survey modes pose challenges to the temporal comparability of data.

The research questions in this book primarily focus on comparing population averages before and during the pandemic. For instance, they investigate whether mental health problems became more prevalent during the pandemic or if household divisions of labour shifted compared with the pre-pandemic period. To ensure the reliability and validity of such comparisons, it is essential to use probability samples that are representative of the target populations and to transparently report the precision of empirical estimates. Furthermore, understanding the pandemic's longer-term effects necessitates data that span multiple, distinct periods throughout its progression.

Because no fully harmonised comparative dataset was readily available, we selected country-specific survey programmes that aligned closely with our methodological requirements. This approach required extensive post-harmonisation of both measurement instruments and data-collection periods, described in detail in Chap. 3. An additional challenge arose from the rapidly evolving nature of the pandemic, where even identical calendar periods varied significantly across countries owing to, for instance, variations in infection rates and the timing of restrictions. To address this, we established four distinct pandemic periods, within which corresponding country-specific intervals were identified for analysis (see Chaps. 2 and 3). Although the duration of these periods may vary slightly between countries, comparisons remain valid as long as the data fall within the same defined pandemic phase, even if collection was not simultaneous.

Pandemic Periods and the Data Set

In this book, we focus not only on the immediate, short-term effects of the pandemic but also on its longer-term implications. However, maintaining rigorous causal identification imposes certain limitations on this approach. First, capturing longer time periods introduces the challenge of panel attrition. Second, other societal developments, crises, or political events may influence social life during the same timeframe. For example, the Russian invasion of Ukraine in spring 2022, along with the subsequent energy crisis and high inflation in Western European countries, is likely to have affected many of the areas of social life under investigation, such as labour markets, anxiety, or political attitudes. Therefore, we limit our analyses to the period up until May 2022.

Konechni and Recchi (Chap. 2) present a detailed summary of pandemic governance across the four countries structured into a three-act periodisation of the crisis from February 2020 to May 2022. The first phase saw governments implementing lockdowns and furlough schemes, marking a dramatic shift in state intervention to cushion the impact of the epidemiological and economic crises. Despite initial resistance, national lockdowns became unavoidable in all four countries, leading to an unprecedented expansion of state responsibilities and economic support for individuals and businesses. In the second phase, governments adopted targeted non-pharmaceutical interventions, including local lockdowns and digital track-and-trace applications. While these innovations proved ineffective in curbing the subsequent COVID-19 waves, they nonetheless advanced public health infrastructures and governmental capacities for monitoring citizens. The third phase marked a shift to individualised pandemic management through the rollout of vaccines. Policies transitioned from regulating public spaces to influencing individual behaviours, introducing ethical considerations surrounding vaccine uptake, such as balancing coercion with persuasion. Throughout these phases, technological advancements were accompanied with persistent tensions between individual rights and collective duties, which influenced public policy decisions and societal responses. This chapter underscores the interplay between unique national contexts and shared challenges, particularly the balance between state authority and individual freedoms, which emerged as a recurring theme across France, Germany, Italy, and the UK.

Each chapter employs a methodological approach that analyses a backbone dataset with harmonised main indicators across countries, supplemented by more specific and in-depth measurements drawn from independent national surveys. These supplemental analyses are designed to remain as parallel as possible across the countries. The chapters focus on four distinct time points: the pre pandemic period, the initial shock in spring 2020, the subsequent lockdowns from winter 2020 to spring 2021, and a final period of decline in spring 2022. Chapter 2 provides the essential background information on pandemic governance across the four countries. Notably, this approach allows us to examine both the reasons behind the timing of unique measures adopted by each country, and areas where convergence occurred (see Chap. 3 for details).

Summary of Key Findings

Chapter 4 investigates health and wellbeing during the COVID-19 pandemic across France, Germany, Italy, and the UK, uncovering both cross-country differences and within-populations disparities shaped by personal circumstances. The pandemic often exacerbated pre-existing inequalities in physical health, mental health, and subjective wellbeing. In terms of self-reported health, the UK and Germany showed relative stability, whereas Italy experienced a notable decline, reflecting the severe impact of the crisis there. Interestingly, France initially exhibited an improvement in self-reported health during early stages—a phenomenon described as the 'eye of the hurricane' paradox (Recchi et al., 2020)—before experiencing a subsequent decline. Mental health challenges, including anxiety, depression, and loneliness, rose significantly across all countries, disproportionately affecting vulnerable groups such as those facing financial hardship. In addition, younger adults, women, ethnic minorities, and parents with young children were particularly susceptible to adverse health conditions. These findings underscore the pandemic's uneven burden, highlighting how societal vulnerabilities were amplified during this time of crisis. A consistent finding was that experiencing Covid-19 symptoms was associated with poorer mental and physical health across all countries.

Chapter 5 explores gender inequalities in unpaid care work during the pandemic as a possible explanation for observed health differences. The findings reveal persistent disparities, with women consistently undertaking more housework and childcare than men across all countries and at every point during the pandemic. Gender gaps in housework were most pronounced during the initial lockdown, particularly in Italy, Germany, and the UK, where two-thirds of partnered women reported bearing the majority of household responsibilities. Despite assumptions that lockdown conditions might encourage greater gender equality in unpaid care work, these disparities remained remarkably resistant to change, underscoring the deeply entrenched nature of gendered patterns in household duties.

Chapter 6 delves into labour market dynamics, particularly the capacity for and adoption of remote work during the pandemic. The findings reveal that remote work was predominantly accessible to higher-skilled workers, with the UK leading in both the adoption and the persistence of remote working practices. In contrast, lower-skilled jobs offered fewer opportunities for teleworking. Furlough schemes played a vital role in cushioning job losses, with Germany's job retention schemes proving especially effective. France and the UK, meanwhile, experienced sharper initial declines in employment but recovered over time. Notably, remote working appears to signify a lasting shift in employment practices, with potential implications for gender differences (Chap. 4) and mental health outcomes (Chap. 7).

Accordingly, Chap. 7 examines health and wellbeing impacts associated with the rapid adoption of remote work during the pandemic. While remote working offered benefits such as flexibility, autonomy, and reduced commuting, it also introduced challenges such as blurred work–life boundaries, increased stress, and reduced social interactions. Although there is evidence of initial negative effects on mental health, particularly in terms of loneliness, this chapter finds no persistent negative impact of remote work on physical health, mental health, or overall wellbeing. Notably, however, mothers experienced greater negative impacts on wellbeing than fathers, underscoring the enduring influence of traditional gender roles in caregiving responsibilities—roles that proved particularly challenging to reconcile in remote work. These findings highlight the complex and varied consequences of remote work, emphasising the importance of ongoing empirical monitoring and the potential need for tailored policy interventions.

Chapter 8 discusses the pandemic's impact on political support and societal attitudes towards liberal democracy. During the initial phases, there was a temporary increase in political support for institutions—described as a 'rally-round-the-flag' effect—driven by heightened uncertainty. However, this consensus quickly dissolved as pre-existing political polarisation re-emerged. At the outset, collectivist and anti-liberal orientations briefly gained prominence but later declined, largely in response to robust social protection policies. These developments highlight the critical role of social welfare measures and cultural contexts in shaping public attitudes during crises.

Chapter 9 focuses on the effects of these social policy responses, investigating how COVID-19 employment protection measures shaped public support for unemployment benefits. The study finds that support for unemployment protection increased among those who experienced job loss. Interestingly, attitudes among those in job retention schemes—who endured comparable income losses to those who lost their job—resembled those among individuals with continuous employment. This suggests that attitudinal shifts were driven more by perceived risks of job loss than immediate material conditions alone. These findings challenge traditional perspectives on welfare attitudes, highlighting the importance of perceived vulnerability. Moreover, they underscore the critical role of social policies and job retention schemes in maintaining public support for the welfare state.

Our comparative analysis reveals more commonalities than differences in how COVID-19 affected social life across the four countries. This outcome can be attributed to similarities in demographic composition, political structures, and social systems. Crucially, these underlying commonalities also shaped their COVID-19 governance. EU membership, which facilitated the coordination of certain policy responses, further contributed to this alignment. While these similarities are evident globally, they are particularly pronounced within the wider European context.

To address this limitation, Chap. 10 examines Sweden's distinct response to COVID-19, characterised by voluntary compliance rather than strict lockdowns. Sweden's approach involved fewer restrictions, relying heavily on individual responsibility and self-regulation. While these measures led to distinct immediate social dynamics compared with other European countries, patterns of social inequalities—such as those related to health, unpaid care work, and unemployment risk—shifted moderately during the pandemic but returned to pre-pandemic levels afterwards. This analysis highlights that, despite Sweden's less coercive strategy, long-term structural inequalities remained largely unaffected.

Conclusion

As previously noted, one surprising finding—especially in hindsight—is the temporary nature of changes in aggregate public opinions, political perspectives, and work orientations during the pandemic. Despite substantial practical constraints on behaviour, working life, and the increased health and labour market risks, these attitudes quickly returned to pre-COVID levels. Similarly, the physical and mental health of the general population demonstrated remarkable resilience, with no permanent shifts observed. Furthermore, labour markets recovered swiftly, with furlough schemes effectively preventing a widespread and sustained rise in unemployment. This evidence suggests that governments succeeded in enabling their populations to navigate the turbulence of the pandemic by maintaining continuities in healthcare, employment, and social protection. In essence, the COVID-19 crisis served as a robust stress test for European welfare states, reaffirming their viability and critical role as stabilising mechanisms during periods of profound upheaval.

One of the major lasting changes observed during the pandemic was the widespread adoption of remote work. With more time spent at home, hours devoted to housework and childcare increased, particularly during lockdowns. Although fathers contributed more to childcare and housework, the primary burden remained disproportionately on women and mothers. During the pandemic, women reported better physical health but poorer mental health than men—a disparity probably driven by the increased childcare demands placed on them. Our analysis also reveals that remote work did not affect health and wellbeing negatively overall, either in the short or longer term. However, fathers appeared to benefit more from working remotely, while mothers experienced a greater share of negative aspects. From a policy perspective, key findings include the need to restructure working lives to allow remote work, which has the potential to foster more family and social time. The pandemic experience also highlighted the critical role of childcare and educational institutions in supporting families and mitigating gendered burdens.

Based primarily on general population surveys, our methodological approach is not ideally suited for identifying vulnerabilities among comparatively small groups. Although each chapter addresses inequalities and potentially vulnerable populations, the reliance on population surveys runs the risk of overlooking groups that are disproportionately affected. This issue is particularly significant for children and adolescents, who are entirely excluded from population surveys through design, as are migrants and individuals with lower levels of education, who are typically underrepresented in general population surveys. Similar limitations exist for other hard-to-reach populations, such as individuals residing in hospitals or elderly care facilities, those with pre-existing medical conditions, and incarcerated persons. As such, the scope of our conclusions regarding the stability of attitudes and behaviours, and the surprising resilience observed across various aspects of social life, is inherently limited to a broader perspective.

The pandemic disrupted two long-term trends in Western societies relating to the individual management of space and time. Regarding space, since the 1960s (Recchi, 2016; Deutschmann, 2022), the majority of citizens of developed societies have enjoyed an unprecedented period of control over their living environments through increased mobility. The radius of their movements—locally, nationally and internationally—has expanded significantly, surpassing anything available to previous generations. This rise of human mobility had been uninterrupted for over half a century until 2020. As for time, individuals' lives have become increasingly constrained by social expectations and pressure for 'acceleration' (Rosa, 2013). Driven largely by capitalist imperatives, this acceleration has permeated work structures as well as leisure time, generating increasingly higher levels of stress in the population (Hobsbawm, 2022). In 2020–2021, COVID-related mobility restrictions reversed this trend, forcing individuals to slow down their pace of everyday life. While these reversals were not permanent, they may have imparted lasting lessons. There are evident in the growing embrace of telework and the so-called Great Resignation (Gandhi & Robison, 2021) that followed the pandemic. Although facilitated by the unusually generous welfare provisions of the period, these phenomena reflect both the extraordinary capacity of human adaptability to changing circumstances and, perhaps, the underlying fatigue associated with late capitalist work–life arrangements.

References

Aarts, E., Fleuren, H., Sitskoorn, M., & Wilthagen, T. (2021). *The new common: How the COVID-19 pandemic is transforming society*. Springer Nature.

Bambra, C., Lynch, J., & Smith, K. E. (2021). *The unequal pandemic: COVID-19 and health inequalities*. Policy Press.

Bordoni, C. (2022). *Post society: Social life after the pandemic*. John Wiley & Sons.

Börner, S., & Seeleib-Kaiser, M. (Eds.). (2023). *European social policy and the COVID-19 pandemic: Challenges to national welfare and EU policy*. Oxford University Press.

Börsch-Supan, A., Abramowska-Kmon, A., Andersen-Ranberg, K., Brugiavini, A., Chłoń-Domińczak, A., Jusot, F., Laferrère, A., Litwin, H., Smolic, S., & Weber, G. (2023). *Social, health, and economic impacts of the COVID-19 pandemic and the epidemiological control measures*. De Gruyter.

Burns, R. B. (2023). *The human impact of the COVID-19 pandemic: A review of international research*. Springer.

Cooper, H., & Szreter, S. (2021). *After the virus: Lessons from the past for a better future*. Cambridge University Press.

Deutschmann, E. (2022). *Mapping the transnational world: How we move and communicate across borders, and why it matters*. Princeton University Press.

Gandhi, V., & Robison, J. (2021, July 22). The 'Great Resignation' is really the 'Great Discontent'. *Gallup*. https://www.gallup.com/workplace/351545/great-resignation-really-great-discontent.aspx

Grasso, M., Klicperová-Baker, M., Koos, S., Kosyakova, Y., Petrillo, A., & Vlase, I. (2021). The impact of the coronavirus crisis on European societies: What have we learnt and where do we go from here? Introduction to the COVID volume. *European Societies, 23*(S1), S2–S32. https://doi.org/10.1080/14616696.2020.1869283

Hobsbawm, J. (2022). *The nowhere office: Reinventing work and the workplace of the future*. Hachette UK.

Lange, E. L., & Shullenberger, G. (Eds.). (2024). *COVID-19 and the left: The tyranny of fear*. Routledge.

Liebe, U. (2022). Survey data must be top-notch to tackle societal crises. *Nature, 606*(7914), 463. https://doi.org/10.1038/d41586-022-01636-y

Lupton, D. (2022). *COVID societies: Theorising the coronavirus crisis*. Routledge.

Parolin, Z. (2023). *Poverty in the pandemic: Policy lessons from COVID-19*. Russell Sage Foundation.

Recchi, E. (2016). Space, mobility and legitimacy. In *Oxford Research Encyclopedia of Politics*. Oxford University Press. https://doi.org/10.1093/acrefore/9780190228637.013.8

Recchi, E., Ferragina, E., Helmeid, E., Pauly, S., Safi, M., Sauger, N., & Schradie, J. (2020). The 'eye of the hurricane' paradox: An unexpected and unequal rise of well-being during the Covid-19 lockdown in France. *Research in Social Stratification and Mobility, 68*, 100508. https://doi.org/10.1016/j.rssm.2020.100508

Rosa, H. (2013). *Social acceleration: A new theory of modernity*. Columbia University Press.

Searight, H. R. (Ed.). (2023). COVID-19: Health disparities and ethical challenges across the globe . Springer InternationalPublishing.

CHAPTER 2

The Three Acts of Pandemic Governance: A Comparison Between France, Germany, Italy, and the UK

Bartholomew Konechni and Ettore Recchi

By the end of 2019, it seemed that many of the threats that had shaken Europe and its institutions following the 2008–2009 recession were settling down. The monetary crises that hit southern European economies—endangering the integrity of the single currency and economic union more generally—had been calmed through a series of bailouts (Tooze, 2018, pp. 319–446), although the uneasy inheritance of austerity remained (Armingeon et al., 2022; Perez & Matsaganis, 2018; Walter et al., 2020). The wave of European populism, which at one time looked as though it might engulf the European Union's political project, appeared to have

B. Konechni (✉)
Sciences Po Paris, Paris, France
e-mail: bartholomew.konechni@sciencespo.fr

E. Recchi
Centre for Research on Social Inequalities (CRIS), CNRS, Sciences Po, Paris, France
e-mail: ettore.recchi@sciencespo.fr

E. Naumann et al. (eds.), *Social Life during COVID-19 in France, Germany, Italy and the UK*,
https://doi.org/10.1007/978-3-031-99349-7_2

been cowed (Jones, 2019). In France, Emmanuel Macron had decisively defeated Marine Le Pen in the 2017 presidential election, although he continued to face strong resistance within the country from the Gilets Jaunes movement (Bendali et al., 2019; Durovic, 2019). In Germany and the UK, the promise of insurgent parties never fully materialised, with the AfD and UKIP remaining peripheral players in the national politics of their respective countries. Even Brexit, an issue that had plagued the EU since the referendum of 2016, seemed largely resolved thanks to the Conservative's landslide victory in December 2019 and the subsequent passage of the *European Union (Withdrawal Agreement) Act* in January 2020 (Sobolewska & Ford, 2020). In Italy, despite Lega Nord's meteoric rise in the 2018 general election, their sudden and largely unexplained departure from government in August 2019 left them isolated and a declining force in the opinion polls (Giuffrida, 2019).

However, it was at the base of the Italian Alps—where Lega Nord had its historical stronghold as a secessionist party—that a new danger was brewing to challenge the temporary respite of European nations. Having travelled halfway across the world from China, the arrival of COVID-19 presented a new threat to the existing social, political, and economic order of European countries. Beginning with just a handful of municipalities in northern Italy at the end of February 2020 (Celotto, 2020; Sanfelici, 2020), a very old technique of governance was about to make a dramatic return: quarantine. Europe had not experienced widespread confinement measures since the cholera outbreaks of the late nineteenth century (Snowden, 2019). But once set in motion, the adoption of lockdown measures spread across the continent with alarming speed. By 9 March 2020, Italy's localised lockdowns had been extended into a national lockdown. In France, President Macron followed suit by announcing the imposition of a quarantine on 16 March 2020. Despite early reservations, both Germany and the UK would also implement national confinement measures on 22 and 23 March 2020, respectively, although both granted regional governments significantly greater flexibility in determining the specific methods of implementation than France and Italy did.

This book explores the consequences of the COVID-19 crisis for European societies by drawing on individual-level panel data from France, Germany, Italy, and the UK. This chapter seeks to place that analysis into a wider context, examining how the pandemic transformed modes of governance in these four countries between February 2020 and May 2022, when the pandemic was at its peak. To that end, the chronology of the crisis will be recounted in three acts.

To begin, this chapter will examine how early on in the pandemic the role of the state was dramatically reconfigured, in terms of both the political and economic relationship between individuals and the institutions which govern their lives. This section will explore how governments initially resisted coercive measures, but then gradually adopted lockdowns one after another for lack of more effective alternatives. Equally, we will show how governments' decisions to restrict citizens to their homes necessitated a historic expansion in state spending and economic support both to individuals and businesses.

The second section will examine attempts by governments to experiment with public policy and introduce more limited measures during later stages of the pandemic, namely locally targeted lockdowns and track-and-trace mobile apps. Although recognising that these attempts largely ended in failure from an epidemiological standpoint, we seek to emphasise that many of these innovations became important parts of each country's public health infrastructure, enabling them to better monitor citizens.

The final section of this chapter combines the scientific and political stories of the vaccine, the ultimate weapon through which the COVID-19 crisis was ended. We highlight the technological triumph of the mRNA vaccines, uniquely capable of providing protection against COVID-19. However, we also underline how this scientific advancement moved the focus of public policy from regulating public space to controlling individual bodies, raising new moral questions for policymakers.

In charting the history of the pandemic, this chapter seeks to achieve two goals. First, we argue that the COVID-19 crisis should not be understood as a single event, but rather as a process that requires periodisation. As the technical means available to governments to combat the pandemic evolved, as the instruments at their disposal became more refined, so too did the challenges facing societies change. From a first period when governments resorted to absolute and disruptive lockdowns, to a second period when nations developed apps and regionally targeted measures, to a third period when the solutions became individualised through the delivery of the vaccine, the material and social obstacles to combating the pandemic mutated. The second goal of this chapter is to show that, in spite of those changes, one important tension remained: the conflict between individual rights and collective duties. We highlight not only the material but also the normative hurdles that states had to overcome in fighting the pandemic, highlighting the initial vacillation of states during the early stages of the pandemic, the often desperate attempts to avoid subsequent lockdowns, and the bitter arguments about the enforcement of the vaccine.

Act 1: The State Unbound

Although a dramatic return of the state was the eventual conclusion of the COVID-19 crisis, in February 2020 this was not considered a *fait accompli* by policy makers. When the first cases began to appear in northern Italy, the government's initial response was to call on citizens to adopt hygienic practices. Coercion was not yet in the window of possibilities. The Italian government, headed by Giuseppe Conte, declared a largely symbolic state of national emergency on 31 January 2020, being hesitant to accept that more forceful measures would be a necessary element in fighting the pandemic (Bosa et al., 2022; Bull, 2021). The initial hope was that citizens could be made co-responsible for the pandemic's management. It quickly became clear that relying on citizens to change their behaviour autonomously would prove to be an insufficient remedy to the crisis (Gatto et al., 2020; Sebastiani et al., 2020).

Serious clusters of the virus were identified in ten municipalities of Lombardy on 21 February 2020. Almost as soon as the Italian government introduced measures to restrict movement in and out of these areas, a new cluster had appeared outside of Lombardy in Vo', a municipality close to Venice (Sanfelici, 2020). Aware that public authorities were losing control, the Conte government in Rome sought to instigate a full lockdown across the affected areas, establishing the 'red zones', which covered about 50,000 people across Italy's industrial heartland. From 23 February, schools, universities, public venues, and workplaces (except those engaged in the production and distribution of essential goods) were all closed, with another six Italian regions being forced to shut schools and universities on 25 February (Bull, 2021). The Italian government hoped that these measures could be contained to a few affected regions. However, the challenge of enforcing this localised lockdown proved to be insurmountable, with citizens continuing to make illegal trips despite police efforts to prevent them (Bonini et al., 2020).

COVID-19 was spilling out beyond the red zones. To re-establish authority, the Italian government significantly expanded the geographic scope of confinement measures. On 1 March, the new 'yellow zones' were introduced, covering remaining parts of the regions of Emilia Romagna, Lombardy, and Veneto, alongside the provinces of Pesaro, Urbino, and Savona. On 4 March, schools and universities were closed across the entire country. In an act of increasing desperation, the red zones were expanded to include all of Lombardy and 14 other surrounding provinces on 8 March, covering approximately 16 million people, around one-quarter of the Italian population. However, a press leak of these plans resulted in thousands fleeing south just 24 hours before this expansion came into effect, with dramatic scenes ensuing at train stations across northern Italy (Bull, 2021). Having depleted their options and with hospitals admissions rising swiftly, the Italian government submitted to a national lockdown on 11 March, originally planned to end on 3 April 2020 but which continued until 3 June 2020.

In France, authorities looked upon their Italian neighbours with concern but were not yet ready to adopt the same forceful measures. Much like Italy, France hoped that with intelligent public policy design, the virus' spread could be effectively curtailed. However, unbeknownst to public authorities, France was merely on a delayed epidemiological timeline to Italy, with their first COVID-19 later—on 25 February 2020 (Bergeron et al., 2020)—but with an equally striking effect once it began—with total COVID deaths hitting around 10,000 by early April (see Fig. 2.1).

Clusters of the virus had been identified in the north of France, particularly in the l'Oise, but the situation did not immediately seem as dire as that in Italy. On 6 March, Olivier Veran, the French Health Minister, announced the adoption of the '*plan blanc*', which allowed hospitals to postpone non-essential surgery to accommodate more COVID-19 patients (ibid.). Equally, the government attempted to limit the extent of public gatherings by banning meetings of more than 5000 people from 8 March onwards. But as the situation continued to deteriorate, the government adopted progressively harsher measures. On 12 March 2020, President Macron announced the closure of schools, which Jean-Michel Blanquer, the Minister of Education, initially said would last only until the Easter holidays (Lepelletier, 2020). Similarly, the government tightened earlier restrictions on 14 March and banned all gatherings of over 100 people. With the virus continuing to spread and new cases doubling between 13 and 15 March 2020 (Or et al., 2021), Macron announced the first national lockdown on 16 March, which came into effect the next day (Bergeron et al., 2020).

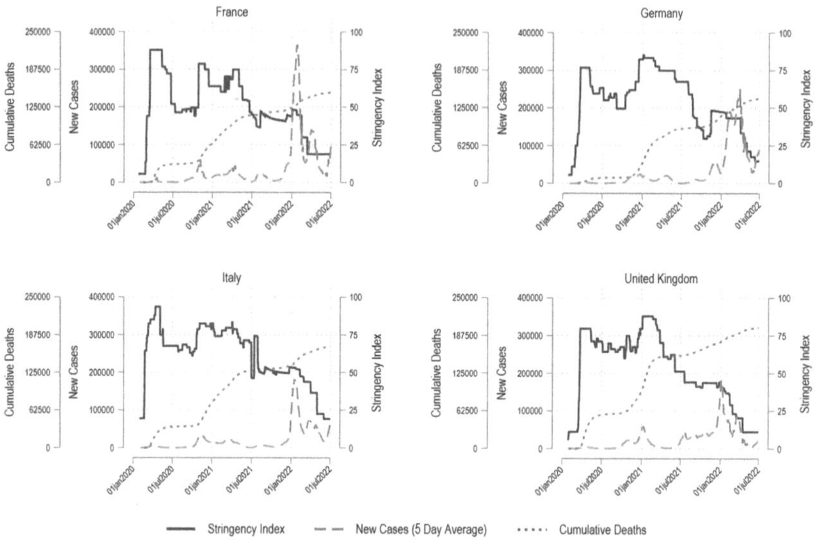

Fig. 2.1 Timeline of COVID-19 new cases, cumulative deaths, and severity of NPIs (summarised by the Oxford-Tracker Stringency Index). (Notes: Cumulative deaths and new cases taken from Mathieu et al. (2021) based on reporting by national governments. Stringency Index taken from Hale et al. (2021) The code for these graphs is an elaboration of the work of Naumann et al. (2020))

The French lockdown was distinct not in its formal provisions but rather in its methods of implementation. Whilst Italy had taken a lax approach to enforcement, France would do the opposite. Within the first day of the lockdown, the French government deployed 100,000 officers to enforce compliance of lockdown rules (Sénat, 2020). In the next week, an additional 22,000 police officers were empowered to issue fines and enforce COVID-19 Non-Pharmaceutical Interventions (NPIs) (Terpstra et al., 2021). Moreover, the French national police launched 535 aerial surveillance missions on their own population (Sénat, 2020). To put the scale of this operation into context, France conducted some 15.5 million controls on individuals and handed out approximately 915,000 fines for breeches of COVID-19 rules in the lockdown's first month (ibid., 38). This means that 2,500 controls and 140 fines per 10,000 residents were conducted. Italy by contrast carried out only 2,100 controls and fined only 50 per 10,000 individuals (Aitkenhead et al., 2022).

As France went headfirst into one of Europe's most strictly enforced lockdowns, Germany and the UK were still hesitating as to how to respond to the pandemic. Deaths were predicted to rise to 500,000 in the UK, but the British government continued to entertain notions of herd immunity as a potential solution to the crisis (Freedman, 2020; Sibony, 2020). On 14 March, the UK government's Chief Scientific Adviser, Patrick Vallance, said in a press conference: 'it's not possible to stop everybody getting it and it's also actually not desirable because you want some immunity in the population. We need to have immunity to protect ourselves from this in the future' (Health and Social Care Committee, 2021, p. 33). He was categorically contradicted two days later by Matt Hancock, the Health Secretary. On 18 March, the UK Prime Minister, Boris Johnson, began to accept that some restrictions on day-to-day life would be necessary and held a press conference to recommend that individuals work from home and avoid contact with those outside of their household. Still at this point, no enforcement mechanisms had been established. Much like France and Italy before them, appeals to citizens proved to be an inadequate response to the crisis at hand. On 23 March 2020, the UK entered a national lockdown. However, unlike France and Italy, the UK granted significant flexibility to regional governments in Scotland, Wales and Northern Ireland to establish their own variations of the rules (Health and Social Care Committee, 2021).

The reaction was more fragmented in Germany. The federal government equivocated over what action to take, with Chancellor Angela Merkel emphasising the seriousness of the virus, yet refraining from presenting any specific policy measures during her press conference on 11 March 2020. As a consequence, the individual German states began to take their own unilateral action to combat the virus, something totally unseen in the three other nations (Kuhlmann et al., 2021). Fourteen out of the sixteen states declared that they would close schools and nurseries on 13 March. Markus Söder, Minister-President of Bavaria, declared a state of emergency on 16 March and introduced limitations on public movement and the opening hours of many businesses. Söder would then harden Bavaria's partial lockdown on 20 March by imposing a night-time curfew, a strategy which was quickly followed by Saarland (Vampa, 2021).

On 22 March, the German federal government finally met with state-level leaders to agree a shared COVID-19 strategy. The more prohibitive approach previously adopted by Bavaria and Saarland was not replicated nationally. Instead it was agreed that a common standard would be set amongst all states, which included the banning of gatherings of more than two people over the following two weeks, enforcing social distancing in public, and closing down non-essential businesses. However, this agreement left open the possibility for states and local government to pursue harsher methods, which enabled significant variation of policy within Germany. For example, following the meeting, Saxony joined Bavaria and Saarland in imposing a night-time curfew (Vampa, 2021). Equally, municipalities began to act more autonomously. On 1 April, the city of Jena in Thuringia introduced a compulsory mask mandate, initially just for cases when social distancing could not be maintained, but subsequently made compulsory for public transport, shops, food deliveries, and offices from 6 April (Mitze et al., 2020). This decision was followed by other German municipalities over the course of April 2020—namely Landkreis Rottweil, Main-Kinzig-Kreis, Wolfsburg, Braunschweig, and Nordhausen—before being adopted by the remaining states between 20 and 29 April (Mitze et al., 2020).

The eventual conclusion, which all four of these countries arrived at, combating the pandemic through lockdowns, precipitated the most severe economic downturn since World War II. In early April 2020, the International Monetary Fund (IMF) predicted that gross domestic product (GDP) would diminish by more than 6% among advanced economies. But the warnings were much worse for European economies, with predictions that the UK would see a 6.5% drop in GDP, Germany and France would experience a 7% decline, and Italy a 9% reduction (Gopinath, 2020). How, then, could European nations avert this seemingly inevitable consequence of a policy solution to which there seemed to be few palatable alternatives? The answer was twofold. First, governments would have to accept large increases in public spending, expanding the fiscal remit of the government in ways unseen since the 2008 financial crisis (see Fig. 2.2) to avoid the permanent closure of many otherwise viable businesses and prevent workers from losing their livelihoods. Second, policymakers would have to exercise their regulatory power to soften the economic crisis ahead, covering issues as diverse as the repayment of loans, the right to evict tenants from their apartments, and the extension of parental leave from work.

Ironically, the UK, which was the slowest to accept lockdown measures, was the first to take decisive action on the economic front. Rishi Sunak, who had become Chancellor of the Exchequer only a month before, presented a new budget on 11 March 2020. In response to the still emerging

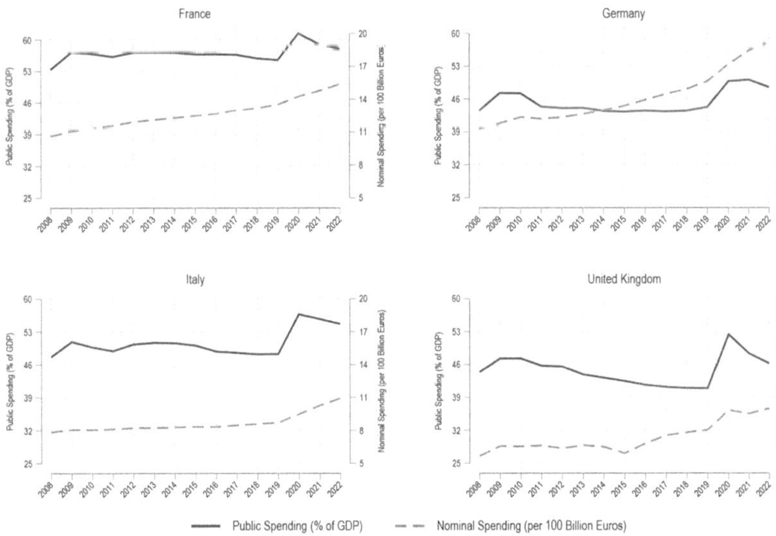

Fig. 2.2 State expenditures in France, Germany, Italy, and the UK: 2008–2020

crisis, Sunak announced £30 billion of additional spending, which would include statutory sick pay for all those advised to isolate (even if they had not shown any symptoms), a yearlong suspension on all business rates below £51,000, the establishment of a £500 million hardship fund to be administered by local authorities, and a new scheme offering small- and medium-sized businesses loans of up to £1.2 million to provide temporary financial stability (Sawyer, 2021).

The British government would soon have to go beyond these stop-gap measures, introducing two major policies designed to weather the country through a longer crisis. The first was the introduction of the Coronavirus Job Retention Scheme, which guaranteed that any worker who was furloughed as a result of the COVID-19 crisis would have 80% of their income paid by government (Wiggan & Grover, 2022). The second measure involved a temporary increase of Universal Credit and the Working Tax Credit alongside an expansion in eligibility for the Local Housing Allowance (Sawyer, 2021), providing lower-income households with approximately an additional £1040 annually. These measures together led the UK to see the largest relative increase in public spending of any of the countries under consideration in this book, leaping from 40.9% of GDP in 2019 to 52.4% in 2020.

During the UK's rapidly evolving approach, Italian policymakers were also presenting their plan. On 17 March 2020, the government introduced the *Decreto Cura Italia* (the Cure Italy Decree), serving as the cornerstone of Italy's economic response to the crisis (Berardi et al., 2020). Much like the UK's plan, Italy brought forward a series of spending proposals (Di Bartolomeo et al., 2022; Moreira et al., 2021). The Italian government allowed businesses to apply to the security funds to support furloughed employees, albeit within a nine-week cap. In addition, €600 indemnity payments were provided to workers who could not look after their children due to illness. A last-resort fund was also set up for workers impacted by COVID-19, with an anticipated budget of €300 million. But in contrast to the UK's plans, Italy sought to implement the majority of its changes through regulation. The *Decreto Cura Italia* suspended the right of landlords to evict their tenants and granted parents an additional 15 days of annual leave. Most dramatically, the Italian government brought in a debt holiday for individuals and small businesses, relieving them of the obligation to repay most substantial loans from banks until 30 September 2020. This highlights a fundamental difference between the UK and Italy: while the UK emphasised spending their way out of the crisis, Italy instead chose to buffer economic collapse through regulation.

To an even greater extent than Italy, France lent on regulation to cushion the impact of the pandemic (Achard, 2022). This is partly attributed to France's position as the highest spender of these four economies, which left it with less fiscal flexibility. The French government sought to protect small- and medium-sized businesses that were not able to pay their rent and utility bills through preventing companies and landlords from cutting them off or evicting them. The moratorium on winter evictions (*trêve hivernale*), which normally lasts from 1 November until 31 March of each year, was extended until 10 July 2020. Equally, the government announced a debt holiday similar to the Italian one. This is not to say, however, that France took no fiscal measures to combat COVID-19. Most notably, the existing furlough scheme—which had been in place since 1918 although was often underutilised—was expanded to cover the vast majority of workers and renumerate most at 70% of their income (Givord & Silhol, 2020; Lambert et al., 2021).

Germany was the most cautious country in its economic response to the pandemic. The German government widened access to its pre-existing furlough scheme, albeit modestly. Previously, firms were required to demonstrate that 30% of their workers would lose their jobs without urgent support to be able to access the furlough scheme; now this threshold was lowered to 10%. Like France and Italy, Germany sought to protect those who fell into rent debts by banning evictions until 30 June 2020 (Ungerer, 2020). Equally, a suspension on penalties for non-repayment of debts, water, and electricity bills was put in place until 1 July 2020 (Hinterlang et al., 2023). However, unlike the UK, Germany opted against increasing its existing benefits. Instead, the government introduced a new supplemental payment (*Kinderzuschlag*) to the pre-existing child benefit scheme (*Kindergeld*), specifically for unemployed parents (Cantillon et al., 2021).

By May 2020, the pandemic's initial shock had passed, and society had survived. Both the UK and Italy experienced COVID-19 fatalities well above 26,000, while in France approximately 24,000 people had died. Germany managed significantly better, with roughly 6,000 COVID-19 related deaths during the pandemic's first wave (WHO, 2020a). However, the true impact of the pandemic extended beyond these mortality figures, ushering in profound transformations in the dynamics between the state and its citizens.

To grapple with the crisis, states expanded both politically and economically. In the political sense, governments began to control aspects of their citizens' lives which had been previously untouched. Prior to 2020, in the context of liberal democracies, it was unimaginable that a government would dictate to its citizens who they could see, where they go could, when they could leave their homes, and how they must interact with one another. The pandemic marked a clear redefinition of the balance between individual citizens' rights and the duty of states to ensure their safety and security.

Out of these political choices came an economic necessity. Governments had to have an expanded role within the economy to manage the consequences of shutting down large parts of business and working life. Some, notably the UK, chose to do this by spending more through raising the basic level of state benefits, creating new schemes to ensure job retention, and providing bridging loans to small- and medium-sized businesses. Other nations chose to expand their role in the economy through regulatory power by imposing debt holidays, establishing eviction moratoriums, and guaranteeing the rights of particular groups of workers. However, as these countries embarked on radical programmes to curtail COVID-19's spread, they were soon faced with the challenge of dismantling their initial response to the crisis, searching for more moderate paths forward.

Act 2: Experiments in Public Policy

One by one, European countries started to progressively lift the lockdowns rules they had put in place in March 2020 as the virus began to recede. In the United Kingdom, individuals were allowed to return to workplaces if they couldn't work from home on 10 May 2020; a phased reopening of schools began on 1 June; non-essential shops and places of worship were allowed to reopen 15 June; and by 23 June even social distancing rules were being relaxed (Holt & Murray, 2022). France followed a similar path (Achard, 2022), officially ending lockdown on 11 May with some schools being allowed to reopen; reopening churches from 18 May; dropping the requirement that individuals not travel more than 100 kilometres from their home on 28 May; and allowing the reopening of bars and restaurants in most of the country and then in Paris on 28 May and 14 June respectively. Italy took a somewhat less gradual if delayed approach (Marziano et al., 2021), allowing almost all businesses and religious centres to reopen on 18 May, with the exception of indoor sports facilities which wouldn't reopen until 25 May and theatres which would have to wait until 15 June. Italy equally moved quickly to reinstate free movement, allowing unrestricted travel within regions on 18 May and then also across region on 3 June. Germany, ever the federalist of the group, took a more staggered approach across region, with different states reopening at different points, but over a broadly similar timeline.

Long before the second wave of COVID-19 started to emerge in Europe between September and October 2020, governments were developing more effective strategies for combatting the virus. Mobile phones, sitting in every citizen's pocket, presented an obvious tool for pandemic management. Europe was hugely behind other world regions when it came to using information technology to manage the pandemic (Kim, 2020; Singh et al., 2020): China integrated health monitoring into the WeChat app from February 2020, South Korea adopted a system of wearable wristbands which monitored the movements of quarantined individuals with virtual ringfences, and Singapore released the first national contact tracing app based on Bluetooth technology at the end of March 2020. Despite early concerns—especially within the French government

(Untersinger, 2020)—about the data protection consequences of adopting contact tracing technology to fight the virus, by autumn 2020 such apps had been implemented across Europe and would become an essential part of the response to COVID-19's second wave.

In June 2020, Italy, Germany, and France all launched contact-tracing apps to support the easing of COVID-19 restrictions, similar to the one initially developed in Singapore (Blasimme et al., 2021). Italy began with a trial of its app, *Immuni*, in four regions on 1 June 2020—Abruzzo, Apulia, Liguria, and Marche—and then swiftly expanded its rollout nationwide on 15 June. Germany released its app, *Corona-Warn-App*, on 16 June 2020, exploiting the same underlying protocol as the Italian app, the *Google/Apple Exposure Notification* (GAEN). France launched their app, *StopCovid*, earlier than Germany, on 2 June 2020. However, France experienced a much slower uptake of its COVID-19 app, with only 2 million downloads by mid-October 2020 in comparison to 20 million in Germany (Bellier, 2020). As a result, the French app was updated and relaunched on 22 October 2020 under the name *TousAntiCovid* (Reynaud, 2020).

The UK was more delayed in adopting a COVID-19 app, namely because it abandoned its first attempted app in favour of working with Google and Apple directly (Neville et al., 2020). The initial app took a data first approach, close to what the French had done, particularly in terms of its use of a centralised database. The second app, which eventually won out, had a privacy first approach, similar to that of Italy and Germany, with GAEN as its basis. The switch seemed to be driven not so much out of moral concerns over holding citizens' data in government hands, but rather out of technical necessity. Initial trials of the first app on the Isle of Wight in May 2020 were racked with technical difficulties, raising serious questions about the compatibility between the UK's in-house app and a large number of mobile devices (Selby, 2020). Although the first app was not immediately abandoned, the technical difficulties were never satisfactorily resolved and by September 2020—first in Scotland on 14 September, then followed by England and Wales on 24 September—the United Kingdom released a contact tracing app to the general public based on GAEN (Blasimme et al., 2021).

Whether or not these apps were effective as a method of containing the virus' spread is a question of debate (Bae et al., 2020; Kondylakis et al., 2020; Singh et al., 2020; Timmers et al., 2020; Zamberg et al., 2020). However, what is clear is that on their own they proved to be an insufficient means by which to stop the virus once the autumn arrived. In order to fight the pandemic, governments would return to the idea which Italy had unsuccessfully attempted at the start of the pandemic, regional lockdowns, in the hope that this time they could be effectively implemented.

The UK was the first country to begin experimenting with localised restrictions again. After a local spike, the city of Leicester was temporarily locked down on 29 June 2020, with non-essential shops being closed as before (Triggle, 2020a). A month later, as Leicester came out of lockdown, restrictions were being tightened in many parts of northern England—principally in Greater Manchester, East Lancashire, and West Yorkshire— where visiting elderly relatives was banned on 31 July 2020 (Gallagher, 2020). These minimal measures implemented during the summer foreshadowed a disorganised patchwork of rules that emerged in the autumn. On 21 August, Oldham, Pendle, and Blackburn saw a further tightening of restrictions (having already been included in the toughening of rules in northern England) while neighbouring Wigan, Rossendale, and Darwen had their restrictions loosened (Department of Health and Social Care, 2020). On 1 September, restrictions were introduced in Glasgow, East Renfrewshire, and West Dunbartonshire, prohibiting individuals living in different households from meeting with one another, but kept schools and businesses open (Scottish Government, 2020). In the small towns of Caerphilly and Bolton, a lockdown was imposed on 8 September, which prevented individuals from leaving these areas and mandated face masks inside shops (Hartley, 2020; Murphy et al., 2020).

To add to the increasingly complex geography of COVID-19 rules, the governments of Wales, Northern Ireland, and Scotland began to chart their own paths. Following Nicola Sturgeon's—Scotland's First Minister—call for a zero-COVID policy in the UK (Torjesen, 2020), Scotland announced its own independent lockdown on 22 September—which banned indoor meetings between different households but allowed up to six people from two different households to meet outside—with harsher restrictions coming into place on 7 October. In Northern Ireland, the government announced a four-week circuit breaker lockdown, beginning on 16 October 2020, which allowed no more than ten people from up to two households to gather, closed all inside activities, and shut down all hospitality with the exception of takeaways (Mahase, 2020). Similarly, in Wales, the First Minister—Mark Drakeford—announced a two-week lockdown on 19 October, shutting down all non-essential businesses and moving all secondary schools online, but electing to keep primary schools open (Morris, 2020).

England, meanwhile, charted its own path by introducing a three-tiered system on 13 October, with varied rules for different parts of the country (Davies et al., 2021). Tier 1 regions faced few restrictions, save for limiting the number of people who could meet inside from different households to six. Tier 2 regions had the same rules with the addition of restrictions on travel between areas. The severest rules were found in Tier 3 regions, with the majority of non-essential businesses being shut altogether. Despite efforts to avoid a full-scale lockdown, Boris Johnson announced a four-week confinement period throughout England beginning on 5 November. Having lost its national unity during the virus' second wave, the United Kingdom would never truly rediscover it, with differences in both the content of NPIs designed to stop COVID-19 and the extent of punishment for breaking the rules varying through the country for the rest of the pandemic (Morphet, 2021; Richards et al., 2022; Warner et al., 2021).

The UK was not alone in attempting to adopt localised measures. France also sought to experiment with more targeted NPIs during the second and third waves of COVID-19, although it is important to emphasise that these measures were always directed from the centre with local and regional government excluded from the policymaking process. This began not with closures and lockdowns, but rather with masks. Although the wearing of masks had already been made compulsory inside buildings on 10 July 2020, it also became compulsory outside on 28 August 2020 but only within the departments of Seine-Saint-Denis, Hauts-de-Seine, Val-de-Marne and Paris (Béguin, 2020). Similarly, the introduction of curfew in France began not with the whole country, but rather with the region of Ile-de-France and eight other urban areas—namely Aix-Marseille, Grenoble, Lille, Lyon, Montpellier, Rouen, Saint-Étienne, and Toulouse—being put under curfew on 17 October (Mégarbane et al., 2021). On 20 March 2021, France even attempted a localised lockdown in sixteen of the ninety-six metropolitan departments (Gatinois, 2021).

In the case of France, these localised measures were almost always brief preludes to the same rules being generalised nationwide. Efforts at imposing a region-specific curfew in October 2020 were abandoned by the end of the month in favour of returning to a national lockdown (Faye, 2020). Similarly, the attempt to impose a localised lockdown in March 2021 ended with the enforcement of the third national lockdown on 3 April 2021 (Dumiot et al., 2021). In spite of this underlying tendency to adopt nationwide rules, minor instances of local variation did persist even in

France, the prime example of this being the regular changes the French government made to the hours during which curfew applied at the local level (Sliman, 2021).

Italy too brought in localised measures during the autumn of 2020. But unlike France, it managed to sustain them into the long term. Between 14 October and 15 November, Italy sought to curtail COVID-19 without the use of lockdowns, opting instead to extend the use of facemasks inside, reduce bars' and restaurants' opening hours, alongside reducing the maximum capacity of recreational facilities (Manica et al., 2021). However, similar to England, Italy adopted a three-tiered system to manage the COVID-19 crisis on 6 November. All tiers faced restrictions on spatial mobility, with the yellow and orange tiers having a 10 p.m. curfew put in place, whilst the red regions had a total stay-at-home mandate with travel in and out of the region banned. In yellow and orange zones, non-essential shops were allowed to remain open during the working week; in red zones all businesses, save for essential industries, were shut down. Throughout the country, secondary schools and universities went online. In the red zones, distance learning was introduced for some primary school students, although the youngest pupils were always kept in classes. Italy never truly returned to a national lockdown after this point, and although regions flexibly changed status, the tier system remained with Italy until the end of the crisis.

Germany, in contrast to the first wave, was much more unified in its national policy. On 28 October, following a meeting with the leaders of the states, Merkel announced that the nation would enter a partial lockdown with restaurants, bars, and theatres closing, while schools and most other businesses were to stay open (Connolly, 2020a). Throughout November, the federal government worked to build consensus on stricter lockdown measures, such as compulsory masks in school and greater limits on social interactions. However, doubts over lockdowns' continued efficacy hindered progress, causing these plans to advance slowly (Oltermann, 2022). On 1 December, Merkel was able to negotiate a nationwide policy that allowed five people from different households to meet at a time, with the exception of Christmas Day, when up to ten people could gather (Connolly, 2020b). However, this policy quickly proved to be insufficient in managing COVID. Bavaria and Saxony were the first to announce that they would pursue much stricter measures, including a night-time curfew. The other states followed as the number of deaths and hospitalisations began to rise again, and by 13 December a total lockdown was implemented across the country. Essential shops and schools were closed, New Year's Eve parties were banned, and the Christmas Day exemptions were reduced such that only four individuals from different households could meet (not including children aged under 14). In spite of these renewed restrictions, almost half of all German fatalities occurred in December 2020—16,718 out of 33,071—forever tarnishing Germany's pandemic record (Warren et al., 2021).

A natural question arises from this second act of the COVID-19 crisis in Europe: were the post-May 2020 attempts at managing the virus ultimately a failure? Was this a story of hubris, where European policymakers relaxed their vigilance after the first wave, consigning their countries to a perpetual battle with the disease? Or was this a tale of ingenuity, where policymakers engaged with an iterative process to devise innovative solutions that balanced epidemiological protection with minimal disruption to wider society?

In the short term the answer is probably the former. European societies experienced a second and much more powerful surge in COVID-19 related fatalities during the autumn of 2020 (see Fig. 2.1). By the end of December 2020 (WHO, 2020b), the United Kingdom and Italy had each garnered over 70,000 COVID-19 fatalities in total (an increase of about 44,000 since the end of the first wave in May 2020), France had a cumulative COVID-19 death-toll of around 60,000 (up by 36,000 since May), and even Germany—which previously had managed to keep the death toll extremely low—had seen almost 30,000 deaths due to COVID-19 (an increase of 24,000 since the first wave). It is evident that, taken together, the measures adopted during this period were unable to stop a second and even third wave from emerging. However, with the fullness of time it is possible to make a richer assessment of what this sombre period did for the fight against COVID-19.

This second period of the crisis offered innovations in public policy which were essential for the later rollout of the vaccine. Despite their initial failure, the apps that were developed as track-and-trace technology would be repurposed as vaccine passports in 2021. It is easy to look upon this period as one of wasted opportunity, of policy makers attracted by the false promise of complex policy's ability to nudge human behaviour (Pierre, 2020). However, such a perspective ignores the fact that these efforts served as crucial steppingstones to an eventual resolution of the pandemic crisis.

Act 3: The Vaccine Dilemma

At the beginning of the pandemic, it was unclear whether a vaccine would or even could be developed. The vast majority of vaccines take between five and ten years to release (Excler et al., 2021). For many of the world's most adaptive diseases—particularly the common cold—a successful vaccine has never been found (Simancas-Racines et al., 2017). It is therefore no small feat that scientists were able to develop not one but four successful vaccines, which were subsequently approved by the European Medicines Agency (EMA) by Christmas 2020.

In recounting the story of the vaccines' arrivals, it is important to recognise that this narrative is as much about political will as it is about technical triumph. It is therefore useful to remember that not all of these vaccines used exactly the same technology and as such had different histories. The Pfizer-BioNTech and Moderna vaccines used mRNA methods, while the Oxford-AstraZeneca and Janssen vaccines used more traditional carrier methods (Rotshild et al., 2021). The mRNA vaccines proved to be much more effective. The Pfizer-BioNTech and Moderna vaccines were 95 and 94% effective respectively. By contrast, the Oxford-AstraZeneca and Janssen vaccines were 81 and 55% effective (Tregoning et al., 2021). The mRNA vaccines could also be manufactured much faster than traditional vaccines, enabling them to be adapted to respond to the rapidly evolving COVID-19 crisis (Zhang et al., 2020). As a result, mRNA vaccines gained widespread popularity across Western societies, making them the focus of this discussion.

Despite their seemingly remarkable success, the mRNA vaccines presented governments with a serious challenge. These vaccines had a shelf-life of approximately six months, but only if kept in highly controlled environments below freezing (–80°C for Pfizer-BioNTech and –20°C for Moderna). Once taken outside into normal temperatures, the life expectancy of both vaccines fell dramatically, becoming unusable beyond 30 days at most (Uddin & Roni, 2021). Governments therefore had to find solutions to two central problems. First, they had to quickly solve the logistical challenge of connecting vaccines with citizens. Second, they had to persuade their populations to take the vaccine today rather than tomorrow, to overcome fears of a new technology and embrace this solution. As far as the organisational question is concerned, these four countries took very similar approaches.

The first to begin this campaign was the UK. Having previously freed itself of European regulatory processes through Brexit, Britain was able to approve the Pfizer-BioNTech vaccine on 2 December 2020 and administer the first dose by 8 December 2020 (Ledford et al., 2020). Margaret Keenan, a 91-year-old woman living in Coventry, was the first person outside clinical trials to be vaccinated and as such became the unsuspecting spearhead of one of the largest public health campaigns in human history (Triggle, 2020b).

The UK had a clear plan to connect citizens to the vaccine efficiently: conversion, prioritisation, and prolongation. The British government ordered the conversion of hundreds of buildings intended for other uses into *ad hoc* vaccine dispensaries: theatres, schools, sports hall, churches, etc. This was achieved with huge success, such that, at one point, every person in the UK lived within 16 kilometres of a vaccine centre (Baraniuk, 2021). Second, the UK adopted a nine-tier vaccine prioritisation list of every person on the NHS based on age and pre-existing health conditions. Given that the NHS is the UK's primary healthcare provider, this included almost every citizen. Letters were sent out inviting individuals for a vaccination at a specified local centre as appointments became available (Warren & Lofstedt, 2022). Third, the UK made the unconventional decision to disregard the advice of manufacturers and prolong the amount of time individuals had to wait between different doses of the vaccine, running the risk of reducing their long-term efficacy. This decision was made to give as many people as possible the first dose, offering some immunity (Tregoning et al., 2021). Despite this somewhat unorthodox approach, the UK's vaccination programme was successful. From early January to the end of March 2021, the number of people who had received a first vaccine rose from 3% to 40%, and by late June this number had risen even further to over 65%.

Germany, France, and Italy all began their vaccination campaigns within three weeks of the UK, on 26 December 2020 in Germany and on 27 December 2020 in Italy and France following approval by the EMA. These three countries opted for simplified criteria of prioritisation compared with the UK. In France, a three-tier system was adopted that prioritised residents of care homes over the age of 75 alongside those who worked in care homes. The elderly population outside retirement homes were then treated, and finally the rest of the population. Germany used a similar system of prioritisation organised predominately by age, with some exceptions for medical professionals (Warren & Lofstedt, 2022). By contrast,

Italy prioritised vaccine dissemination primarily by occupation rather than age (Oliani et al., 2022): all healthcare workers and individuals aged over 80 were to be vaccinated first, then followed by teachers, police officers, pharmacists, and veterinarians, and then others potentially at risk of contamination, before finally the rest of the population.

The arguments over vaccine prioritisation on the European continent—whether to protect the vulnerable or the productive—were important in demonstrating a different set of policy targets amongst governments. However, these decisions were not decisive in defining the outcome of the vaccine rollout. All three of the continental European countries under consideration here faced one major challenge during the early stages of vaccine rollout: procurement. Unlike the UK, which, owing to Brexit, had never participated in the common purchasing of vaccines with its European neighbours, EU countries had failed to reserve their vaccines ahead of time. Even before the vaccine was developed or approved, the UK had already bought 190 million doses in July 2020 (enough for 140% of its population), while the EU had bought zero (Gleißner et al., 2021). This resulted in mainland European countries facing the same slowdown as the UK during the summer, without having benefitted from the same early surge in vaccine uptake. By the end of March only 13% of the French population and 12% of the populations in Germany and Italy had received a first dose of the vaccine. By the end of June, the situation had greatly improved, but all three of these countries still remained significantly behind the UK in terms of the proportion of the population that had received the first dose: France at 58%, Germany at 56%, and Italy at 51% (Mathieu et al., 2021).

Whether slow or fast, organised or disorganised, all four countries ended up with the same fundamental problem after delivering the vaccine programme for a few months. Once the first group of willing vaccine receivers had been treated, governments were left trying to convince the unwilling minority to comply. Sitting in medical centres and refrigerators, shelf-life ticking down, all European governments were faced in the summer with the question of how to get the remaining 35–49% of their populations to accept the vaccine and thus close the final chink in Europe's public health defences (Fig. 2.3).

On 15 March 2021, the House of Commons' Petition Committee gathered—some in person and others online—to debate exactly this question. Still riding high on the wave of early vaccinations, there was a growing consciousness that the early uptake was slowing down. The petition up

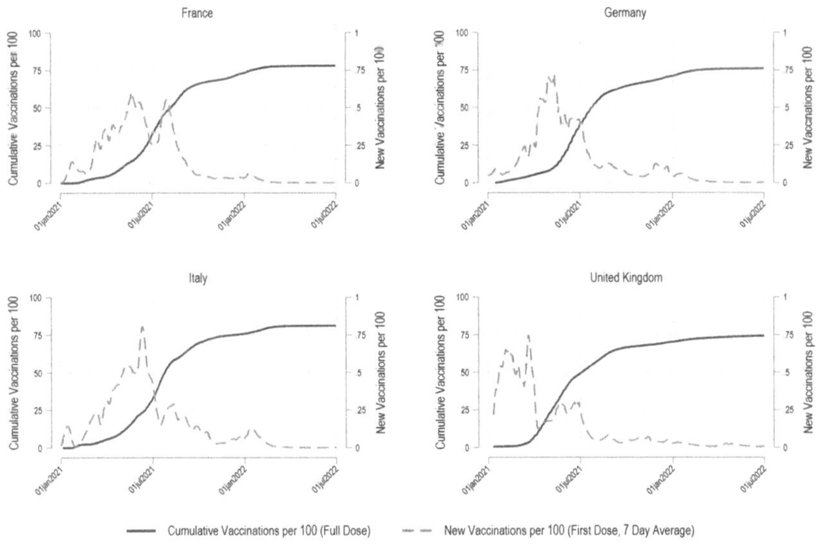

Fig. 2.3 Timeline of COVID-19 vaccinations

for debate was a motion asking the government to rule-out vaccine passports in all forms in the UK, even were the rate of vaccinations to slow. The debate sauntered on for an hour and a half in total, culminating with a response from the government's Paymaster General, Penny Mordaunt, in which it was affirmed that the government was considering all options but taking the members' views under advisement. In many ways this was an inconsequential moment deep in the halls of Westminster. However, it succeeded in encapsulating the arguments about the role of coercion in the future of vaccine implementation, perhaps never more clearly than when Steve Baker—a Conservative backbencher and former chair of the European Research Group—took to the floor ten minutes into the debate:

> Effectively making vaccines mandatory by implication through COVID status certification could be counterproductive. The evidence from across Europe shows that if people feel compelled to take vaccines, it puts them off. It would implement, of course, a checkpoint society. It would mean passes for the pub—if you want your pint, Sir David,[1] you will have to show your

[1] Here the 'Sir David' in question is Sir David Amess, Conservative Member of Parliament for Southend West until his assassination in 2021, who chaired this meeting of the Petition Committee.

> papers. I did not think that is the society that we wished to live in. A surveillance state would be instituted. There would be mission creep. Passes would be irreversible and divisive, and of course they would infringe on the autonomy of the individual. (Hansard, 2021)

Baker made two fundamental arguments here: an empirical conjecture that injunctions would hamper the vaccine's uptake, and a normative assertion that vaccine passports would constitute an authoritarian form of social control. In relation to his first point, there was real uncertainty over whether vaccine mandates would encourage greater uptake. If individuals were sufficiently averse to the prospect of the vaccine, then maybe no penalty could assuage their doubts. Even more troubling, mandates might harden existing scepticism towards the vaccine. With regard to the second point, many countries feared that by shifting from general lockdown measures to individual and potentially discriminatory forms of control represented by vaccine certificates, society would tip into an unacceptable and ultimately unjustifiable level of state coercion. These two debates shaped the final chapter of the pandemic, as governments were called to grapple with their unruly vaccine-sceptic minorities.

At the core of this isssue was the problem of vaccine hesitancy. It is challenging to determine with great certainty why significant portions of the population across these different countries were so slow to receive the vaccine. But, broadly, there appears to have been two problem groups in the population from the policymakers' points of view (MacDonald, 2015): delayers and refusers. Refusers were clearly the more challenging group, often denying the seriousness or even existence of COVID-19, seeing the vaccine—particularly the mRNA vaccines—as a harmful means of social control rather than a remedial measure (Chirumbolo, 2021; Hitti & Weissman, 2021). By contrast, delayers' motivations were less clear, their hesitancy seemingly unconnected to ideological impulses (Navarre et al., 2021; Schwarzinger et al., 2021). The challenge for policy makers was therefore to craft a policy to encourage or enforce vaccine uptake for both groups, counterbalancing concerns about government overreach.

France was the first to take decisive action. Macron gave a national address on 12 July 2021 to announce a battery of new measures to enforce the vaccine. First, he declared that vaccines would become compulsory for anyone working in hospitals, clinics, or retirement homes (Pallas, 2022).

Second, the President brought forward the domestic use of the *passe sanitaire*—a document which was already being used to facilitate international travel and could be integrated into the pre-existing TousAntiCovid app on mobile phones—which would now be required to enter bars, clubs, restaurants, theatres, and other public events (Le Coz, 2021; Slama, 2022). There would be two ways to acquire the *passe sanitaire*. Either an individual could complete a negative COVID test 24 hours before its use, or individuals could get the certificate through receiving two doses of the vaccine. The consequence of this was that individuals now effectively needed to present evidence of having been vaccinated not only to go through international borders but also in everyday life, thus creating a huge disincentive against delaying or refusing. It was still uncertain whether these new measures would prove effective. Would individuals respond to this intervention by choosing to be vaccinated or, as Baker predicted, would opposition become more entrenched?

In the short run, it seemed that the French plan worked. The number of daily vaccinations rose sharply following Macron's announcement, with more than four million people getting their first shot and more than six million appointments being made between his speech and the end of July 2021 (Hart, 2021). Moreover, the rate of new vaccinations remained above the forecasted level for many months after this (Mills & Rüttenauer, 2022).

Italy quickly followed France's example. On 22 July 2021, the Italian government introduced their own plan for quasi-compulsory vaccines using the *certificazione verde*. As with France, this was a pre-existing system for the regulation of international travel, built into the Italian COVID-19 app, and necessary for entry into train stations, restaurants, hotels, bars, and indoor sporting facilities (Spitale et al., 2022). Importantly, Italy also gave the option of a temporary *certificazione verde*, which lasted 48 hours following a negative COVID-19 test. However, Italy swiftly went much further than France—where the vaccine was never made compulsory to enter education or to go to most places of work—by making the vaccine obligatory for all workers on 15 October 2021. These supplementary measures allowed employers to dismiss employees if they did not receive the vaccine within five days and instituted fines of up to €1,500 for businesses found to have unvaccinated staff (Cuzzocrea, 2021). Like in France, the intial adoption of quasi-compulsory vaccine certificates was highly effective in encouraging vaccine uptake. For the 30 days following the initial implementation of domestic vaccine passport on 22 July, around

1,300 extra individuals were getting vaccinated daily, compared to similar countries (Mills & Rüttenauer, 2022).

Germany too would come to adopt measures disincentivising vaccine refusal or delay, but with far less impact. On 23 August 2021, Germany initiated its 3G rule: *geimpft, genesen, getestet* (vaccinated, recovered, tested). This required individuals to show that they had been fully vaccinated, had recently recovered from, or had received a negative test in the last 48 hours to be granted access to hospitals, retirement homes, restaurants, indoor public events, and hair/beauty salons. The implementation of this rule proved far less effective than its French and Italian counterparts in increasing the rate of vaccinations, with studies suggesting that it either had no or a significantly smaller effect (Karaivanov et al., 2022). Why this should be the case is not entirely clear but Mills and Rüttenauer (2022) have suggested that the policy was less effective because at the time of implementation most of those who were in principle willing to take the vaccine had already done so. Equally it is true to say that Germany never went as far in truly enforcing uptake of the vaccine, with plans for compulsory vaccinations for medical staff being scuppered by Marcus Soder, who refused to enforce the proposal in Bavaria.

Meanwhile the UK remained the most sceptical towards the enforcement of compulsory vaccine passports for domestic use. Even though the country had the technical capacity to implement vaccine passports—through a vaccine app—the UK government never made the vaccine a requirement for daily activities. The devolved governments did attempt to implement some measures similar to those in France, Italy, and Germany. The Scottish Parliament passed a bill to enforce vaccine certificates for nightclubs from 1 October 2021 onwards (Christie, 2021) and Wales followed suit from 5 October 2021, passing by a narrow majority of one vote in the Senedd (Morris, 2021). Northern Ireland agreed to enforce vaccine passes from 13 December in a broader set of businesses, including restaurants, bars, and other hospitality venues. However, the plans were abandoned in the following month after strong opposition from the powerful Democratic Unionist Party (McCormack, 2022). Despite these limited measures on a regional basis, the notion of compulsory vaccines never gained momentum in the UK, becoming trapped between conflicting ideologies, particularly on the part of Conservative backbenchers such as Steve Baker.

These different approaches to encouraging vaccine uptake provoke a question. Did the enforcement of the vaccine result in higher rates of vaccination? The results are mixed in the short term. France and Italy saw a clear rise in uptake of the vaccine, while the impacts in Germany were much weaker (Mills & Rüttenauer, 2022; Karaivanov et al., 2022). In the long run, these policies had a minimal effect, as, by mid-2022, the countries with higher levels of stringency did have greater vaccine uptake. As a brief example, by June 2022 (Mathieu et al., 2021) 81% of people had been fully vaccinated in Italy, 78% in France, 76% in Germany, and 74% in the UK. Whether or not this difference represents the long-term consequence of compulsory vaccine certificates remains up for debate. Ultimately, this final act of the pandemic underscores an undeniable truth: beyond the epidemiological scoreboard, evaluations of pandemic policies depend on normative questions about the role of the state and extent to which personal freedoms should be sacrificed for collective goals. It is not the task of this chapter to resolve such questions, but only to highlight that the evaluation of public policy is intrinsically intertwined with moral considerations.

Epilogue

This chapter charts the course of the COVID-19 crisis: the two years between February 2020 and May 2022 when Europe was engaged in a prolonged battle against a biological enemy. This story has many dimensions: epidemiological, political, economic, and behavioural. As such, there is not a straightforward narrative that neatly draws together all of these events. We have focused on tracing the sequence of policy responses in four countries, with the aim of highlighting commonalities and differences among them, as well as continuities and discontinuities within each of them. In spite of this complexity, there are three takeaways that emerge from this analysis.

First, the timing of policy did not only depend on epidemiological trends but also on the technological capacity of governments to respond to the crisis. Early on, governments reacted to the virus' spread with an almost on-the-hour urgency and 'pragmatism' (Boin & Lodge, 2021). However, as the pandemic continued, states became more proactive, developing tools which enabled them to break from the calendar of the disease. What distinguishes each of the three periods presented in this chapter are the means that governments had at their disposal to combat the virus. In the first period, governments had only imprecise instruments with which to mitigate COVID-19's consequences: lockdowns, furlough programmes, debt holidays, the closure of schools and other meeting places. In the second period, governments attempted to hone their response through better identifying impacted individuals via track-and-trace apps. Ultimately, these attempts proved to be insufficient in protecting communities from the new waves which arrived in autumn and winter. However, in the final period, governments built on their previous innovations—most notably the COVID-19 apps—to deliver the vaccine. The vaccine became the critical tool to liberate society from the necessity of confinement measures every time the virus surged, breaking the cycle between policy responses and the virus' ebb and flow.

Second, there were policy differences between the four countries but these were often expressed not so much in the content of their response to the pandemic as in how policies were implemented, revealing dimensions of public policies that are not new at all (McConnell & Stark, 2021). Most prominently, variation between countries was often dependent on the degree of policy centralisation, with France being the most extreme while Germany championed a principle of subsidiarity. The strictness of enforcement was also a significant difference. Throughout the pandemic, France sought to develop a powerful apparatus of enforcement, while nations such as the UK were content to be flexible with the governance of their citizens. It would also be remiss not to mention levels of public spending which proved to be a significant difference between nations, with the UK deploying the most generous effort and Germany the most cautious. Aside from minor differences in timing of certain NPIs, the array of regulations implemented—lockdowns, social distancing, mask mandates, testing, contact tracing, limits to association, and ultimately vaccination campaigns—were consistent across all cases. In retrospect, policy variations between countries, which bewildered observers in the early stage of the pandemic (Capano et al., 2020), have diminished over time, particularly when nations share many institutional and socioeconomic similarities (differences are possibly larger when comparing with other continent, as demonstrated by China's Zero-COVID approach [Mei, 2020]). This reflects a tendency towards *policy isomorphism*—partly thanks to the EU's coordinating role in certain areas, formally and informally (Schomaker et al., 2021)—and *path dependency*, recognising that each country's response was influenced by its existing institutions and norms.

Third, despite differences both between and within countries, there remains a common thread which binds together these different periods and experiences of the COVID-19 crisis. Namely, the tension of balancing individual rights and collective duties. The inescapable reality that individuals alone could not overcome the epidemiological challenge facing Europe in February and March 2020 necessitated an expansion of state coercive power unimaginable prior to the pandemic. This began with generalised and indiscriminate measures, namely lockdowns. But as the tools became more refined, the locus of coercion moved from geographical space to individual bodies. The creation of apps to identify the ill and then the subsequent enforcement of vaccines through those same apps pushed the nature of enforcement from being general to particular, from being concerned with society at large to being targeted at individuals. As this evolution in COVID-19 policy took place, so too did the tension between the interests of individuals and society grow. For most of the pandemic this tension did not produce significant policy differences. However, in the final act, the debate around vaccine enforcement brought these two impulses of liberal democratic societies to a head. As nations adopted divergent policies to encourage or coerce late-stage vaccine uptake, they revealed how far political communities were willing to go in bringing an end to this devastating crisis.

References

Achard, C. (2022). Le travail social en France au défi de la crise sanitaire. Ruptures, permanences et (dis)continuités. *Écrire le social, 4*(1), 54–65. https://doi.org/10.3917/esra.004.0054

Aitkenhead, E., Clements, J., Lumley, J., Muir, R., Redgrave, H., & Skidmore, M. (2022). *Policing the pandemic.* The Police Foundation. https://www.police-foundation.org.uk/2017/wp-content/uploads/2010/10/policing_the_pandemic_final.pdf

Armingeon, K., de la Porte, C., Heins, E., & Sacchi, S. (2022). Voices from the past: Economic and political vulnerabilities in the making of next generation EU. *Comparative European Politics, 20*(2), 144–165. https://doi.org/10.1057/s41295-022-00277-6

Bae, Y. S., Kim, K. H., Choi, S. W., Ko, T., Jeong, C. W., Cho, B. L., Kim, M. S., & Kang, E. K. (2020). Information technology–based management of clinically healthy COVID-19 patients: Lessons from a living and treatment support center operated by Seoul national university hospital. *Journal of Medical Internet Research, 22*(6), e19938. https://doi.org/10.2196/19938

Baraniuk, C. (2021). Covid-19: How the UK vaccine rollout delivered success, so far. *BMJ, 372*, n421. https://doi.org/10.1136/bmj.n421

Béguin, F. (2020). Covid-19: le port du masque obligatoire à Paris et dans la petite couronne. *Le Monde.fr*. Retrieved September 27, 2022, from https://www.lemonde.fr/planete/article/2020/08/27/port-du-masque-21-departements-classes-en-rouge-objectif-de-1-million-de-tests-les-principales-annonces-de-jean-castex_6050094_3244.html.

Bellier, U. (2020). StopCovid: quatre mois après son lancement, une appli à la peine, maintenue sans grande conviction. *Le Monde.fr*. Retrieved September 21, 2022, from https://www.lemonde.fr/pixels/article/2020/10/03/stopcovid-quatre-mois-apres-son-lancement-une-appli-a-la-peine-maintenue-sans-grande-conviction_6054604_4408996.html.

Bendali, Z., Challier, R., Sudda, M. D., Fillieule, O., & Aldrin, P. (2019). Le mouvement des Gilets jaunes: un apprentissage en pratique(s) de la politique ? *Politix, 128*(4), 143–177. https://doi.org/10.3917/pox.128.0143

Berardi, C., Antonini, M., Genie, M. G., Cotugno, G., Lanteri, A., Melia, A., & Paolucci, F. (2020). The COVID-19 pandemic in Italy: Policy and technology impact on health and non-health outcomes. *Health Policy and Technology, 9*(4), 454–487. https://doi.org/10.1016/j.hlpt.2020.08.019

Bergeron, H., Borraz, O., Castel, P., & Dedieu, F. (2020). *Covid-19: une crise organisationnelle*. Presses de Sciences Po. https://doi.org/10.3917/scpo.berge.2020.01

Blasimme, A., Ferretti, A., & Vayena, E. (2021). Digital contact tracing against COVID-19 in Europe: Current features and ongoing developments. *Frontiers in Digital Health* 3. Retrieved September 21, 2022, from https://www.frontiersin.org/articles/10.3389/fdgth.2021.660823.

Boin, A., & Lodge, M. (2021). Responding to the COVID-19 crisis: A principled or pragmatist approach? *Journal of European Public Policy, 28*(8), 1131–1152. https://doi.org/10.1080/13501763.2021.1942155

Bonini, C., Bocci, M., Ciriaco, T., Foschini, G., Mensurati, M., Tonacci, F., Visetti, G., & Zunino, C. (2020). L'Ora Zero. L'inchiesta Sulla Notte in Cui Il Covid Si è Preso l'Italia. *La Repubblica*.

Bosa, I., Castelli, A., Castelli, M., Ciani, O., Compagni, A., Galizzi, M. M., Garofano, M., Ghislandi, S., Giannoni, M., Marini, G., & Vainieri, M. (2022). Response to COVID-19: Was Italy (un)prepared? *Health Economics, Policy and Law, 17*(1), 1–13. https://doi.org/10.1017/S1744133121000141

Bull, M. (2021). The Italian Government response to Covid-19 and the making of a prime minister. *Contemporary Italian Politics, 13*(2), 149–165. https://doi.org/10.1080/23248823.2021.1914453

Cantillon, B., Seeleib-Kaiser, M., & van der Veen, R. (2021). The COVID-19 crisis and policy responses by continental European welfare states. *Social Policy & Administration, 55*(2), 326–338. https://doi.org/10.1111/spol.12715

Capano, G., Howlett, M., Jarvis, D. S. L., Ramesh, M., & Goyal, N. (2020). Mobilizing policy (in)capacity to fight COVID-19: Understanding variations

in state responses. *Policy and Society, 39*(3), 285–308. https://doi.org/10.1080/14494035.2020.1787628
Celotto, A. (2020). *La quarantena dei diritti. Come una pandemia può sospendere le nostre libertà*. Historica Edizioni.
Chirumbolo, S. (2021). Vaccination hesitancy and the "Myth" on mRNA-based vaccines in Italy in the COVID-19 era: Does urgency meet major safety criteria? *Journal of Medical Virology, 93*(7), 4049–4053. https://doi.org/10.1002/jmv.26922
Christie, B. (2021). Covid-19: Vaccine passports approved in Scotland despite criticism. *BMJ, 374*, n2229. https://doi.org/10.1136/bmj.n2229
Connolly, K. (2020a). Germany to impose new Coronavirus rules amid record rise in cases. *The Guardian*. Retrieved September 27, 2022, from https://www.theguardian.com/world/2020/oct/28/germany-set-to-impose-new-coronavirus-rules-amid-record-rise-in-cases.
Connolly, K. (2020b). Germany to impose tighter Covid rules after highest daily death rate. *The Guardian*. Retrieved September 27, 2022, from https://www.theguardian.com/world/2020/nov/25/germany-to-decide-next-round-of-covid-restrictions.
Cuzzocrea, A. (2021). Green Pass obbligatorio per tutti approvato in Cdm. Dal 15 ottobre, stipendio sospeso dopo 5 giorni per chi entra senza. *la Repubblica*. Retrieved October 27, 2022, from https://www.repubblica.it/politica/2021/09/16/news/green_pass_governo_cabina_regia_cdm_lavoro-318034459/.
Davies, N. G., Barnard, R. C., Jarvis, C. I., Russell, T. W., Semple, M. G., Jit, M., John, W., & Edmunds. (2021). Association of Tiered restrictions and a second lockdown with COVID-19 deaths and hospital admissions in England: A modelling study. *The Lancet. Infectious Diseases, 21*(4), 482–492. https://doi.org/10.1016/S1473-3099(20)30984-1
Department of Health and Social Care. (2020). More targeted action in local areas to curb the spread of Coronavirus. *GOV.UK*. Retrieved September 23, 2022, from https://www.gov.uk/government/news/more-targeted-action-in-local-areas-to-curb-the-spread-of-coronavirus.
Di Bartolomeo, G., D'Imperio, P., & Felici, F. (2022). The fiscal response to the Italian COVID-19 crisis: A counterfactual analysis. *Journal of Macroeconomics, 73*, 103447. https://doi.org/10.1016/j.jmacro.2022.103447
Dumiot, V., Sarlandie, C., & de La Robertie. (2021). Faire face à la crise: la Covid-19, un nouveau défi pour l'efficacité de l'action publique. *Gestion et management public, 94*(4), 37–48. https://doi.org/10.3917/gmp.094.0037
Durovic, A. (2019). The French elections of 2017: Shaking the disease? *West European Politics, 42*(7), 1487–1503. https://doi.org/10.1080/01402382.2019.1591043

Excler, J.-L., Saville, M., Berkley, S., & Kim, J. H. (2021). Vaccine development for emerging infectious diseases. *Nature Medicine, 27*(4), 591–600. https://doi.org/10.1038/s41591-021-01301-0

Faye, O. (2020). Reconfinement de toute la France dès jeudi soir, écoles ouvertes, attestation « pour ceux qui travaillent »... les pistes pour endiguer l'épidémie. *Le Monde.fr*. Retrieved September 27, 2022, from https://www.lemonde.fr/politique/article/2020/10/28/covid-19-emmanuel-macron-reflechit-a-imposer-un-reconfinement-au-niveau-national_6057621_823448.html.

Freedman, L. (2020). Strategy for a pandemic: The UK and COVID-19. *Survival, 62*(3), 25–76. https://doi.org/10.1080/00396338.2020.1763610

Gallagher, J. (2020). Coronavirus: Visiting people at home banned in parts of Northern England. *BBC News*. Retrieved September 23, 2022, from https://www.bbc.com/news/uk-53602362.

Gatinois, C. (2021). Covid-19: le gouvernement sous le feu des critiques après la mise en place des nouvelles règles de confinement. *Le Monde.fr*. Retrieved September 27, 2022, from https://www.lemonde.fr/planete/article/2021/03/21/covid-19-le-gouvernement-sous-le-feu-des-critiques-apres-la-mise-en-place-des-confinements-locaux_6073915_3244.html.

Gatto, M., Bertuzzo, E., Mari, L., Miccoli, S., Carraro, L., Casagrandi, R., & Rinaldo, A. (2020). Spread and dynamics of the COVID-19 epidemic in Italy: Effects of emergency containment measures. *Proceedings of the National Academy of Sciences, 117*(19), 10484–10491. https://doi.org/10.1073/pnas.2004978117

Giuffrida, A. (2019). Italy's Matteo Salvini calls for fresh elections as coalition fractures. *The Guardian*. Retrieved September 6, 2022, from https://www.theguardian.com/world/2019/aug/09/italys-matteo-salvini-calls-for-fresh-elections-as-coalition-fractures.

Givord, P., & Silhol, J. (2020). *Confinement: Des Conséquences Économiques Inégales Selon Les Ménages*. Insee. https://www.insee.fr/fr/statistiques/4801313#consulter

Gleißner, W., Follert, F., Daumann, F., & Leibbrand, F. (2021). EU's ordering of COVID-19 vaccine doses: Political decision-making under uncertainty. *International Journal of Environmental Research and Public Health, 18*(4), 2169. https://doi.org/10.3390/ijerph18042169

Gopinath, G. (2020). The great lockdown: Worst economic downturn since the great depression. *IMF Blog*. Retrieved September 27, 2022, from https://blogs.imf.org/2020/04/14/the-great-lockdown-worst-economic-downturn-since-the-great-depression/.

Hale, T., Angrist, N., Goldszmidt, R., Kira, B., Petherick, A., Phillips, T., ... & Tatlow, H. (2021). A global panel database of pandemic policies (Oxford COVID-19 Government Response Tracker). *Nature Human Behaviour, 5*(4), 529–538.

Hansard. (2021). Vaccine passports - Hansard - UK Parliament. Retrieved October 31, 2022, from https://hansard.parliament.uk//commons/2021-03-15/debates/8D4B8782-7BA5-475B-A48A-370859B78209/VaccinePassports.

Hart, R. (2021). Vaccine passports spur explosion in vaccinations—and protests—as Europe cracks down on vaccine holdouts. *Forbes*. Retrieved October 25, 2022, from https://www.forbes.com/sites/roberthart/2021/07/27/explosion-in-vaccinations-and-protests-follow-health-pass-announcements-as-europe-cracks-down-on-vaccine-holdouts/.

Hartley, N. (2020). Coronavirus: Wales' first local lockdown starts in Caerphilly. *BBC News*. Retrieved September 23, 2022, from https://www.bbc.com/news/uk-wales-54064915.

Health and Social Care Committee. (2021). *Coronavirus: Lessons Learned to Date, Sixth Report of the Health and Social Care Committee and Third Report of the Science and Technology Committee of Session 2021–22*. House of Commons. HC 92. https://committees.parliament.uk/publications/7496/documents/78687/default/

Hinterlang, N., Moyen, S., Röhe, O., & Stähler, N. (2023). Gauging the effects of the German COVID-19 fiscal stimulus package. *European Economic Review, 154*, 104407. https://doi.org/10.1016/j.euroecorev.2023.104407

Hitti, F. L., & Weissman, D. (2021). Debunking mRNA vaccine misconceptions—An overview for medical professionals. *The American Journal of Medicine, 134*(6), 703–704. https://doi.org/10.1016/j.amjmed.2021.02.004

Holt, L., & Murray, L. (2022). Children and Covid 19 in the UK. *Children's Geographies, 20*(4), 487–494. https://doi.org/10.1080/14733285.2021.1921699

Jones, E. (2019). Populism in Europe: What scholarship tells us. *Survival, 61*(4), 7–30. https://doi.org/10.1080/00396338.2019.1637125

Karaivanov, A., Kim, D., Lu, S. E., & Shigeoka, H. (2022). COVID-19 vaccination mandates and vaccine uptake. *Nature Human Behaviour*, 1–10. https://doi.org/10.1038/s41562-022-01363-1.

Kim, M. (2020). South Korea is watching quarantined citizens with a smartphone app. *MIT Technology Review*. Retrieved September 21, 2022, from https://www.technologyreview.com/2020/03/06/905459/coronavirus-south-korea-smartphone-app-quarantine/.

Kondylakis, H., Katehakis, D. G., Kouroubali, A., Logothetidis, F., Triantafyllidis, A., Kalamaras, I., Votis, K., & Tzovaras, D. (2020). COVID-19 mobile apps: A systematic review of the literature. *Journal of Medical Internet Research, 22*(12), e23170. https://doi.org/10.2196/23170

Kuhlmann, S., Hellström, M., Ramberg, U., & Reiter, R. (2021). Tracing divergence in crisis governance: Responses to the COVID-19 pandemic in France, Germany and Sweden Compared. *International Review of Administrative Sciences, 87*(3), 556–575. https://doi.org/10.1177/0020852320979359

Lambert, A., Girard, V., & Guéraut, E. (2021). Socio-economic impacts of COVID-19 on working mothers in France. *Frontiers in Sociology, 6*, 732580. https://doi.org/10.3389/fsoc.2021.732580

Le Coz, P. (2021). Éthique et vaccination. *Études, 4286*(10), 35–44. https://doi.org/10.3917/etu.4286.0035

Ledford, H., Cyranoski, D., & Van Noorden, R. (2020). The UK has approved a COVID vaccine—here's what scientists now want to know. *Nature, 588*(7837), 205–206. https://doi.org/10.1038/d41586-020-03441-8

Lepelletier, P. (2020). Blanquer annonce la fermeture des écoles «au moins jusqu'aux vacances de printemps». *Le Figaro*. Retrieved January 31, 2022, from https://www.lefigaro.fr/politique/blanquer-annonce-la-fermeture-des-ecoles-au-moins-jusqu-aux-vacances-de-printemps-20200313.

MacDonald, N. E. (2015). Vaccine hesitancy: Definition, scope and determinants. *Vaccine, 33*(34), 4161–4164. https://doi.org/10.1016/j.vaccine.2015.04.036

Mahase, E. (2020). Covid-19: Experts recommend two week circuit break to reduce transmission in the UK. *BMJ, 371*, m4038. https://doi.org/10.1136/bmj.m4038

Manica, M., Guzzetta, G., Riccardo, F., Valenti, A., Poletti, P., Marziano, V., et al. (2021). Impact of tiered restrictions on human activities and the epidemiology of the second wave of COVID-19 in Italy. *Nature Communications, 12*(1), 4570. https://doi.org/10.1038/s41467-021-24832-z

Marziano, V., Guzzetta, G., Rondinone, B. M., Boccuni, F., Riccardo, F., Bella, A., Poletti, P., Pezzotti, P., Brusaferro, S., Rezza, G., Iavicoli, S., Ajelli, M., & Merler, S. (2021). Retrospective analysis of the Italian exit strategy from COVID-19 lockdown. *Proceedings of the National Academy of Sciences, 118*(4), e2019617118. https://doi.org/10.1073/pnas.2019617118

Mathieu, E., Ritchie, H., Ortiz-Ospina, E., Roser, M., Hasell, J., Appel, C., Giattino, C., & Rodés-Guirao, L. (2021). A global database of COVID-19 vaccinations. *Nature Human Behaviour, 5*(7), 947–953. https://doi.org/10.1038/s41562-021-01122-8

McConnell, A., & Stark, A. (2021). Understanding policy responses to COVID-19: The stars haven't fallen from the sky for scholars of public policy. *Journal of European Public Policy, 28*(8), 1115–1130. https://doi.org/10.1080/13501763.2021.1942518

McCormack, J. (2022). Covid-19: NI to scrap vaccine passports in pubs and restaurants. *BBC News*. Retrieved Ocotber 28, 2022, from https://www.bbc.com/news/uk-northern-ireland-60044349.

Mégarbane, B., Bourasset, F., & Scherrmann, J.-M. (2021). Is curfew effective in limiting SARS-CoV-2 progression? An evaluation in France based on epidemiokinetic analyses. *Journal of General Internal Medicine, 36*(9), 2731–2738. https://doi.org/10.1007/s11606-021-06953-9

Mei, C. (2020). Policy style, consistency and the effectiveness of the policy mix in China's fight against COVID-19. *Policy and Society, 39*(3), 309–325. https://doi.org/10.1080/14494035.2020.1787627

Mills, M. C., & Rüttenauer, T. (2022). The effect of mandatory COVID-19 certificates on vaccine uptake: Synthetic-control modelling of six countries. *The Lancet Public Health, 7*(1), e15–e22. https://doi.org/10.1016/S2468-2667(21)00273-5

Mitze, T., Kosfeld, R., Rode, J., & Wälde, K. (2020). Face masks considerably reduce COVID-19 cases in Germany. *Proceedings of the National Academy of Sciences, 117*(51), 32293–32301. https://doi.org/10.1073/pnas.2015954117

Moreira, A., Léon, M., Moscarola, F. C., & Roumpakis, A. (2021). In the eye of the storm…again! Social policy responses to COVID-19 in Southern Europe. *Social Policy & Administration, 55*(2), 339–357. https://doi.org/10.1111/spol.12681

Morphet, J. (2021). *The impact of COVID-19 on devolution* (1st ed.). Bristol University Press. https://doi.org/10.2307/j.ctv1k03sjr

Morris, S. (2020). Wales to go into national two-week "firebreak" Covid lockdown. *The Guardian*. Retrieved September 23, 2022, from https://www.theguardian.com/world/2020/oct/19/wales-to-go-into-national-firebreak-covid-lockdown

Morris, S. (2021). Wales introduces compulsory Covid pass for nightclubs and sports events. *The Guardian*. Retrieved October 28, 2022, from https://www.theguardian.com/politics/2021/oct/05/wales-introduces-compulsory-covid-pass-for-nightclubs-and-sports-events.

Murphy, S., Walker, P., & Butler, P. (2020). Tighter restrictions introduced in Bolton to curb Coronavirus. *The Guardian*. Retrieved September 23, 2022, from https://www.theguardian.com/world/2020/sep/08/tighter-restrictions-to-be-introduced-in-bolton-to-curb-coronavirus.

Naumann, E., Möhring, K., Reifenscheid, M., Wenz, A., Rettig, T., Lehrer, R., Krieger, U., Juhl, S., Friedel, S., Fikel, M., Cornesse, C., & Blom, A. G. (2020). COVID-19 policies in Germany and their social, political, and psychological consequences. *European Policy Analysis, 6*(2), 191–202. https://doi.org/10.1002/epa2.1091

Navarre, C., Roy, P., Ledochowski, S., Fabre, M., Esparcieux, A., Issartel, B., Dutertre, M., Blanc-Gruyelle, A.-L., Suy, F., Adelaide, L., Pariset, C., Kisterman, J. P., Champagne, H., & Saison, J. (2021). Determinants of COVID-19 vaccine hesitancy in French hospitals. *Infectious Diseases Now, 51*(8), 647–653. https://doi.org/10.1016/j.idnow.2021.08.004

Neville, S., Bradshaw, T., & Warrell, H. (2020). UK starts to build second contact tracing app. *Financial Times*.

Oliani, F., Savoia, A., Gallo, G., Tiwana, N., Letzgus, M., Gentiloni, F., Piatti, A., Chiappa, L., Bisesti, A., Laquintana, D., & Castaldi, S. (2022). Italy's rollout of COVID-19 vaccinations: The crucial contribution of the first experimental mass vaccination site in Lombardy. *Vaccine, 40*(10), 1397–1403. https://doi.org/10.1016/j.vaccine.2022.01.059

Oltermann, P. (2022). Germany's plan for vaccination mandate losing momentum. *The Guardian*. Retrieved October 27, 2022, from https://www.theguardian.com/world/2022/feb/14/germany-plan-general-covid-vaccination-mandate-losing-momentum-bundestag-debate-march.

Or, Z., Gandré, C., Zaleski, I. D., & Steffen, M. (2021). France's response to the Covid-19 pandemic: Between a rock and a hard place. *Health Economics, Policy and Law, 1–13*. https://doi.org/10.1017/S1744133121000165

Pallas, C. (2022). Alerte ! Soignants…. *VST - Vie sociale et traitements, 154*(2), 37–42. https://doi.org/10.3917/vst.154.0037

Perez, S. A., & Matsaganis, M. (2018). The political economy of austerity in Southern Europe. *New Political Economy, 23*(2), 192–207. https://doi.org/10.1080/13563467.2017.1370445

Pierre, J. (2020). Nudges against pandemics: Sweden's COVID-19 containment strategy in perspective. *Policy and Society, 39*(3), 478–493.

Reynaud, F. (2020). Covid-19: ce que change TousAntiCovid, la nouvelle application de suivi des cas contacts. *Le Monde.fr*. Retrieved September 21, 2022, from https://www.lemonde.fr/pixels/article/2020/10/22/covid-19-ce-que-change-tousanticovid-la-nouvelle-application-de-suivi-des-cas-contacts_6057003_4408996.html.

Richards, D., Warner, S., Smith, M. J., & Coyle, D. (2022). Crisis and state transformation: Covid-19, levelling up and the UK's incoherent state. *Cambridge Journal of Regions, Economy and Society, rsac038*. https://doi.org/10.1093/cjres/rsac038

Rotshild, V., Hirsh-Raccah, B., Miskin, I., Muszkat, M., & Matok, I. (2021). Comparing the clinical efficacy of COVID-19 vaccines: A systematic review and network meta-analysis. *Scientific Reports, 11*(1), 22777. https://doi.org/10.1038/s41598-021-02321-z

Sanfelici, M. (2020). The Italian response to the COVID-19 crisis: Lessons learned and future direction in social development. *The International Journal of Community and Social Development, 2*(2), 191–210. https://doi.org/10.1177/2516602620936037

Sawyer, M. (2021). Economic Policies and the Coronavirus Crisis in the UK. *Review of Political Economy, 33*(3), 414–431. https://doi.org/10.1080/09538259.2021.1897254

Schomaker, R. M., Hack, M., & Mandry, A.-K. (2021). The EU's reaction in the first wave of the Covid-19 pandemic between centralisation and decentralisation, Formality and Informality. *Journal of European Public Policy, 28*(8), 1278–1298. https://doi.org/10.1080/13501763.2021.1942153

Schwarzinger, M., Watson, V., Arwidson, P., Alla, F., & Luchini, S. (2021). COVID-19 vaccine hesitancy in a representative working-age population in France: A survey experiment based on vaccine characteristics. *The Lancet Public Health, 6*(4), e210–e221. https://doi.org/10.1016/S2468-2667(21)00012-8

Scottish Government. (2020). Restrictions introduced across West of Scotland. Retrieved September 23, 2022, from http://www.gov.scot/news/restrictions-introduced-across-west-of-scotland/.

Sebastiani, G., Massa, M., & Riboli, E. (2020). Covid-19 epidemic in Italy: Evolution, projections and impact of government measures. *European Journal of Epidemiology, 35*(4), 341–345. https://doi.org/10.1007/s10654-020-00631-6

Selby, J. (2020). NHS Start building second contact tracing app days after tests began on first. *inews.co.uk*. https://inews.co.uk/news/coronavirus-latest-nhs-build-second-covid-19-contact-tracing-app-with-apple-google-426092 (September 21, 2022).

Sénat. (2020). Deuxième rapport d'étape sur la mise en oeuvre de l'état d'urgence sanitaire. Commission des Lois. https://www.senat.fr/fileadmin/Fichiers/Images/commission/lois/MI_Covid19/Mission_suivi_urgence_Covid-19_Deuxieme_rapport_etape.pdf

Sibony, A.-L. (2020). The UK COVID-19 response: A behavioural irony? *European Journal of Risk Regulation, 11*(2), 350–357. https://doi.org/10.1017/err.2020.22

Simancas-Racines, D., Franco, J. V. A., Guerra, C. V., Felix, M. L., Hidalgo, R., & Martinez-Zapata, M. J. (2017). Vaccines for the common cold. *The Cochrane Database of Systematic Reviews, 2017*(5), CD002190. https://doi.org/10.1002/14651858.CD002190.pub5

Singh, H. J., Leon, D. C., & Yap, K. (2020). Mobile health apps that help with COVID-19 management: Scoping review. *JMIR Nursing, 3*(1), e20596. https://doi.org/10.2196/20596

Slama, S. (2022). Le pass sanitaire, instrument conjoncturel ou révélateur du futur ? *Journal du Droit de la Santé et de l'Assurance - Maladie (JDSAM), 31*(1), 97–99. https://doi.org/10.3917/jdsam.221.0097

Sliman, G. (2021). Impact d'un an de Covid. *Les Tribunes de la santé, 68*(2), 37–50. https://doi.org/10.3917/sevel.068.0037

Snowden, F. (2019). *Epidemics and society*. Yale University Press. https://doi.org/10.2307/j.ctvqc6gg5

Sobolewska, M., & Ford, R. (2020). *Brexitland: Identity, diversity and the reshaping of British politics*. Cambridge University Press. https://doi.org/10.1017/9781108562485

Spitale, G., Biller-Andorno, N., & Germani, F. (2022). Concerns around opposition to the green pass in Italy: Social listening analysis by using a mixed meth-

ods approach. *Journal of Medical Internet Research, 24*(2), e34385. https://doi.org/10.2196/34385
Terpstra, J., de Maillard, J., Salet, R., & Roché, S. (2021). Policing the Corona crisis: A comparison between France and the Netherlands. *International Journal of Police Science & Management, 23*(2), 168–181. https://doi.org/10.1177/1461355720980772
Timmers, T., Janssen, L., Stohr, J., Murk, J. L., & Berrevoets, M. A. H. (2020). Using eHealth to support COVID-19 education, self-assessment, and symptom monitoring in the Netherlands: Observational Study. *JMIR mHealth and uHealth, 8*(6), e19822. https://doi.org/10.2196/19822
Tooze, J. A. (2018). *Crashed: How a decade of financial crises changed the world.* Allen Lane.
Torjesen, I. (2020). Covid-19: Should the UK be aiming for elimination? *BMJ, 370*, m3071. https://doi.org/10.1136/bmj.m3071
Tregoning, J. S., Flight, K. E., Higham, S. L., Wang, Z., & Pierce, B. F. (2021). Progress of the COVID-19 vaccine effort: Viruses, vaccines and variants versus efficacy, effectiveness and escape. *Nature Reviews Immunology, 21*(10), 626–636. https://doi.org/10.1038/s41577-021-00592-1
Triggle, N. (2020a, June 30). Leicester lockdown tightened as Coronavirus cases rise. *BBC News.* Retrieved September 23, 2022, from https://www.bbc.com/news/uk-england-leicestershire-53229371.
Triggle, N. (2020b, August 12). Covid-19 vaccine: First person receives Pfizer Jab in UK. *BBC News.* Retrieved October 19, 2022, from https://www.bbc.com/news/uk-55227325.
Uddin, M. N., & Roni, M. A. (2021). Challenges of storage and stability of mRNA-based COVID-19 vaccines. *Vaccines, 9*(9), 1033. https://doi.org/10.3390/vaccines9091033
Ungerer, J. (2020). Coronavirus measures in private law: Comparison of Moratoria in the United Kingdom and Germany. *Oxford University Comparative Law Forum.* Retrieved September 12, 2022, from https://ouclf.law.ox.ac.uk/coronavirus-measures-in-private-law-comparison-of-moratoria-in-the-united-kingdom-and-germany/.
Untersinger, M. (2020). 'StopCovid, une application de traçage passée en deux mois de l'idée dystopique à l'Assemblée'. *Le Monde.fr.* Retrieved September 21, 2022, from https://www.lemonde.fr/pixels/article/2020/04/27/stopcovid-une-application-de-tracage-passee-en-deux-mois-de-l-idee-dystopique-a-l-assemblee_6037924_4408996.html.
Vampa, D. (2021). COVID-19 and territorial policy dynamics in Western Europe: Comparing France, Spain, Italy, Germany, and the United Kingdom. *Publius: The Journal of Federalism, 51*(4), 601–626. https://doi.org/10.1093/publius/pjab017

Walter, S., Ray, A., & Redeker, N. (2020). Distributive conflict and interest group preferences in deficit countries. In S. Walter, A. Ray, & N. Redeker (Eds.), *The politics of bad options: Why the Eurozone's problems have been so hard to resolve*. Oxford University Press. https://doi.org/10.1093/oso/9780198857013.003.0003

Warren, S., Richards, D., Coyle, D., & Smith, M. J. (2021). English devolution and the Covid-19 pandemic: Governing dilemmas in the shadow of the treasury. *The Political Quarterly, 92*(2), 321–330. https://doi.org/10.1111/1467-923X.12989

Warren, G. W., & Lofstedt, R. (2022). COVID-19 vaccine rollout management and communication in Europe: One year on. *Journal of Risk Research, 25*(9), 1098–1117. https://doi.org/10.1080/13669877.2021.2001674

WHO. (2020a). *Coronavirus Disease (COVID-19), Situation report – 102*. World Health Organization, Geneva. https://www.who.int/docs/default-source/coronaviruse/situation-reports/20200501-covid-19-sitrep.pdf?sfvrsn=742f4a18_4.

WHO. (2020b). *Weekly epidemiological update - 29 December 2020*. World Health Organization, Geneva. https://www.who.int/publications/m/item/weekly-epidemiological-update%2D%2D-29-december-2020.

Wiggan, J., & Grover, C.. (2022). The politics of job retention schemes in Britain: The Coronavirus job retention scheme and the temporary short time working compensation scheme. *Critical Social Policy*. https://doi.org/10.1177/02610183221086515.

Zamberg, I., Manzano, S., Posfay-Barbe, K., Windisch, O., Agoritsas, T., & Schiffer, E. (2020). A mobile health platform to disseminate validated institutional measurements during the COVID-19 outbreak: Utilization-focused evaluation study. *JMIR Public Health and Surveillance, 6*(2), e18668. https://doi.org/10.2196/18668

Zhang, N.-N., Li, X.-F., Deng, Y.-Q., Zhao, H., Huang, Y.-J., Yang, G., Huang, W.-J., et al. (2020). A thermostable mRNA vaccine against COVID-19. *Cell, 182*(5), 1271–1283.e16. https://doi.org/10.1016/j.cell.2020.07.024

CHAPTER 3

Survey Design and Data

Simona Guglielmi, *Piotr Marzec*, *Elias Naumann*, *and Andrew Zola*

Introduction

The COVID-19 pandemic prompted governments to devise strategies to curb the virus's spread but also to address its potential impacts for public health, the economy, and democratic systems. Research on the societal impact of the pandemic was crucial for policymakers to make informed decisions during the crisis (Adams-Prassl et al., 2020; Arpino et al., 2021;

S. Guglielmi
Department of Social and Political Sciences, University of Milan, Milano, Italy
e-mail: simona.guglielmi@unimi.it

P. Marzec
Institute for Social and Economic Research, University of Essex, Colchester, UK
e-mail: p.marzec@essex.ac.uk

E. Naumann (✉)
GESIS Leibniz Institute for the Social Sciences, Mannheim, Germany
e-mail: Elias.Naumann@gesis.org

A. Zola
Centre for Research on Social Inequalities (CRIS), CNRS, Sciences Po, Paris, France
e-mail: andrew.zola@sciencespo.fr

E. Naumann et al. (eds.), *Social Life during COVID-19 in France, Germany, Italy and the UK*,
https://doi.org/10.1007/978-3-031-99349-7_3

Möhring et al., 2021). In the field of social sciences, however, non-pharmaceutical measures taken to control the spread of the virus directly limited methods available for collecting survey data.

Prior to the pandemic, most surveys that aimed to chart social change relied on probability samples and face-to-face, interviewer-administered surveys, which were often gathered at long intervals of one to two years. As such, with a quickly evolving situation at the start of 2020, a higher frequency of data collection was needed. Also, contact restrictions made in-person survey administration nearly impossible and many surveys were forced to switch to self-administration. To quickly gather the information needed, social scientists increased data collection by designing surveys (Busemeyer, 2023; Fetzer et al., 2021) with harmonised questionnaires, usually online. However, these large and sometimes international data-collection projects usually did not rely on probability-based samples. Pre-existing or pre-planned survey projects also supported research on the pandemics' consequences by including specifically designed question modules in their questionnaires (Kapteyn et al., 2020; Kühne et al., 2020). However, these were often national datasets.

Our comparative study builds on these approaches by utilising four country-specific panel surveys, three of which are grounded in pre-existing longitudinal protocols. Each of these survey programmes increased their data-collection frequency during the COVID-19 pandemic to track short-term changes. However, a key trade-off of our approach lies in the reliance on post-harmonisation to ensure comparability across countries' results. In this chapter, we present the four datasets and detail the post-harmonisation with regard to the field periods and the measurement of core concepts.

The Surveys in Four Countries: Study Design

France: Coping with COVID-19 (CoCo) and Étude Longitudinal par Internet pour les Sciences SOciales (ELIPSS)

The *Coping with COVID-19* survey (*CoCo*: Recchi et al., 2021) was designed to capture the social experiences from the onset of the pandemic in France (Recchi et al., 2020). For this, the study relied on the pre-existing *Étude Longitudinal par Internet pour les Sciences Sociales* (*ELIPSS*), a probability-based online panel of individuals. This sample is representative of the French metropolitan population aged between 18 and 79 years with fixed addresses and working knowledge of the French language. *ELIPSS* has been operating since 2012 at Sciences Po and is similar to other probability-based online panels in Europe, including the *LISS* panel in the Netherlands, the *German Internet Panel*, and the *GESIS* panel in Germany (Blom et al., 2016).

In its pilot phase from 2012 to 2016, *ELIPSS* began with a sample of 1039 respondents drawn from a random sample of 4500 households included in the 2011 census, conducted by the *Institut national de la statistique et des études économiques* (INSEE). One individual within the household aged between 18 and 75 years old was then chosen to be contacted. Recruitment initially took place via postal outreach, which one-half of those contacted offered a €10 incentive as an experimental recruitment design. Non-responding individuals were followed up through letters, telephone calls, and in-person visits. Recruitment was expanded after this pilot phase, and in 2016 a further 2500 respondents were added to the panel. All respondents recruited in 2012 and 2016 were offered a tablet with 3G or 4G network connection for responding to the questionnaires. This ensured that the panel avoided bias related to incomplete internet coverage (Couper, 2000) in a population where about 10% of households did not have internet connection as of 2019 (Crédoc, 2019). Although no direct financial incentive was offered for questionnaire responses, participants were allowed to keep their tablets. Two stratified recruitment rounds have been conducted since this point, in 2020 and 2023, which ensured the panel's ongoing neutral representation of the French metropolitan population.

By 2020, respondents engaged in approximately ten questionnaires annually, each requiring about 20 minutes to complete. These efforts yielded an average response rate (RR) of around 80%. Most *ELIPSS* questionnaires are open for two to four weeks, with reminder emails sent to non-respondents. Detailed socio-demographic and economic information about respondents is gathered annually by ELIPSS. The majority of other surveys are constructed by external researchers working on specific projects.

The *CoCo* project launched in March 2020 as a targeted study using the *ELIPSS* panel. It was a collaborative effect between the Center for Research on Social Inequalities and the Centre de Données Socio-Politiques, both affiliated with Sciences Po, and received funding from the Agence Nationale de la Recherche (ANR).

A total of 1404 panellists were invited to participate in the project, through eight waves administered between March 2020 and April 2021 during the most severe epidemiological crises in France: five in the spring of 2020 during and after the first lockdown, two in the autumn of 2020 before and during the second lockdown, and one in the spring of 2021 during the third lockdown. The questionnaires were open for one week, with two reminder messages sent during each wave. Each round of the study asked core questions focusing on objective and subjective health, employment status and location, and opinions about COVID-19 policies. These core inquiries were supplemented by rotating thematic questions that provided deeper insight on topics such as health and wellbeing, work practices, household relations and division of labour, and socio-political opinions. Participation rates varied between 67% in fourth wave and 76% in the first wave, with the lower participation in the late spring of 2020 attributed to the high frequency of surveys conducted in that period.

The sample of respondents marginally underrepresents individuals living in single households, in households in the Paris region, in households with individuals aged over 60 and under 25 years, and individuals with few qualifications. To address these biases, the surveys contain post-stratification weights calculated using information taken from the census on age, gender, highest level of education, area of residence (ZEAT), and nationality.

Germany: The Mannheim Corona Study (MCS) and the German Internet Panel (GIP)

The German data are taken from the *Mannheim Corona Study* (*MCS*) and its parent study, the German Internet Panel (*GIP*). The *MCS* is a longitudinal, probability-based online survey with a daily-rotating panel design, conducted between 20 March and 10 July 2020. It draws its foundation from the *GIP*, a probability-based online panel representing Germany's general population.

The *GIP* was first implemented in 2012 and has undergone three recruitment rounds, in 2012, 2014, and 2018 (Blom et al., 2016; Cornesse et al., 2022). Eligible respondents were drawn from population registers, with the target population comprising individuals aged 16–75 years who resided in Germany at the time of recruitment. Respondents were contacted through in-person visits in 2012 and 2014, and by post in 2018. Those who agreed to participate were invited to complete bi-monthly *GIP* surveys, conducted exclusively online. In the first two recruitment rounds, sample units without internet access were provided with equipment to participate in such web surveys (Blom et al., 2016; Cornesse & Schaurer, 2021). The average duration of the standard *GIP* survey waves are 20–25 minutes. Respondents receive a conditional incentive of €4 for each completed questionnaire, with an additional bonus of €10 for completing all six survey waves in a year, or €5 if only one wave is missed. The incentive is credited to their panel accounts and paid out twice a year as online vouchers, bank transfers, or charitable donations, depending on the panel member's preference. *GIP* members officially remain members of the panel unless they explicitly opt out. They can rejoin the surveys at any wave, even after missing consecutive waves.

In September 2012, the *GIP* recruited 1483 respondents, corresponding to a RR of 18.5% at panel registration. The 2014 recruitment round rose to a RR of 21%, adding 3209 respondents to the panel. The final recruitment round in 2018 further increased with rate of 24.1%, adding 2990 respondents. In January 2020, 4575 respondents participated in the final pre-COVID wave of the *GIP*, corresponding to a completion rate of 58.9%. As is common across many other panel studies, respondents drop off over time. The cumulative completion rate of the *GIP* gradually declined from 58.9% in January 2020, to 57.1% in January 2021, registering at 52.2% in January 2022, and finally reached 48.8% in January 2023.

During the early stages of the COVID-19 pandemic in Germany, the *MCS* was deployed to study the societal impact of the pandemic from an interdisciplinary perspective. For the *MCS*, the *GIP* sample was divided into eight random sub-samples (Blom et al., 2020; Cornesse et al., 2022). The first seven sub-samples were then each assigned to a day of the week. Across the following 16 weeks, panel members in these sub-samples were invited via email to participate in a short survey distributed the corresponding allocated day. After receiving the invitation, participants had 48 hours to complete the survey. The eighth sub-sample served as a control group to study the impact of the data-collection process. The average duration of each survey was eight minutes, and respondents received a conditional incentive of €2 on completion of each survey, which was credited to their *GIP* panel accounts.

On average, there were 3419 participants in the *MCS* data collection per week. The average RR was 62.4% across data-collection weeks, whereas the daily RR ranged from 59.2% on Fridays to 65.7% on Mondays (Blom et al., 2020). Because the *MCS* was integrated with the *GIP*, previous *GIP* data were available for the *MCS* sample, which included detailed socio-demographic information. As a result, the regular *GIP* waves during 2020 and subsequent years can be used for comparative analysis.

Although achieving high RRs is important, ensuring the accuracy of data—specifically, how effectively the sample represents the German population—is equally significant. Blom et al. (2020) report that the *MCS* sample contained a low bias compared with distributions from official statistics, namely the German *Mikrozensus*, with regard to age, gender, education, household size, marital status, region, and citizenship. However, non-German citizens were underrepresented in the *MCS*, appearing here at a rate of 3.1% compared with 12.8% in the *Mikrozensus*. In addition, the youngest age group, 16–29 years, and individuals with lower levels of education were slightly underrepresented. The youngest age group appeared at 17.2% in *MCS* vs. 20.9% in *Mikrozensus*, and the proportions of those with lower educational attainments were 26.2% in *MCS* and 31.0% in *Mikrozensus*. Gender, household size, marital status, and geographic region were closely aligned with the distributions in the target population.

The regular *GIP* waves collect data on individual attitudes and preferences that informed political and economic decision-making processes. The *GIP* covers topics such as attitudes towards policies, politics, the welfare state, German and EU politics, health, social inequality, education, employment, and key socio-demographic information. Similarly, the *MCS* maintained a broad interdisciplinary approach, covering topics such as changes to employment and financial situations, childcare arrangements, satisfaction with selected politicians, attitudes towards democratic processes, the frequency of social interactions, and indicators of physical and mental health.

Italy: The ResPOnsE COVID-19 Project

The *ResPOnsE* COVID-19 project (Response of Italian Public Opinion to the COVID-19 Emergency) was launched in March 2020 with the aim of creating a research infrastructure to monitor public opinion during the COVID-19 emergency in Italy. Developed by the spsTREND 'Hans Schadee' laboratory in collaboration with the SWG research institute, this project is part of the Departments of Excellence 2018–2022 initiative, promoted by the Ministry of University and Research and funded by the Cariplo Foundation. The survey comprised four rounds of data collection conducted between April 2020 and December 2021, gathering over 30,000 interviews using Computer Assisted Web Interviewing (CAWI).

The four survey waves were distributed as follows. The first wave took place from 6 April to 6 July 2020, gathering approximately 15,000 interviews with a RR of 46.6%. The second wave occurred from 21 December 2020 to 2 January 2021, comprising approximately 3000 interviews and a RR of 47%. The third wave was conducted from 17 March to 16 June 2021, and collected around 9300 interviews, and achieved a significantly higher RR of 76.9%. The fourth and final wave occurred from 10 November to 22 December 2021, gathering approximately 3000 interviews, with a RR of 67.1%. The total number of interviews collected over the course of the project was 31,122. Moreover, the survey included an oversampling for the Lombardy region, resulting in an additional 1124 cases in the third wave. By concentrating on Lombardy, the initial epicentre of the pandemic in Italy, the study enabled a more in-depth regional analysis.

In order to study opinion trends in the post-pandemic period, Waves 5 and 6 were also conducted, from 7 November to 22 December 2022, and from 6 June 2023 to 6 July 2023, respectively. Approximately 60% of participants were interviewed at least twice between the first and sixth surveys, thus allowing for a longitudinal analysis of intra-individual variations, which occurred across 2020–2023.

The first, third, fourth, and fifth waves were structured using a Rolling Cross-Section (RCS) design and included a panel design. This methodology divides the sample into smaller subgroups, which are then sequentially released over a given period—specifically, two to three months per wave in this instance. On any given day, a specific subgroup is invited to participate in the survey, and individuals may also respond in the following days. In the RCS waves, an average of 100–150 interviews were conducted each day, corresponding to approximately 1000 interviews per week in the first wave, and around 700 interviews per week in the third and fourth waves. By contrast, the second wave's data collection was concentrated within a single week. This design allowed for the daily samples to be mutually independent, ensuring that the estimates were comparable across days and optimised for studying trends of time-sensitive phenomena such as public opinion. Moreover, approximately 60% of participants were interviewed again between the first, third, and fourth waves, enabling a longitudinal analysis of intra-individual changes across 2020–2021. This hybrid design captured cross-sectional snapshots and longitudinal data, allowing for a comprehensive examination of the evolution of public attitudes concerning the changing dynamics of the pandemic (Vezzoni et al., 2020).

The survey consisted of a central questionnaire and thematic modules. The questionnaire included a core set of questions repeated in all four waves, organised into 11 thematic sections that covered topics such as trust in institutions, compliance with health measures, and attitudes towards vaccination. This structure enabled researchers to track changes of opinion over time. In contrast, the thematic modules varied across waves and focused on specific issues relevant to each phase of the pandemic, such as the economic impact of lockdown measures or opinions on the vaccination campaign. This combination of continuous core content and adaptive thematic modules made it possible to analyse both long-term trends and specific short-term phenomena.

The target population for the survey was Italian residents aged above 18 years. Owing to limitations on time and resource, probabilistic sampling was not feasible. Instead, the sample was sourced from an online community maintained by SWG, a private research institute. The sample reflected the distribution of the Italian adult population by gender and region of residence. To correct for potential sampling biases, the sample was stratified in accordance with Italian National Institute of Statistics (ISTAT) macro-areas of residence and controlled for gender and age quotas. Post-stratification weights were also applied to adjust the sample, ensuring that it aligned with the population structure. These weights, alongside the data files, are available for download.

To enhance the survey's analytic capacity, the dataset was supplemented with macro-level variables providing daily data on the health emergency. This included the number of COVID-19 infections and deaths at both the national and regional levels on the day of each interview. These macro-level variables were sourced from official records and are publicly available through the *COVID-19 dati andamento nazionale* repository. The integration of these data allows researchers to contextualise individual responses within broader concerns of pandemic, facilitating a more detailed understanding of the evolution of public opinion response to the crisis.

In sum, the *ResPOnsE* COVID-19 project provides a detailed overview of Italian public opinion throughout the pandemic. Through combining cross-sectional with longitudinal data, the survey offers a unique opportunity to explore not only how opinions changed over time but also how individual-level factors drove these changes. The extensive dataset allows for the analysis of long-term impacts on various dimensions of Italian public opinion, such as trust in institutions (Guglielmi et al., 2020), democratic support (Pedrazzani et al., 2021), acceptance of freedom restrictions (Ladini & Maggini, 2022), endorsement of conspiracy theories (Vezzoni et al., 2021), religious behaviour (Molteni et al., 2020), and gender roles (Kulic et al., 2020). The project's methodological rigour and comprehensive scope make it a valuable resource for policymakers and researchers aiming to comprehend and address public attitudes during the pandemic and in its aftermath. The English version of the *ResPOnsE* COVID-19 dataset, including data from the first to the fourth wave, can be freely accessed on the dataverse UNIMI repository (Vezzoni et al., 2023).

The UK: Understanding Society

Understanding Society, also known as the *UK Longitudinal Household Survey* (*UKHLS*), aims to explore how life is changing in the UK by providing high-quality survey data. The project has been running since 2009 and builds on and works with the *British Household Panel Survey*, which ran from 1991 to 2009 (ISER, 2023). The study design is comparable to panel surveys in other countries, such as the *German Socio-Economic Panel* (*SOEP*), the US *Panel Study of Income Dynamics* (*PSID*), and the Australian Household Income and *Labour Dynamics in Australia* (*HILDA*).

The study includes multiple sample components that function together to provide a large, representative sample of data for the UK. The first wave took place across 2009–2010 and gathered the following samples:

- *The General Population Sample* (*GPS*): a combination of a clustered and stratified probability sample of approximately 24,000 households in the UK in 2009–2010, and a simple random sample of households living in Northern Ireland selected with a selection probability twice as high as that of the GB sample, resulting in approximately 2000 households.
- *Ethnic Minority Boost Sample* (*EMBS*): households where at least one individual has an ethnic minority background selected from areas of high ethnic minority concentration in 2009–2010, which accounted for approximately 4000 households.

In Wave 2, spanning 2010–2011, the surviving sample of British Household Panel Survey members who were willing to participate in the

UKHLS joined the study (approximately 8000 households). In Wave 6 (2014–2015), the *Immigrant and Ethnic Minority Boost Sample* (IEMBS) was introduced to enhance the representation of these communities. This addition included 2900 households where at least one individual with an ethnic minority background or was born outside the UK. All of the samples were drawn as probability samples of postal addresses.

The adults of each household are interviewed yearly. They report on their current situation and any changes to their and their children's personal circumstances since the previous interview. One resident also details the specific household circumstances. Youth respondents aged 10–15 years self-report in a separate questionnaire. The questionnaires cover a wide range of topics, including key research areas such as employment, income, health and mental wellbeing, ethnicity and immigration, and family and household dynamics. Other topics are covered more regularly, for example, political views, attitudes and voting behaviour, neighbourhood cohesion, and national identity.

The fieldwork period of this approach is spread over two years owing to the significant size and complexity of the sample design. Until Wave 7, the study was primarily based on CAPI (Computer-Assisted Personal Interviewing) interviews, with some CATI (Computer-Assisted Telephone Interviewing) interviews, typically totalling a few hundred per wave. A higher proportion of individuals were offered web interviews from Wave 8, in which respondents were sent a link to a self-completion web questionnaire. However, 20% of the sample was specifically allocated for face-to-face interviews. During the COVID-19 pandemic, face-to-face interviewing was suspended and the survey switched entirely to web and telephone interviews. CAPI interviews were reintroduced in 2022, with a change to their administration: rather than allocating 20% of the sample for CAPI, assignments are based on the estimated probability of response to web interviews. Households with a low probability of responding online are assigned to CAPI.

The Understanding Society data are published with weights that account for unequal selection probabilities, differential nonresponse, and potential sampling error. Given the study's complexity and sample design, reporting a single RR figure is impractical. Detailed information about RRs can be found in the RR tables (ISER, 2023, response rates tables 1–50, p. 20).[1]

[1] For further details about the study including incentives, consent, and guidance on mixed-mode analysis, see the main survey user guide (Institute for Social and Economic Research,

When the pandemic started there was an urgent need for high-quality and up-to-date survey data that capture how UK residents were experiencing the crisis (Institute for Social and Economic Research, 2021). Utilising the existing samples and survey infrastructure, the Understanding Society team designed an independent survey addressing these needs. Specifically, this was the Understanding Society COVID-19 survey.

The survey was based on a 20-minute web questionnaire,[2] combining questions from the main survey with questions unique to the COVID-19 survey, such as questions about COVID-19 symptoms and healthcare utilisation. Because the COVID-19 survey utilised a sub-sample of the main Understanding Society survey, respondent information can be linked through a unique individual identifier provided for each participant. This feature reduced anticipated time taken to complete the questionnaire by omitting questions in the COVID-19 survey that could be linked from the main survey, such as age and education. To ensure that the COVID-19 sample is representative of the UK population, similar to the *UKHLS* survey, the data must be adjusted using the provided weight. This process accounts for unequal selection probabilities and addresses differential nonresponse.

The survey began in April 2020 and was distributed monthly across Waves 1–4. This was modified to a bi-monthly schedule from September 2020 to March 2021 (Waves 5 to 8), concluding with a post-lockdown final wave in September 2021. The eligible sample included all individuals older than 16 years of age by April 2020 in households from all *UKHLS* samples (*GPS*, *EMBS*, *BHPS*, *IEMBS*) who participated in Wave 8 or 9 of the main survey. In Waves 1–4, all members of these households were invited to participate. From the fifth wave, eligibility was limited to those who had completed at least one partial interview in any of the first four web surveys. From Wave 6 onwards, this criterion was modified to exclude respondents who had completed only the initial interview and none thereafter. The sample size and RR (full interview) were as follows: Wave 1: n = 17,312, RR = 39.5%; Wave 2: n = 14,607, web RR = 34.6%, telephone RR = 19.2%; Wave 3: n = 13,917, RR = 33.0%; Wave 4: n = 13,577, RR = 32.3%; Wave 5: n = 12,696, RR = 30.2%; Wave 6: n = 12,168, web RR = 28.1%, telephone RR = 51.1%; Wave 7: n = 11,797, RR = 28.1%; Wave 8: n = 12,509, RR = 29.8%; Wave 9: n = 12,572, RR = 30.1%. (ISER, 2021, Tables 6.3 and 6.4).

2023) and other topic-specific user guides, FAQs, training videos, publications based on the study, visit www.understandingsociety.ac.uk.

[2] Several hundred telephone additional interviews were conducted in Waves 2 and 6.

Periodisation

To allow for a comparison between chronology of countries, we combined the field periods of the different surveys. One clear limitation of this methodology is the availability of data. As there was no consistency of approaches between surveys, field periods overlap only slightly. But even if all countries had collected data at exactly the same moment, the fast-evolving pandemic would have made such comparisons challenging in any case; for example, infection waves and respective lockdown policies started some weeks earlier in one country than in the others.

Based on the number of new cases and the stringency of lockdown measures (Fig. 3.1), we identified four pandemic periods and linked the respective survey data from each of the countries. This enables each chapter to focus on a distinct timeframe of actions and attitudes, rather than specifying months of the year, which differ between countries.

We used the data that were collected closest to the onset of the pandemic to cover the pre-pandemic period (Table 3.1). For France and the UK, we use data from 2019 from the ELLIPSPS Annual Survey Wave 7 (for France) and from the *UKHLS* main survey Waves 10 and 11 (for UK). Much of the German data from the pre-pandemic period originate

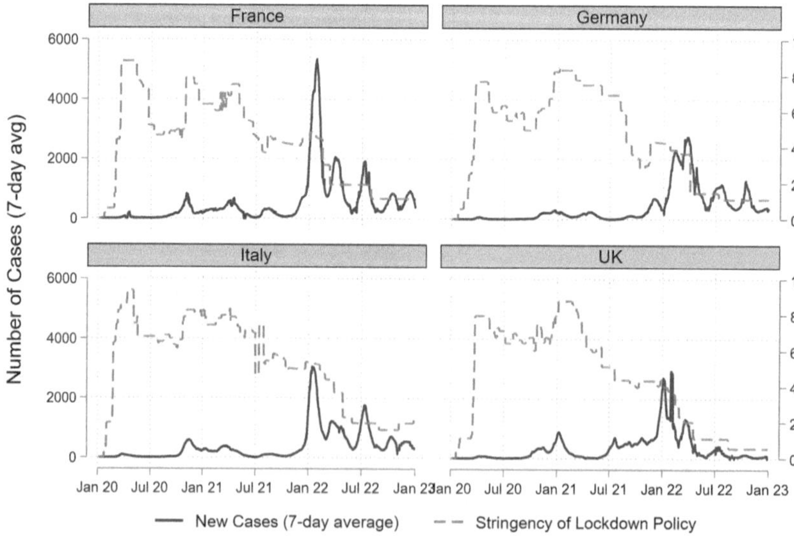

Fig. 3.1 Lockdown policies and COVID-19 incidence, 2020–2022

Table 3.1 Target population and field periods

	France	*Germany*	*Italy*	*UK*
Target population	18+-year-old residents of France (in households)	16+-year-old residents of Germany	18+-year-old residents of Italy	All 16+-year-old residents of UK (in households)
Periods and field times				
Pre-pandemic	2019 (ELIPSS Annual Survey, Wave 7	2019 (GIP, Waves 29–44)	*N/A*	2019 (UKHLS main survey, Waves 10-11)
Shock	Apr–May 2020	Mar–Jul 2020 (MCS)	Apr–Jul 2020 (ResPOnsE, Wave 1)	May 2020 (UKHLS COVID19, Wave 2)
Reprise	April 2021 (COCO, Wave 8)	Jan–Jul 2021 (GIP, Waves 51–54)	Mar–Jun 2021, (ResPOnse, Wave 3)	Mar 2021 (UKHLS COVID19, Wave 8)
Demise	Oct–Nov 2022 (CoCo, Waves 9 & 10)	May–Sept 2022 (GIP, Waves 59 & 61)	Nov–Dec 2021, (ResPOnse, Wave 4)	Sep 2021 (UKHLS COVID19, Wave 9)

from *GIP* waves collected during 2019. However, for some indicators, data are available for January 2020 also.

All countries experienced an initial period of shock in spring 2020. Heavy lockdowns were imposed from late March and brought public life to a halt (see also Chap. 2). Because all four countries gradually lifted restrictions during summer 2020, we used data collected between the end of March 2020 and July 2020 to capture this period.

Summer 2020 saw low rates of infection, which led to a relaxation of restrictions. However, all four countries experienced a period of increased infections during winter 2020 and spring 2021. This period witnessed cases rise and countries faced a second and third wave of COVID-19 infections, with peaks in autumn 2020 and between January 2021 and March 2021. In response, the severity of lockdown measures rose again around December 2020 and remained as such until June 2021. We capture this period of Reprise with data from April 2021 (*CoCo*, Wave 8) in France, *GIP* data covering the period January–July 2021 for Germany (*GIP*,

Waves 51–54), Italian data collected between March and June 2021 (*ResPOnse*, Wave 3), and the *UKHLS* Wave 8 from March 2021.

With the widespread availability of vaccines in the latter half of 2021, COVID 19's Demise period began. Despite peaks in cases, lockdown policies were eventually and gradually lifted. To capture potential medium-term effects of the pandemic, we rely on data collected between September 2021 and September 2022 (see Table 3.1).

Dependent Variables

Health and Wellbeing

There is extensive research into the measurement of health and wellbeing. Indeed, there are many instruments to chart different aspects of wellbeing and mental health, such as Beck-Inventory, GHQ, PHQ, and WEMWBS, which have held up to criticism. However, the most accurate and comprehensive measures are not suitable for inclusion in standardised quantitative social science surveys of large samples owing to time constraints. Such measures form just one of the many aspects that tend to be measured in these surveys. The amount of time allocated is limited so as to not ask too much of the respondents, therefore discouraging them from participating. As a result, most surveys include only one or two questions to measure each concept. While most of these concepts were measured in the four surveys used, the questions were not the same and items differed in question wording and/or in response options. Consequently, we have attempted to harmonise our indicators ex post. We acknowledge that this approach has its limitations. Therefore, chapters of this book standardise values and analyse separate models for each country.

To gain a more detailed picture of the impact of the pandemic on health and wellbeing across and within the four countries, Chaps. 5 and 7 examine a broad set of indicators. The measures included are physical health, depression and anxiety, loneliness, and life satisfaction and happiness.

Physical health can be measured in variety of manners: all-cause mortality, psychological distress indicators, disease prevalence or incidence, to name just a few. Scholars warn against concentrating on any single factor, condition, or health dimension. However, focusing on a specific factor can help us to understand the root cause of a social health problem but it cannot aid the evaluation of the manner in which social structures reproduce health inequalities (specifically, the social stratification of labour market organisation and educational system). For example, in some countries, educated women smoke more than less educated women. This does not mean, however, that social inequalities in health are lower, which is to say that less educated women are ill more frequently and die earlier. 'Therefore, it's important not only to identify specific pathways producing health inequalities but also not to lose sight of the overall impact of social conditions on health' (Phelan et al., 2010). A common solution is the use of a generic, but multidimensional indicator, as self-rated health. Perceived, self-reported, or self-assessed health is an approximate but theoretically fruitful indicator of an individual's general health. There is some scientific literature to support this idea: 'people are excellent judges of their own underlying state of health and future prospects' (Drever et al., 2004, p. 590).

The measure of perceived health is widely considered a reliable indicator of actual health conditions in socio-epidemiological literature (see, among others, Jylhä, 2009). Essentially, it functions as a latent construct that 'mixes the personal experience of acute and chronic symptoms, and different situations of psycho-physical status, such as fatigue, backache and headaches' (Sarti & Espinola, 2018, p. 92). Moreover, numerous empirical studies have observed the correlation between self-reported health and clinical observations, covering morbidity, physical disability, and health behaviours. In addition, the World Health Organization (WHO) recommends self-reported health as the most suitable for comparative purposes, and as such it is highly relevant within the framework of this book. The specific topic in all surveys relies on a similar wordings of questions and response scales range from 1–5 (with the higher value denoting better health) across all countries (see Table 3.2). Indicators should be comparable across countries, despite minor differences in the UK's method of collection.

The American Psychological Association (APA)'s Dictionary of Psychology describes mental health as 'a state of mind characterized by emotional wellbeing, good behavioural adjustment, relative freedom from anxiety and disabling symptoms, and a capacity to establish constructive relationships and cope with the ordinary demands and stresses of life'. Other, comparable studies have investigated social determinants of mental health and the 'complex interplay of individual, family, community and structural determinants', as well as the bi-directional relationship with physical health. Notably, the role of challenging life experiences such as unemployment, marital dissolution, parental separation, deterioration of

Table 3.2 Health and wellbeing measures

	France	*Germany*	*Italy*	*UK*
Self-rated health				
Question text	Would you say that, overall, your health is:	How is your health in general? Would you say it is…	Think about present days. Would you say that, overall, your health is…	In general, would you say your health is…
Response option	5 Very good 4 Good 3 Fairly good 2 Bad 1 Very bad	5 Very good 4 Good 3 Fair 2 Bad 1 Very bad	5 Very good 4 Good 3 Fairly good 2 Bad 1 Very bad	5 Excellent 4 Very good 3 Good 2 Fair 1 Poor
Note that although the question wording was similar and response scales varied from 1 to 5 in the same direction (higher value is better health) across all countries, the labels was a little different for UK				
Life satisfaction				
Question text		How satisfied are you with the following areas of your life? …With my work …With my family		On a scale of 1–7, where 1 is very dissatisfied and 7 is very satisfied, how satisfied are you with your life overall?
Response option		Scale from 0 to 10 with 0 'completely dissatisfied' and 10 'completely satisfied'		Scale from 0 to 7 with 0 'completely dissatisfied' and 7 'completely satisfied'
Question wording and response scales varied across Germany and UK, so items were standardised and centred around country-specific mean at pre-COVID				
Happiness				
Question text	In the past two weeks, have there been times when you felt happy?		On a 0–10 scale, how happy are you?	Have you recently been feeling reasonably happy, all things considered?

(*continued*)

Table 3.2 (continued)

	France	*Germany*	*Italy*	*UK*
Response option	1 Never 2 Rarely 3 Sometimes 4 Often 5 Permanently		0 Not happy at all – 1 2 .... 10 Very happy	1 More so than usual 2 Same as usual 3 Less so than usual 4 Much less than usual
Question wording and response scales varied, so items were standardised and centred around country-specific mean at pre-COVID				
Anxiety				
Question text	In the past two weeks, have there been times when: - You felt really nervous?	Please say how you feel right now... ...I am nervous. ... I am worried that something could go wrong?	In the past week, how often have you experienced: Feeling nervous, anxious, or agitated	
Response options	1 Never 2 Rarely 3 Sometime **4 Often** **5 Permanently**	1 Not at all 2 A little bit **3 Somewhat** **4 Very**	1 Rarely 2 Sometimes (once or twice) **3 Frequently (3–4 times)** **4 Most of the time**	
As the question wording and response scales varied across countries, the responses were dichotomised, by considering the two highest value responses (shown here in bold) as being anxious, otherwise not.				

(*continued*)

Table 3.2 (continued)

	France	*Germany*	*Italy*	*UK*
Depression				
Question text	In the past two weeks, have there been times when you felt sad and dejected?	In the last seven days, how often have you… … felt down, depressed or hopeless? … had little interest or pleasure in doing things?	In the last seven days, how often have you felt depressed?	The next questions are about how you have been feeling over the last few weeks….Have you recently been feeling unhappy or depressed?
Response option	1 Never 2 Rarely 3 Sometimes **4 Often** **5 Permanently**	1 Never 2 1–2 days **3 3–4 days** **4 5–7 days**	1 Rarely 2 Sometimes (once or twice) **3 Frequently (3–4 times)** **4 Most of the time**	1 Not at all 2 No more than usual **3 Rather more than usual** **4 Much more than usual**
As the question wording and response scales varied across countries, the responses were dichotomised, by considering the two highest value responses (shown here in bold) as being depressed, otherwise not.				
Loneliness				
Question text	In general, would you say that you feel…?	In the last seven days, how often have you felt lonely?	In the last four weeks, how often did you feel lonely?	In the last seven days, how often have you felt lonely?
Response option	1 Very surrounded 2 Rather surrounded **3 Rather alone** **4 Very alone**	1 never 2 1–2 days **3 3–4 days** **4 5–7 days**	1 Hardly ever or never 2 Some of the time **3 Often**	1 Rarely 2 sometimes (once or twice) **3 frequently (3–4 times)** **4 most of the time**
As the question wording and response scales varied across countries, the responses were dichotomised, by considering the highest value responses (shown here in bold) as being lonely, otherwise not.				

physical health, and increased financial stress have been studied in detail (Sbarra et al., 2011; Auersperg et al., 2019; Arena et al., 2023). The pandemic not only represented a challenging life experience but was also marked by disruption, and in some cases a pause in the access to mental health care services.

In this book, we focus on depression and anxiety, two of the most commonly studied mental health indicators in social sciences. The APA's Dictionary of Psychology defines depression as 'a negative affective state, ranging from unhappiness and discontent to an extreme feeling of sadness, pessimism, and despondency, which interferes with daily life. Various physical, cognitive, and social changes also tend to co-occur, including altered eating or sleeping habits, lack of energy or motivation, difficulty concentrating or making decisions, and withdrawal from social activities. It is symptomatic of a number of mental health disorders'. Anxiety is defined as 'an emotion characterized by apprehension and somatic symptoms of tension in which an individual anticipates impending danger, catastrophe, or misfortune. The body often mobilizes itself to meet the perceived threat: Muscles become tense, breathing is faster, and the heart beats more rapidly'.

Survey items measuring depressive feelings were generated independently within each of the four countries. Survey questions and response scales align only partially (Table 3.2). To synthesise these data, we standardised them in a manner that records whether respondents felt 'sad and dejected' (France), 'down, depressed or hopeless' (Germany), 'depressed' (Italy), or 'unhappy or depressed' (UK). The timescale within the question also varies, being anchored retrospectively to 'often or more in the last two weeks' in France, 'three or more days of the last week' in Germany and Italy, and 'recently' in the UK. The least comparable indicator is the UK measure, as it does not refer to a specific time span but rather uses subjective terms instead of a quantifiable scale. As such, respondents who have been through a sustained periods of depression do not appear in our estimates. Individuals might have experienced depression at the time of the interview, but not more so than in the past. Therefore, UK figures should be taken as conservative estimates.

Similarly, the items on anxiety ask whether respondents feel 'nervous' (France), 'worried that something could go wrong' (Germany), or 'nervous, anxious, or agitated' (Italy). As response scales varied between countries, we relied on country-specific information of these indicators to standardise them, assessing whether a respondent was experiencing a clinically defined state of anxiety.

We also consider loneliness in addition to these measures. While not a measure of mental health, it is closely associated with both physical and mental health, and wellbeing. Moreover, owing to pandemics resulting in disruption to social interactions, we hypothesised that levels of loneliness increased during the pandemic. In Germany, Italy and the UK, the question asks how often respondents feel lonely, whereas France phrased this in a different manner. Because response scale only partly overlaps between countries, we depend on country-specific information on these indicators to dichotomise them so that they are supposed to indicate whether a respondent has relevant feelings of loneliness (Table 3.2).

Before the 1960s, psychologists focused on unhappiness or mental health issues. Spurred on by behavioural and social scientists, they entered the field of Subjective Well-Being (SWB) with Wilson's 1967 paper on 'Correlates of avowed happiness' published in the *Psychological Bulletin* (Diener 1984). Diener (1984) summarised the research on SWB or happiness as research that 'is concerned with how and why people experience their lives in positive ways, including both cognitive judgments and affective reactions'. He elaborated further and claimed that 'subjective well-being is a broad category of phenomenon that includes people's emotional responses, domain satisfactions and, global judgments of life satisfaction' (Diener et al., 2009). Understanding individual wellbeing includes both quantifiable measures of physical and mental health, alongside individuals' feelings and beliefs about their health. The importance of subjective wellbeing was internationally recognised in 2012, when the United Nations General Assembly adopted Resolution 66/281. They proclaimed that 20 March was to be observed as annual International Day of Happiness and initiated the annual publication of The World Happiness Report, which has been published yearly since 2013. Ever more countries regularly report average levels of life satisfaction and happiness among their national populations.

The SWB literature distinguishes between hedonic (pleasure-oriented) and eudaimonic (meaning-oriented) dimensions. While Kahneman et al. (1999) emphasises happiness as an affective and cognitive state, Ryan and Deci (2001) highlight wellbeing as a process of personal growth and need fulfilment (meaning-oriented). We measure both aspects and analyse life satisfaction and happiness separately. As the available indicators vary in their phrasing for life satisfaction and response scales for life satisfaction and happiness, we standardised the items within countries and centred individual values around the country-specific average pre-COVID.

Employment Situation

Chapters 6, 7, and 9 focus on changes in employment conditions. The survey asks respondents to indicate which employment situation applied to them at a given point in time, and we distinguish between those in paid work (whether that be employed or self-employed, either full-time or part-time), those in furlough, unemployed individuals, retirees, and those with alternative employment situations, such as students or homemakers. For individuals in paid work, we explore how the place of work has changed over time, noting whether employees worked remotely or on-site, either all or some of the time.

Political Preferences

Chapter 8 focuses on changes in political attitudes during the pandemic. This involves an examination of respondents' perceptions of their respective governments' performances during the pandemic, and collectivist or anti-liberal orientations. We ground this investigation in similar but not identical questions found across countries with the goal of determining the possibility of a 'rallying around the flag' effect, understanding its potential duration, intensity, and heterogeneities across social groups.

Socio-demographic Variables

We also harmonised standard socio-demographic variables (Table 3.3). These include sex (male, female), age categories (18–34, 35–54, 55+ years), migration status noted by the country of birth (not available for Italy), education level (less than a university degree, a university degree and higher), and net monthly household income in three income brackets (< €1500 EUR, €1500–2500, €2500 or more). Income information was not available for Italy, but a measure of financial wellbeing was, which was used instead of income. We also capture the household and family situations through partnership statuses, and whether individuals live with children below the age of 18 years. We further provide information on whether children in the household are younger than ten years, which we correlate to higher care needs. All countries also have information captured regularly as to whether people have been diagnosed or have symptoms of COVID-19. These data allow us to provide a harmonised indicator for infections at the individual level.

Table 3.3 Control variables and moderators

	France	*Germany*	*Italy*	*UK*
Sex	Men, Women			
Age group	<35 years, 35–54 years, 55 years or older			
Immigration status	Born in the country, born outside the country			Born in the country, born outside the country
Partnership status	Has a partner or not			
Whether currently living with children (below the age of 18)	No, living with children less than ten years old, living with children with at least one ten years or older			
Highest educational qualification received	Less than tertiary or no qualifications, Tertiary or higher			
Current employment status	In paid work, short time work or on furlough, unemployed, retired, other (in education, on parental leave, home maker)			
Income (Def 1) Net monthly household income	< 1500 EUR, 1500–2500EUR, 2500EUR or more			< 1500 EUR, 1500–2500EUR, 2500EUR or more
Income (Def 2) How does their family income allow them to live?			Cannot make ends meet, with some difficulty, acceptably, comfortably	
Has been diagnose with or had symptoms of COVID-19	Yes, No			

References

Adams-Prassl, A., Boneva, T., Golin, M., & Rauh, C. (2020). Inequality in the impact of the coronavirus shock: Evidence from real time surveys. *Journal of Public economics, 189*, 104245.

Arena, A., Mobbs, S., Sanatkar, S., Williams, D., Collins, D., Harris, M., Harvey, S., & Deady, M. (2023). Mental health and unemployment: A systematic review and meta-analysis of interventions to improve depression and anxiety outcomes. *Journal of Affective Disorders, 335*, 450–472. https://doi.org/10.1016/j.jad.2023.05.027

Arpino, B., Pasqualini, M., Bordone, V., & Solé-Auró, A. (2021). Older people's nonphysical contacts and depression during the COVID 19 lockdown. *The Gerontologist, 61*(2), 176–186.

Auersperg, F., Vlasak, T., Ponocny, I., & Barth, A. (2019). Long-term effects of parental divorce on mental health – A meta-analysis. *Journal of Psychiatric Research, 119*, 107–115. https://doi.org/10.1016/j.jpsychires.2019.09.011

Blom, A. G., Bosnjak, M., Cornilleau, A., Cousteaux, A.-S., Das, M., Douhou, S., & Krieger, U. (2016). A comparison of four probability-based online and mixed-mode panels in Europe. *Social Science Computer Review, 34*(1), 8–25. https://doi.org/10.1177/0894439315574825

Blom, A. G., Cornesse, C., Friedel, S., Krieger, U., Fikel, M., Rettig, T., Wenz, A., Juhl, S., Lehrer, R., Möhring, K., Naumann, E., & Reifenscheid, M. (2020). High frequency and high quality survey data collection: The Mannheim Corona Study. *Survey Research Methods, 14*(2), 171–178.

Busemeyer, M. R. (2023). Financing the welfare state in times of extreme crisis: Public support for health care spending during the Covid-19 pandemic in Germany. *Journal of European Public Policy, 30*(1), 21–40.

Cornesse, C., Krieger, U., Sohnius, M. L., Fikel, M., Friedel, S., Rettig, T., Wenz, A., Juhl, S., Lehrer, R., Möhring, K., Naumann, E., Reifenscheid, M., & Blom, A. G. (2022). From German internet panel to Mannheim Corona study: Adaptable probability-based online panel infrastructures during the pandemic. *Journal of the Royal Statistical Society Series A: Statistics in Society, 185*(3), 773–797.

Cornesse, C., & Schaurer, I. (2021). The long-term impact of different offline population inclusion strategies in probability-based online panels: Evidence from the German Internet Panel and the GESIS Panel. *Social Science Computer Review, 39*(4), 687–704.

Couper, M. P. (2000). Review: Web surveys: A review of issues and approaches. *The Public Opinion Quarterly, 64*(4), 464–494.

Crédoc. (2019). *Baromètre du numérique. Enquête sur la diffusion des technologies de l'information et de la communication dans la société française en 2019.* https://www.credoc.fr/publications/barometre-du-numerique-2019

Diener, E. (1984). Subjective well-being. *Psychological Bulletin, 95*(3), 542–575.

Diener, E., Helliwell, J., Lucas, R., & Schimmack, U. (2009). *Well-being for public policy.* Oxford University Press.

Drever, F., Daran, T., & Whitehead, M. (2004). Exploring the relation between class, gender, and self-rated general health using the new socioeconomic classification: A study using data from 2001 census. *Journal of Epidemiology and Community Health, 58*, 590–596.

Fetzer, T., Hensel, L., Hermle, J., & Roth, C. (2021). Coronavirus perceptions and economic anxiety. *Review of Economics and Statistics, 103*(5), 968–978.

Guglielmi, S., Dotti Sani, G. M., Molteni, F., Biolcati, F., Chiesi, A. M., Ladini, R., Maraffi, M., Pedrazzani, A., & Vezzoni, C. (2020). Public acceptability of containment measures during the COVID-19 pandemic in Italy: How institutional confidence and specific political support matter. *International Journal of Sociology and Social Policy, 40*(9/10), 1069–1085. https://doi.org/10.1108/IJSSP-07-2020-0342

Institute for Social and Economic Research. (2021). *Understanding society COVID-19 user guide.* Version 10.0, October 2021: University of Essex, Colchester.

Institute for Social and Economic Research. (2023). *Understanding society: Waves 1–13, 2009–2022 and harmonised BHPS: Waves 1–18, 1991–2009*, User Guide, 06 December 2023. University of Essex, Colchester.

Jylhä, M. (2009). What is self-rated health and why does it predict mortality? Towards a unified conceptual model. *Social Science & Medicine, 69*(3), 307–316.

Kahneman, D., Diener, E., & Schwarz, N. (Eds.). (1999). *Well-being: Foundations of hedonic psychology.* Russell Sage Foundation.

Kapteyn, A., Angrisani, M., Bennett, D., De Bruin, W. B., Darling, J., Gutsche, T., Liu, Y., Meijer, E., Perez-Arce, F., Schaner, S., Thomas, K., & Weerman, B. (2020, June). Tracking the effect of the COVID-19 pandemic on the lives of American households. *Survey Research Methods, 14*(2), 179–186.

Kühne, S., Kroh, M., Liebig, S., & Zinn, S. (2020). The need for household panel surveys in times of crisis: The case of SOEP-CoV. *Survey Research Methods, 14* (2), 195–203. Southampton: European Survey Research Association.

Kulic, N., Dotti Sani, G.M., Strauss, S. & Bellani, L. (2020). Economic disturbances in the COVID-19 crisis and their gendered impact on unpaid activities in Germany and Italy. *European Societies.* https://doi.org/10.1080/14616696.2020.1828974

Ladini, R., & Maggini, N. (2022). The role of party preferences in explaining acceptance of freedom restrictions in a pandemic context: The Italian case. *Quality & Quantity.* https://doi.org/10.1007/s11135-022-01436-3

Möhring, K., Naumann, E., Reifenscheid, M., Wenz, A., Rettig, T., Krieger, U., Friedel, S., Finkel, M., Cornesse, C., & Blom, A. G. (2021). The COVID-19 pandemic and subjective well-being: Longitudinal evidence on satisfaction with work and family. *European Societies, 23*(S1), S601–S617.

Molteni, F., Ladini, R., Biolcati, F., Chiesi, A. M., Dotti Sani, G.M., Guglielmi, S., Maraffi, M., Pedrazzani, A., Segatti, P. & Vezzoni, C. (2020). Searching for comfort in religion: Insecurity and religious behaviour during the COVID-19 pandemic in Italy. *European Societies.* https://doi.org/10.1080/14616696.2020.1836383

Pedrazzani, A., Maraffi, M., Guglielmi, S., Biolcati, F., Chiesi, A. M., Dotti Sani, G. M., Ladini, R., Molteni, F., Segatti, P., & Vezzoni, C. (2021). Is democracy effective against Coronavirus? An analysis of citizens' opinions in Italy.

Partecipazione e Conflitto, 14(1), 176–201. https://doi.org/10.1285/i20356609v14i1p176
Phelan, J. C., Link, B. G., & Tehranifar, P. (2010). Social conditions as fundamental causes of health inequalities: Theory, evidence, and policy implications. *Journal of Health and Social Behavior, 51*(1_suppl), S28–S40. https://doi.org/10.1177/0022146510383498
Recchi, E., Ferragina, E., Godechot, O., Helmeid, E., Pauly, S., Safi, M., Sauger, N., Schradie, J., Tittel, K., & Zola, A. (2020). *Living through Lockdown: Social Inequalities and Transformations during the COVID-19 Crisis in France.* Zenodo. https://doi.org/10.5281/zenodo.3978023
Recchi, E., Ferragina, E., Safi, M., Sauger, N., & Schradie, J. (2021). *Coping with Covid-19: Social distancing, cohesion and inequality in 2020 France* [Dataset]. Centre des Données Socio-Politiques (CDSP).
Ryan, R. M., & Deci, E. L. (2001). On happiness and human potentials: A review of research on hedonic and eudaimonic well-being. *Annual Review of Psychology, 52*(1), 141–166.
Sarti, S., & Espinola, S. R. (2018). Health inequalities in Argentina and Italy: A comparative analysis of the relation between socio-economic and perceived health conditions. *Research in Social Stratification and Mobility, 55*, 89–98.
Sbarra, D. A., Law, R. W., & Portley, R. M. (2011). Divorce and death: A meta-analysis and research agenda for clinical, social, and health psychology. *Perspectives on Psychological Science, 6*(5), 454–474. https://doi.org/10.1177/1745691611414724
Vezzoni, C. Chiesi, A.M., Biolcati, F., Dotti-Sani, G.M., Guglielmi, S., Ladini, R., Maggini, R., Maraffi, M., Molteni, F., Pedrazzani, A., Segatti, P., Moroni, M., & Piacentini, F. (2023). ResPOnsE COVID-19. Cumulative file: Wave 1 to Wave 4 (English version). https://doi.org/10.13130/RD_UNIMI/W3AFKS.
Vezzoni, C., Dotti Sani, G.M., Ladini, R., Biolcati, F., Chiesi, A.M., Guglielmi, S., Maggini, N., Maraffi, M., Molteni, F., Pedrazzani, A., & Segatti, P. (2021). Where does the Coronavirus come from? On the mechanisms underlying the endorsement of conspiracy theories on the origin of SARS-CoV-2. *Italian Political Science Review*. https://doi.org/10.1017/ipo.2021.19.
Vezzoni, C., Ladini, R., Molteni, F., Dotti Sani, G. M., Biolcati, F., Chiesi, A., Maraffi, M., Guglielmi, S., Pedrazzani, A., & Segatti, P. (2020). Investigating the social, economic and political consequences of Covid-19: A rolling cross-section approach. *Survey Research Methods, 14*(2), 187–194. https://doi.org/10.18148/srm/2020.v14i2.7745

CHAPTER 4

Double Vulnerability? A Cross-Country Comparison of Inequalities in Health, Subjective Wellbeing, and Mental Health During the COVID-19 Pandemic

Alita Nandi, Elias Naumann, Anne McMunn, Ettore Recchi, Francesco Molteni, Giulia Dotti Sani, and Simone Sarti

Introduction

In recent decades, many countries have moved away from national policies focused on the growth of gross domestic product, instead prioritising the wellbeing and living conditions of their citizens (OECD (https://www.

Supplementary Information The online version contains supplementary material available at https://doi.org/10.1007/978-3-031-99349-7_4.

A. Nandi (✉)
Institute for Social and Economic Research, University of Essex, Colchester, UK
e-mail: anandi@essex.ac.uk

E. Naumann et al. (eds.), *Social Life during COVID-19 in France, Germany, Italy and the UK*,
https://doi.org/10.1007/978-3-031-99349-7_4

oecd.org/en/topics/measuring-well-being-and-progress.html), ONS, 2022). This shift embraces a multidimensional approach to wellbeing focussing on both subjective and objective factors, such as employment, income, wealth, education, civic engagement, environmental quality, housing, and health. The COVID-19 pandemic caused a severe and unprecedented disruption to daily life across the world, and the impact was felt across multiple areas.[1] In this chapter, we focus on health, subjective wellbeing and mental health. We examine how these changed during the pandemic in four European societies: France, Germany, Italy, and the UK.

It has been well documented that the pandemic exacerbated existing inequalities in economic prospects as well as health and wellbeing (Platt & Warwick, 2020). In plain terms, some parts of society were doubly affected, feeling the direct impact of the pandemic and, due to their personal circumstances, these effects were experienced more severely. Building on existing research, which tends to focus on single countries, we compare

[1] Internationally accessible repositories of research on the development and impact of the COVID-19 pandemic developed very quickly. Here is a selection: https://www.who.int/emergencies/diseases/novel-coronavirus-2019/global-research-on-novel-coronavirus-2019-ncov; https://www.economicsobservatory.com/; https://publichealthscotland.scot/our-areas-of-work/health-protection/infectious-diseases/covid-19/covid-19-research-repository/; https://www.ons.gov.uk/peoplepopulationandcommunity/healthandsocialcare/conditionsanddiseases

E. Naumann
GESIS Leibniz Institute for the Social Sciences, Mannheim, Germany
e-mail: elias.naumann@gesis.org

A. McMunn
Research Department of Epidemiology & Public Health, University College London, London, UK
e-mail: a.mcmunn@ucl.ac.uk

E. Recchi
Centre for Research on Social Inequalities (CRIS), CNRS, Sciences Po, Paris, France

MPC, European University Institute, Florence, Italy
e-mail: ettore.recchi@sciencespo.fr

F. Molteni • G. Dotti Sani • S. Sarti
Department of Social and Political Sciences, University of Milan, Milano, Italy
e-mail: francesco.molteni@unimi.it; giulia.dottisani@unimi.it; simone.sarti@unimi.it

the changes during the pandemic across these four European countries. We examine the population as a whole, and different sub-groups who may have experienced the pandemic differently, based on factors such as age, gender, ethnicity or minority status, parenthood, key worker status, availability of remote work, access to social support, and pre-existing health conditions. We also analyse whether health and wellbeing had any direct association with experiencing COVID-19 symptoms.

The pandemic disrupted daily life in many different ways that were likely to have had a negative impact on individual health and wellbeing. First, it resulted in a sudden and dramatic interruption of social interactions and reduction or a complete end of many leisure activities. It also increased uncertainties about the future, more so for young people. This was expected to increase levels of loneliness, mental distress, depression, anxiety and stress. Second, the pandemic disrupted work environments and processes. As far as possible, working from home was encouraged or even mandated for large part of the working population (see Chap. 6). While working from home improved work–life balance and reduced commuting times for many, the experience was less positive for individuals inhabiting small or shared apartments with poor internet connection and increasing energy bills. Younger workers and those who had recently joined the workforce were not offered the opportunity to develop their workplace networks and skills through everyday informal interactions. Third, COVID-19 pandemic disrupted the education of children and young people, as learning was made remote, disproportionately affecting very young children, with parents being called to teach their own children. The wellbeing of these children suffered as they were suddenly removed from their peer group and social network. In turn, this negatively affected parents' wellbeing, particularly that of mothers who are often still the primary caregivers, as they were called to manage care responsibilities with work (Chap. 5). Fourth, the pandemic affected individual financial situations: increased employment uncertainty for some fields of work resulted in stress across the population. To summarise, the pandemic disrupted everyone's daily lives, but much more for some than for others.

While these four Western European countries have similar economic, social, and political contexts, policy differences implemented to manage the pandemic differed in both when and how severely they were implemented (see Chap. 2 for details). As such, we expect some impacts of the COVID-19 pandemic to manifest differently between countries and over time.

In this chapter, we draw on a wide set of measures—governed by the availability in the surveys included—to attain a more holistic perspective of the impact of the pandemic on health and wellbeing across and within these four countries. Following the general template of this volume, we use quantitative survey data collected during the pandemic. Aside from Italy, the data were collected from existing pre-pandemic surveys and as such the longitudinal analysis comparing pre-pandemic levels excludes Italy. All estimates are weighted appropriately, and the sample design has been considered when computing standard errors. The health and wellbeing measures included in this chapter are physical health, depression, anxiety, life satisfaction, happiness, and loneliness. Attempts were made to harmonise the measures across the surveys. Where this was not possible, only the country-specific surveys in which the measures were available were examined, such as happiness. The surveys used in the analysis for this chapter are Coping with Covid-19 survey (CoCo, Recchi et al., 2022) for France, Mannheim Corona Study (MCS, Blom et al., 2020) and its parent study, the German Internet Panel (GIP, Blom et al., 2015) for Germany, Response of Italian Public Opinion to the COVID-19 Emergence (ResPOnsE, Vezzoni et al., 2024) for Italy, Understanding Society (University of Essex, 2023) for UK. A detailed discussion about the surveys, datasets, measures included in the analyses, harmonisation issues, and the exact definitions of the time periods and the sample sizes have been provided in Chap. 3.

In the following sections, we discuss our findings of the changes in these measures during the pandemic across countries and sub-groups within these countries. These sections each adopt a similar structure, beginning with a brief, targeted literature review concerning the changes in the health and wellbeing observed during the pandemic, most of which are single-country studies. This is followed by a cross-country comparison over time in which we report descriptive statistics of the measures to demonstrate how these measures evolved over time between the four countries. We report findings from country-specific multivariate analyses of the impacts of the measures to identify vulnerable groups. Each section concludes with an evaluation of how the pandemic may have exacerbated differences between and across these social groups. The chapter ends with a discussion of the key findings.

Self-reported Health in Europe During the COVID-19 Pandemic

The shared focus of many studies on the effects of pandemics is the way in which events of this magnitude uncover and amplify pre-existing health inequalities (Mishra et al., 2021). This is a fundamental idea of social epidemiology which suggests that both the probability of exposure and the outcomes are not random but rather socially patterned. For example, Bambra et al. (2020) reviewed past research on health inequalities during the 1918 Spanish flu pandemic and the H1N1 outbreak in 2009. This revealed prevalent inequalities such as differing mortality rates between high- and low-income countries, more and less affluent neighbourhoods, urban and rural areas, and higher and lower socio-economic groups. Such patterns and associations were also anticipated for the COVID-19 pandemic, as existing inequalities in key health determinants—like employment status, access to essential goods, general working conditions, housing, and healthcare— are known to be associated with 'hypertension, diabetes, asthma, chronic obstructive pulmonary disease (COPD), heart disease, liver disease, renal disease, cancer, cardiovascular disease, obesity and smoking' (Bambra et al., 2020, p. 965), all of which are recognised as risk factors that influence the severity of COVID-19's impact. In addition, Bambra et al. note that the different lockdowns and containment measures probably had an unequal impact correlated to different individual experiences, such as job or income loss, overcrowding, or different access to green and public spaces.

Focusing on the UK, Mishra et al. (2021) and Platt and Warwick (2020) provide an overview of widely known inequalities. They find that deaths related to COVID 19 has been higher among men and the elderly. They also demonstrate that, compared to the White native population, people of all other ethnic groups (aside from the Chinese) were more at risk of being diagnosed with COVID-19 (in the French context, see Khlat et al., 2022), and a higher risk of complications and death with the difference being the highest for Black individuals (2.7 times higher). In addition to comorbidities—which are themselves unequally distributed (for example, they are higher among those living in overcrowded housing without the option of remote working)—Mishra et al. (2021) identify three other critical aspects that might be valuable for studying other contexts: (i) geography, specifically the difference between rural and urban areas, with the former performing better; (ii) socio-economic status, as those experiencing financial hardship show higher mortality rates and children from lower socio-economic backgrounds have higher risks of contracting COVID-19; (iii) groups that are harder to reach by health services—such as the homeless—face disparity in health outcomes including COVID-19. Dukhovnov and Barbieri (2022) find similar results in the United States: COVID-19 mortality rates were 2.58 times higher in the lowest quintile counties than for the highest.

Cross-country Comparison: Evolution over Time

The data on subjective health are analysed through survey interviews, in which participants self-report their general health status. We hypothesised a decline in overall health throughout the progression of the pandemic. However, the situation observed in the four surveys suggests otherwise (see Fig. 4.1). These show: estimated general health scores adjusted for age, gender, education and employment status. Fluctuations in the

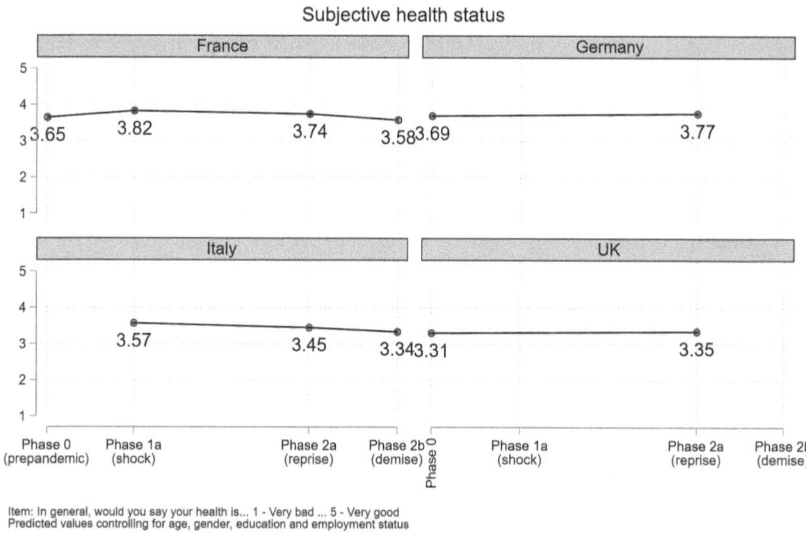

Fig. 4.1 Subjective health status before and during the pandemic: estimated general health status scores reported (Note: Ratings range from 1 (very bad) to 5 (very good), with estimated values adjusted for age, gender, education and employment status)

averages of health status were minimal, with differences never exceeding 0.23 (on a 1–5 scale) as observed in Italy between the initial phase (1a—Shock) and the final (2b—Demise). Not only are the differences negligible, but they also appear in unexpected manners. In this context, Italy is the only country in which a discernible, declining pattern in self-reported health is observed. Conversely, we note relative stability in the UK (3.31 in the pre-pandemic period vs. 3.35 in the Reprise period) and in Germany (3.69 vs. 3.77). The most intriguing case is France, in which we observe an increase in the average subjective health right after the pandemic (+0.17), which is then followed by a gradual decline. This result aligns coherently with the contribution by Recchi et al. (2020a), which investigates wellbeing and gestures to the 'Eye of the Hurricane' paradox: whereby the large majority of individuals who were not seriously infected by the virus could be viewing their current condition in a more positive light than they normally would because they were comparing themselves to the pandemic casualties.

Cross-country Comparison: Identifying Vulnerable Groups

Using a multivariate analysis of self-reported health measures across the four countries individually (see Table A4.1 in the Online Appendix), we identify social groups that were generally more vulnerable to COVID-19. As expected, reports of self-rated health decreases with age for all of the four countries studied. Moreover, in terms of magnitude, the size of this association is the largest compared to the estimated coefficients of the other covariates included in the models. By contrast, the effect of gender is far smaller and varies across countries: in France and Germany females declare marginally better health, while in Italy and the UK the opposite occurs.

Focusing on income, we note that individuals declaring higher incomes report better subjective health across all four countries. As with age, the effects in this case are sizable and in expected directions. Regarding other variables in the models, we find that those who have had COVID-19, the unemployed, individuals without a partner, and those with lower education levels tend to display lower subjective health. The effect on children is varied, with children (both over and under ten years of age) being associated with better health in Germany and the UK, and worse health in Italy, with no effect for children over ten years. Overall, the elderly and the most economically vulnerable are more at risk of negative changes to subjective health. Determining whether these inequalities have increased or decreased during the pandemic will be the focus of the following section.

Cross-country Comparison: Did the Pandemic Exacerbate Group-Level Differences?

A summary of results is presented through a series of graphs, found in Table A4.2 of the Online Appendix. These have been derived from different models in which variables depicting social groups were interacted with health measures within various periods of the pandemic, with the pre-pandemic period as the control. This process excludes Italy for reasons previously stated, and the Shock and Demise periods for Germany and the UK, as self-reported health was not measured in those periods.

Beginning with age, almost all the interaction terms are not statistically significant. This suggests that age differences in subjective physical health remained constant across the pandemic, with the elderly consistently reporting lower levels. Expressed differently, with regard to physical health, the pandemic impacted all age groups in similar manners in all of the four countries under study. The only slight exception to this pattern is the intermediate age group (35–54 years old), which reports slightly better health during the Reprise phase in the UK. However, the size of this effect is nearly negligible (approximately +0.07 on a 1–5 scale).

In the previous analyses, we found that gender was marginally associated with health outcomes. As with age, this limited effect remained constant throughout the entire pandemic period, with only women reporting better health during the Demise period in France.

Some evidence of shifting inequalities across the pandemic periods can be observed when considering income, especially within the UK. Interviewees with middle and high incomes reported better health status in the Reprise period compared to previous periods. This might indicate a possible slight decrease in health inequality in the periods right after the onset of the pandemic.

Mental Health: Depression and Anxiety

At the start of the COVID-19 outbreak, research on the mental health correlated to the pandemic flourished (for a review, see Prati & Mancini, 2021). However, only a very small minority of these studies drew on longitudinal data based on representative samples. The results of these national studies indicate remarkable within- and between-country heterogeneity. A substantial decrease from April to June 2020 was found in the UK (Niedzwiedz et al., 2021; Fancourt et al., 2021). However, the overall level of distress remained above pre-pandemic levels (Daly et al., 2020). Women, particularly those with young children, ethnic minority men and women, young people, and those with high social capital faced higher mental health repercussions (Moreno-Agostino et al., 2022, Gagné et al., 2021b, 2021a; Proto & Quintana-Domeque, 2021; Nandi & Platt, 2021, Xue & McMunn, 2021: Daly et al., 2020).

Researchers also identified differences on the impact on anxiety and depression. For example, in the UK, Kwong et al., 2020, 2021 found that anxiety and depression was higher for younger age groups during the pandemic. However, when compared with pre-pandemic levels, depression changed less and more slowly over time, while anxiety nearly doubled during the pandemic for young adults. This increase in anxiety affected more women and those with pre-existing mental health issues, financial problems, or difficulty accessing mental health information (Ibid.). While self-isolation increased the risk of anxiety and depression, individuals living alone were at a higher risk of depression but not anxiety (Kwong et al., 2021). Evidence from the Netherlands revealed a stability in anxiety and depression across the overall population (van der Velden et al., 2020) and among a subsample of individuals diagnosed with depression prior to the pandemic (Pan et al., 2021).

A systematic review of 48 studies across 204 countries also demonstrated that anxiety and depression increased during the pandemic, disproportionately affecting women (Santomauro et al., 2021). Similar findings were reported in a meta-analysis by Salari et al. (2020). According to a large-scale review of studies carried out by the OECD (2021), depression and anxiety increased in 2020 compared to years prior to this (in 10 out of 13 countries where survey data included these measures available in both periods). They also found that risk factors such as financial insecurity and unemployment increased it during the pandemic while protective factors such as social connections and access to health services reduced it. Similar impacts of higher levels of mild anxiety and depression were recorded in some countries of the Global South: Ethiopia, the Indian states of Andhra Pradesh and Telangana, Peru, and Vietnam (Porter et al., 2021). They also identified similar risk factors (pre-existing health conditions, economic vulnerability, food insecurity, and educational or employment disruption) and protective factors (prior parent and peer relationships).

Among older age groups, a longitudinal and comparative study including two conventional measures of depression (namely, self-reported feelings of depression and sleeping troubles), covering 11 European countries with large representative samples, demonstrated a consistent, cross-national trend of *lesser*—rather than higher—prevalence of depression in the period May–July 2020 compared to previous years (Van Winkle et al., 2021).

Qualitative studies in the UK found that the pandemic increased anxiety levels among young children and adolescents, particularly when they engaged with the news or social media (Lockyer et al., 2020, 2022). While reassurances from parents helped, they still suffered from anxiety. As adolescence is a crucial transitional age, such intense disruption to schooling and social interactions had a severe impact on their anxiety levels. Similar results were recorded in Canada (Lane et al., 2022). Qualitative studies based in the UK and Australia found that parents of very young children reported increased levels of anxiety—particularly health anxiety—and worries regarding the wellbeing of their children (Gibson et al., 2021). Additionally, mothers 'were finding it difficult to balance work commitments and time for family. This suggests that mothers are vulnerable to feeling the mental load of the demands of home-schooling, childcare, domestic tasks and paid employment during the pandemic' (Gibson et al., 2021). Parents of young children also reported higher levels of anxiety (Kwong et al., 2021), but their levels of anxiety were lower if their children maintained a routine (Lees et al., 2022). In such cases, the extent of emotional and behavioural difficulties of the children were also lower (Ibid.).

A comparative study of six countries (Denmark, Estonia, Iceland, Norway, Sweden, and the UK) also found that individuals diagnosed with COVID 19 reported higher levels of depression but not anxiety following the diagnosis. The impact of this reduced over time and was lower for those who had milder symptoms (Magnúsdóttir et al., 2022). Kwong et al. (2021), however, found that among the older age groups, those who suspected or had been tested for a COVID infection reported higher levels of depression and anxiety.

Depression in Europe During the COVID-19 Pandemic

The proportion of individuals reporting feelings of depression over time and across countries is shown in Fig. 4.2. With the benefit of covering all adult cohorts across four countries, our data partly confirm and partly nuance the existing findings. While the method of data and measure harmonisation is discussed in Chap. 3, here, we highlight harmonisation of depression measures as our survey questions concerning depression align only partially, which is important in understanding cross-country differences. To harmonise them, we have transformed them into a binary variable that records whether respondents feel 'sad and dejected' (France), 'down, depressed, or hopeless' (Germany), 'depressed' (Italy), 'unhappy or depressed' (UK). The timeframe of the question also differs, being anchored retrospectively to 'often or more in the last two weeks' in France, 'three or more days of the last week' in Germany and Italy, and 'recently' in the UK. The least comparable indicator is the UK's measure as it does

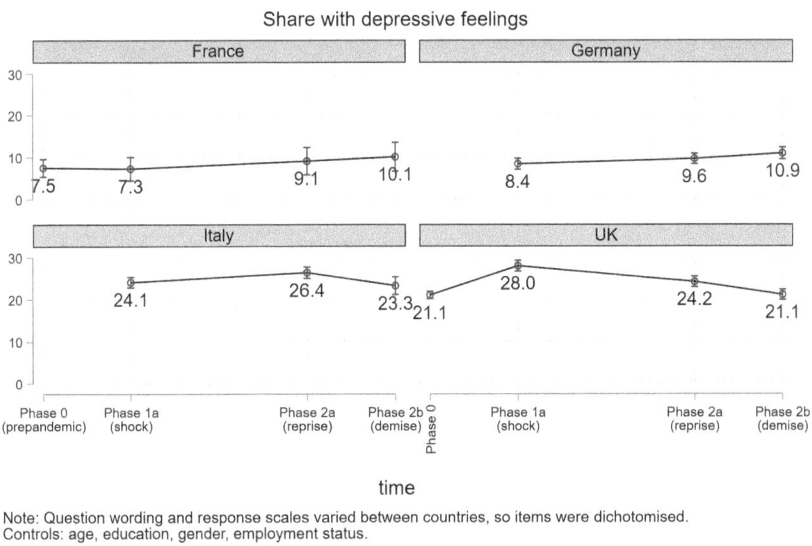

Fig. 4.2 The prevalence of depressive feelings before and during the pandemic: estimated proportion of people reporting depressive feelings. (Note: Questions wordings and response scales varied between countries, so items were dichotomised. Estimated proportions were adjusted for age, education, gender, employment status)

not refer to a specific, measurable time span (instead asking about the 'last few weeks') and is relative to past subjective states ('more, less or the same as usual') rather than to an absolute experience. This means that respondents who have been through a durable depression will not be recorded as feeling depressed because even though they may be depressed at the time of the interview, that may not necessarily be more so than previously. UK figures should therefore be taken as conservative estimates. Despite this limitation we find that the proportion of respondents in the UK who report feeling more depressed than is typical increased from 21.1% pre-pandemic to 28% in Spring 2020, although reverting to pre-pandemic levels at later stages (similar findings were reported in Fancourt et al., 2021; Hajek et al., 2022). The most consistent figures are found in Italy. The proportion of the population who felt depressed for at least half of the previous week oscillates around a 25% during the entire period of observation. A less pessimistic picture emerges in France and Germany: in both countries, there is a slight increase in proportions depressed in 2021, but never more than 10% of the population.

Perhaps not unexpectedly, heterogeneities are higher where depression is a more widespread issue, such as in Italy and the UK (see Table A4.3 in the Online Appendix), while variations are scarcely significant in France. In both Italy and the UK, two groups were particularly exposed to depression during the pandemic: the young and the poor. These results are confirmed by other studies (Hajek et al., 2022). In Italy, individuals younger than 35 have a markedly higher risk of depression than all other age groups. In the UK, this extends to individuals up to 54 year, as with pre-pandemic data, as well as in comparative studies using the Survey of Health, Ageing, and Retirement in Europe (SHARE) panel (Van Winkle et al., 2021). One element of young people's exposure to depression during COVID times is attributable to their precariousness as students, temporary workers, or being out of work. All of these conditions are significantly associated with higher risks of depression across Italy, Germany, and the UK. Having a low income and not having a partner are more common conditions for the young and appear as significant predictors of higher risks of depression. With other conditions remaining the same, contracting COVID-19 also tends to accentuate depression more generally (but significantly so in Italy and the UK). This was notably the case in 2020 and 2021 in Italy, but also in 2022 in the UK. In Italy and the UK, we also find a significant gender effect, with women more exposed to depression. British data indicate that this is in continuity with pre-pandemic statistics (see also Hajek et al., 2022). In Italy, there is also a higher risk for parents of small children, particularly in the Reprise and Demise periods.

Overall, there is a correlation between levels of depression and welfare strength, which the pandemic may have accentuated (see Table A4.4 in the Online Appendix). Leaving aside the senior population, for which retirement systems are consistently strong, France and Germany have more robust labour market protection and public childcare in comparison to Italy and the UK. This is likely to buffer the psychological repercussions of the COVID-19 pandemic. This tentative hypothesis finds some support in other research in societies with less welfare protection, such as Brazil, and shows how the pandemic multiplied the proportion of the generally depressed by a factor of six (Feter et al., 2021).

Anxiety in Europe During the COVID-19 Pandemic

Questions concerning anxiety were not asked in the UK survey, and as such we report analysis results from France, Germany, and Italy. The only data measuring anxiety pre-pandemic is in France. As the question texts and response options varied, these scales were dichotomised (see Chap. 3 for details). Figure 4.3 shows the estimated proportion of individuals who reported anxiety at different points in time, controlling for age, education, gender and employment status. Compared with the Shock period, we anticipated anxiety levels to fall during Reprise and either stay the same or fall during Demise. However, this was not the case. In Germany, compared to the Shock period, the proportion who identified as feeling anxious fell during Reprise, but increased during Demise. In Italy, this proportion slightly increased during Reprise and then fell during Demise. In France, we found that this proportion fell during the Shock period compared to the pre-pandemic, and then steadily increased during the Reprise and Demise periods.

We then conducted a multivariate analysis of the likelihood of feeling anxious during the three pandemic periods. The results are reported in Table A4.5 in the Online Appendix. We note considerable heterogeneity in these experiences. As expected, the likelihood of feeling anxious was higher for younger age groups, aside from in Germany where individuals aged 35–54 years presented the highest risk.

Differences attributed to gender also followed expectations in Germany and Italy, with women more likely than men to feel anxious, while there

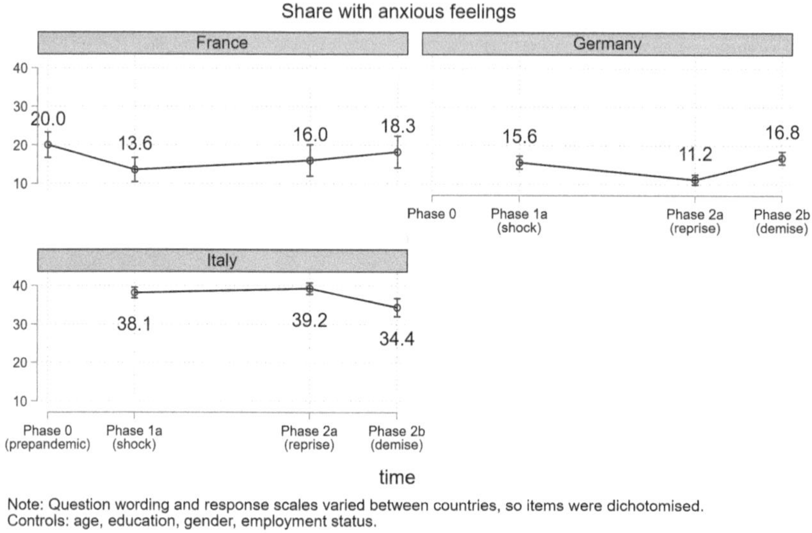

Fig. 4.3 The prevalence of anxious feelings before and during the pandemic: estimated proportion of people reporting anxious feelings. (Note: Questions wordings and response scales between countries, so items were dichotomised. Estimated proportions were adjusted for age, education, gender, employment status)

are no gender difference in France. Existing research in UK and France had shown that women are more likely to be the primary caregivers during home-schooling for children (see Chap. 5), which may have contributed to poorer mental health for women (Xue & McMunn, 2021). Accordingly, we also examined whether individuals with children suffered more than others. While the pandemic may have increased childcare responsibilities, it also enabled a better work–life balance, allowing more time to be spent with children. Theoretically, it was not clear what the overall effect might be. We did not find any statistically significant differences in risk of anxiety between individuals living with their children and those who did not in France and Italy, but found significantly lower levels of anxiety in Germany for those living with children.

As the pandemic disrupted social interactions, those living with a partner were anticipated to report better mental health. This is the case only in Italy.

The correlation of anxiety with economic factors, such as education, employment status, and income, were not always in the expected direction. Education did not result in any difference to mental health in any country. In France, employment status and income levels were not influential either. In Italy, higher income levels and paid employment status were protective against anxiety. In Germany, employment status was preventative, but higher levels of income were not. This possibly reflects better economic protection measures implemented in Germany and France than in Italy.

Interestingly, the foreign-born in Germany were more likely to feel anxious than their German born counterparts. This might be attributed to greater uncertainties during the pandemic driven by different countries imposing new rules of international travel disrupting travel to close family members living in different countries. It is also possible that these differences reflect existing pre-pandemic differences, as immigrants in Germany generally report poorer mental health (Nesterko et al., 2019).

We also examined whether having been diagnosed with COVID-19 or reporting its symptoms resulted in higher levels of anxiety. This was only the case in Italy.

As data concerning anxiety were also collected pre-pandemic in France, we examined whether the differences in the likelihood of feeling anxious between different sub-groups changed during the pandemic as compared to before the pandemic (see Table A4.6 in the Online Appendix). In other words, did the pandemic exacerbate differences in risk of anxiety for some groups? We find that the difference between the oldest and youngest age groups increased during the Reprise phase, mirroring the result for the overall population. It is possible that the youngest age group's anxiety levels increased during the pandemic as the impact of such major disruptions to the economy are more likely to negatively affect those at the beginning of their careers. We also found that before the pandemic parents of children older than ten reported lower levels of anxiety as compared to adults without children. This difference vanished during the pandemic, possibly because of the additional childcare responsibilities which counteracted this positive association.

Life Satisfaction and Happiness in Europe During the COVID-19 Pandemic

For decades, Europe has been world-leading in life satisfaction. However, this fell to its lowest level since 1980 in April 2020 (Allas et al., 2020). A study based on an international sample of volunteers recruited through the internet—one-fifth of whom lived in Europe— reported a 30% reduction in life satisfaction in April 2020 (Ammar et al., 2022). According to the Living, Working and Covid-19 dataset (LWC), levels of life satisfaction in Europe fluctuated over the pandemic from 6.3 during April–May 2020 to 6.7 in June–July as restrictions eased, and then reducing to 5.7 in February–March 2021 as new strains of the virus arose and vaccination was implemented (Eurofound, 2020). Similarly using the LWC, Bachmann et al. (2021) found life satisfaction was negatively associated with the spread of COVID-19 in Northern Europe, but not in Southern or Western Europe. These patterns are attributed to concerns regarding *laissez-faire* attitudes towards lockdown in Northern European countries. On the other hand, Clark and Lepinteur (2021) found that in France, Germany, Italy, Spain, and Sweden, the stringency of their government policy responses reduced life satisfaction during 2020, once the intensity of the pandemic (measured by number of daily deaths) was controlled for. They also found that economic support policies were not associated with life satisfaction. In line with these findings, life satisfaction levels in the spring of 2020 were highest in Sweden which chose not to implement a lockdown (Independent SAGE, 2020).

In the UK, there was a dramatic decline of life satisfaction between March 2020 and March 2021. This was the nation's lowest levels in 11 years after gradually climbing since 2011. The figure slightly improved between March 2021 and March 2022 (UK Office for National Statistics,2022). This pattern was replicated when considering individual changes compared with 2018–19 levels, with life satisfaction hitting its lowest in January 2021 when the UK experienced a second strict lockdown period and its highest levels of pandemic-related deaths (Chao et al., 2021).

Research into life satisfaction during the pandemic does not tend to suggest gender differences, but does find that living with a partner buffered the effects of the pandemic on life satisfaction (Chao et al., 2021; de Pedraza et al., 2020; Institute of Global Health Innovation, 2020). As was the case pre-pandemic, many studies found that employment was protective and job loss, reductions in income, and other job-related changes were associated with greater dissatisfaction (de Pedraza et al., 2020; Institute of Global Health Innovation, 2020; Carlsen et al., 2022). Analysis of the UK found differences by educational qualifications to be marginally smaller during the pandemic than pre-pandemic (Chao et al., 2021). As with loneliness, age patterns in life satisfaction shifted during the pandemic. Life satisfaction tends to be represented as a U-shaped association with regard to age, with lowest levels in the mid-life ages of 40–60 years. However, at least in the early part of the pandemic, life satisfaction levels were lowest in those under age 30 and increased in a linear fashion with age (Institute of Global Health Innovation, 2020). COVID-19 infection rates were associated with declines in life satisfaction in Norway (Carlsen et al., 2022). Countries with higher COVID-19 death rates had lower life satisfaction in Western countries, but this was not the case in Asian countries, where death rates were lower (Institute of Global Health Innovation, 2020).

Cross-country Comparisons: Evolution over Time

Figures 4.4 and 4.5 show the evolution of levels of life satisfaction in Germany and UK and happiness in France, Italy, and the UK before and during the pandemic. These figures show the estimated levels of life satisfaction and happiness adjusted for age, gender, education and employment status. These changed in expected ways—dropped during the pandemic Shock period and recovered during Reprise and Demise periods.[2] Happiness levels in Italy, however, remained constant during the three pandemic phases.

Cross-country Comparison: Identifying Vulnerable Groups

We report the results of the multivariate analysis of life satisfaction and happiness during the pandemic in Table A4.7 in the Online Appendix. We find that life satisfaction and happiness results are very similar in Germany, France and UK but somewhat different in Italy. Across the board, older age groups report lower levels of life satisfaction and happiness, but with the notable exception of Italy where the opposite is found. Women

[2] The happiness question in the UK is worded such that higher values represents lower levels of happiness.

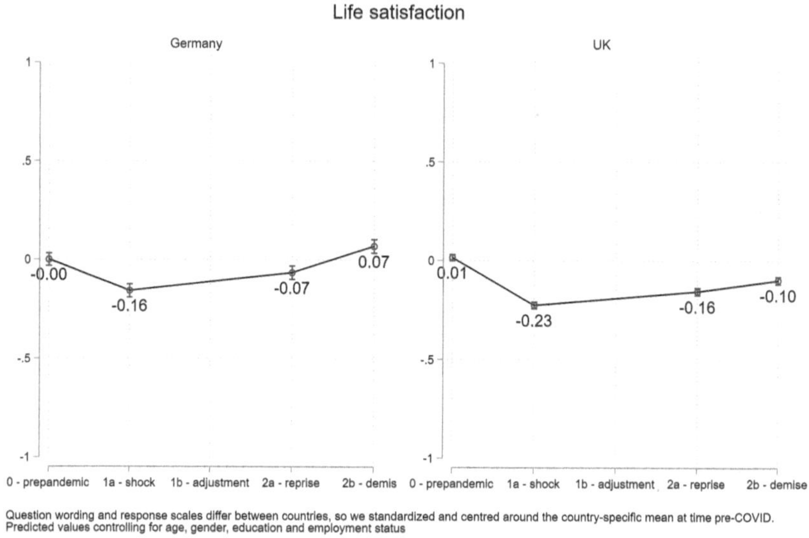

Fig. 4.4 Life satisfaction before and during the pandemic in Germany and the UK: estimated levels of life satisfaction reported (Note: Question wording and response scales varied between countries and so the scores were standardised and centred around the country specific pre-pandemic mean. Estimated levels were adjusted for age, gender, education and employment status.)

reported higher levels of life satisfaction but lower levels of happiness. This may reflect a disproportionate delegation of caring responsibilities which could increase levels of stress, but not adversely affect an overall view of their life.

Life satisfaction and happiness are also higher among those with partners. This is likely due to partnership buffering the negative impacts of social isolation. As with other wellbeing measures, the results for individuals living with children are mixed for reasons discussed earlier. The pandemic allowed individuals to spend more time with their children, make up for lack of other social interactions, but also increased childcare responsibilities owing to home-schooling, particularly for women. We find children aged over ten years in the household led to reduced levels of life satisfaction in Germany and Italy, and very young children reduced levels of happiness in the UK. This result in UK is similar to the patterns observed for women, who have higher childcare responsibilities (see Chap. 5).

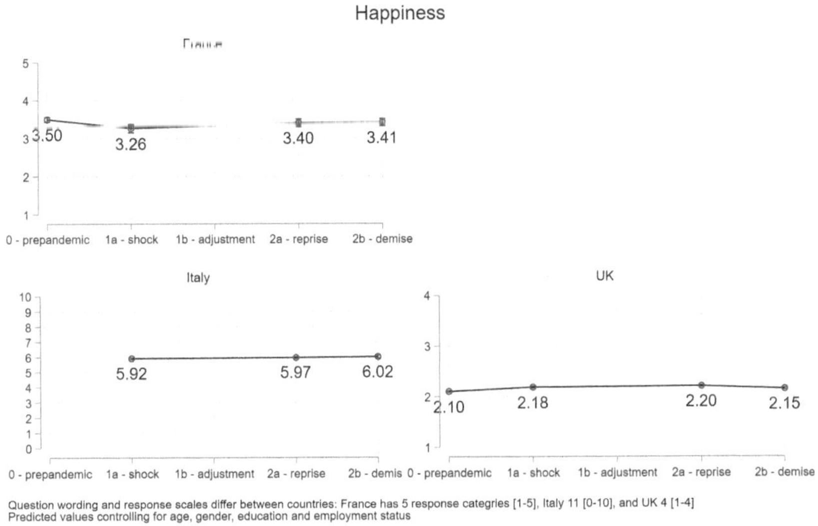

Fig. 4.5 Happiness before and during the pandemic: estimated happiness scores reported (Note: Question wording and response scales varied between countries. Estimated levels were adjusted for age, gender, education and employment status.)

Economic factors also adhered to our expectations. Higher income groups and those in employment reported higher levels of life satisfaction and happiness. The association with education is mixed and varies by country. Individuals with higher levels of education reported lower levels of life satisfaction in Germany but higher levels in the UK. They also reported lower levels of happiness in Italy and UK, but higher levels in France. As cognitive measure of wellbeing adopts a more holistic understanding of one's life than happiness which captures the more immediate experience, the seemingly contradictory results for the UK suggest that the more highly educated were forced to work from home with poorer facilities, resulting in lower happiness. However, they generally enjoy higher incomes and better job satisfaction, which results in higher life satisfaction.

As with all measures of health and wellbeing, experiencing COVID-19 resulted in lower levels of life satisfaction and happiness. These results are only statistically significant in the UK.

Immigrant and ethnic minority status have no influence, except in Germany. Individuals born outside Germany reported lower levels of life satisfaction, however it is possible these differences existed pre-pandemic.

Cross-country Comparison: Did the Pandemic Exacerbate Group-Level Differences?

To analyse group differences observed during the pandemic, we related the time-period variable with different group variables (see Table A4.8 in the Online Appendix). In UK, the results were mixed: the age difference in happiness and life satisfaction between parents and non-parents had decreased by the end of the pandemic, but any other differences increased. In Germany, these differences tended to return to pre-pandemic levels aside from the difference in life satisfaction between households with children ages over ten and non-parents. Overall, the pandemic exacerbated inter-group differences in life satisfaction and happiness in France, partially in the UK, but not in Germany.

Loneliness in Europe During the COVID-19 Pandemic

It is now widely acknowledged that social relationships are a key social determinant of health and wellbeing (Berkman & Krishna, 2014; Holt-Lunstad et al., 2010; Kawachi & Berkman, 2014). In particular, loneliness—defined as a perceived lack of close social ties —has been shown in meta-analyses to predict poor health and mortality as strongly as traditional, risk factors such as smoking and obesity (Holt-Lunstad et al., 2015). In addition, loneliness has been linked with depression (Cacioppo et al., 2006) and a range of health risk factors such smoking, inactivity (Shankar et al., 2011), high blood pressure (Hawkley et al., 2010), inflammation (Walker et al., 2019), and cortisol responses (Steptoe et al., 2004). However, poor health may also itself lead to an increased risk of loneliness, particularly in the context of the COVID-19 pandemic when those with chronic conditions were required to isolate and shield themselves from social contact more so than others without such conditions. According to the Living, Working, COVID-19 survey (LWC), 46% of individuals who reported bad health also reported being lonely for at least half of the time in the past two weeks, compared with 20% of those who reported good health (Baarck et al., 2021). In addition to its importance for health, loneliness is an important aspect of subjective wellbeing in its own right, with many countries making explicit efforts to reduce loneliness in later life (HM Government, 2018; Sandu et al., 2021) and, increasingly, in earlier life too (Lasgaard et al., 2016).

During the pandemic, restrictions on social contact were necessary to reduce the risk of infection. However, this led to potential negative effects on health and wellbeing, particularly for vulnerable groups such as the elderly, who faced increased social isolation and loneliness. This phenomenon has been referred to as the Social Connectivity Paradox (Smith et al., 2020). A recent meta-analysis of 34 longitudinal studies—23 of which were conducted in Europe—found a small but significant increase in loneliness during the pandemic compared to pre-pandemic levels (Ernst et al., 2022). Similarly, Baarck et al. (2021), using data from internet-based volunteer participants from Europe (LWC survey), reported comparable findings. However, a separate study that combined data from seven longitudinal surveys in the UK, Denmark, France, and the Netherlands—including some that used similar volunteer samples—found that loneliness levels were lower during the pandemic compared to pre-pandemic periods (Varga et al., 2021).

Over time, data on the pandemic has become available from large, pre-existing surveys that have used probability sampling techniques. For instance, findings from SHARE, which focuses on individuals aged 50 and older, revealed that 29% of Europeans reported experiencing loneliness (either occasionally or more frequently) between June and August 2020 (Cohn-Schwartz et al., 2022; Santini & Koyanagi, 2021). Of those, 40% stated that their loneliness had worsened during the pandemic (Ibid.). SHARE also indicated that physical distancing itself was linked to a higher likelihood of feeling lonely, but only in Northern Europe. In Austria, for example, Mayer et al. (2022) found higher levels of loneliness across March and June 2020 compared with pre-pandemic SHARE sweeps conducted before the pandemic. Loneliness peaked during strict lockdowns and eased as restrictions were lifted, especially for individuals living alone. Meanwhile, participants in Southern Europe reported feeling lonelier overall, despite more frequent social interactions. Researchers attribute this to cultural differences—southern European countries tend to have stronger expectations of social contact due to their collectivist cultures, whereas Northern European countries lean towards more individualistic social norms (Cohn-Schwartz et al., 2022).

Similar patterns were observed for studies that included younger adults. For example, in Germany, daily diaries written during the first four weeks of the pandemic demonstrated loneliness levels rose for the first two weeks and then decreased slightly across the latter two (Buecker et al., 2020). Evidence from the long-standing German Socioeconomic Panel (GSOEP) similarly showed that loneliness levels increased across the initial lockdown, but then decreased before restrictions were officially eased (Entringer & Gosling, 2022). Two studies found increased levels of loneliness in the spring and summer of 2020 compared to 2019 in the Netherlands (van der Velden et al., 2021; van Tilburg et al., 2021). Conversely, another study that uses a national sample reported no change in loneliness levels during the pandemic in Germany, with approximately a quarter reporting at least some loneliness both before and after (Beutel et al., 2021). A study using the UK Household Longitudinal Study (UKHLS) also found no difference in loneliness in April 2020 compared with 2015–2019 (Niedzwiedz et al., 2021), nor did a survey of Swedish citizens aged 65–71 years who found loneliness remained stable between March 2020 and pre-pandemic levels (Kivi et al., 2021). Surprisingly, a study in Barcelona found loneliness decreased in the first ten days of the pandemic, even for people living alone (Bartrés-Faz et al., 2021).

A consistent finding across studies is that the age profile of loneliness changed during the pandemic. Before the pandemic, older age groups were generally found to experience higher levels of loneliness. However, pandemic-era research consistently indicates that younger people experienced higher levels of loneliness (Baarck et al., 2021; Varga et al., 2021; Buecker & Horstmann, 2021; Beutel et al., 2021). Some studies also suggest that women experienced higher levels of loneliness (Varga et al., 2021; Bu et al., 2020), although not all research supports this trend (Baarck et al., 2021). Several studies identify living alone as a risk factor for loneliness (Atzendorf & Gruber, 2021; Bu et al., 2020), along with being single and childless (Arpino et al., 2022). Economic disadvantage—whether in terms of income, employment, or educational qualifications—increases the risk of experiencing loneliness (Bu et al., 2020; Cohen-Mansfield et al., 2016). Despite the shift in age-related loneliness patterns, other risk factors for loneliness during the pandemic remained largely unchanged from pre-pandemic findings (Hansen & Slagsvold, 2015).

Cross-country Comparisons: Evolution over Time

The measures used to assess loneliness varied across countries, so we dichotomised them for consistency (see Chap. 3 for details). Figure 4.6 illustrates the estimated proportion of individuals experiencing loneliness before and during the pandemic, adjusted for age, gender, education and employment status. We initially expected loneliness to increase during the Shock phase and then decline during Reprise and remain stable or decrease further during Demise, as lockdown restrictions eased. However, these observed patterns did not fully align with these expectations. One partial exception was the UK, where loneliness levels decreased during the Reprise and the Demise periods compared to the Shock phase. In France and the UK—where pre-pandemic data on loneliness was available—there was a decline in loneliness during the initial Shock period. This trend may reflect two contrasting effects: individuals with family members had increased opportunities to spend time with them, while those without close family connections experienced similar levels of loneliness to what they did before the pandemic.

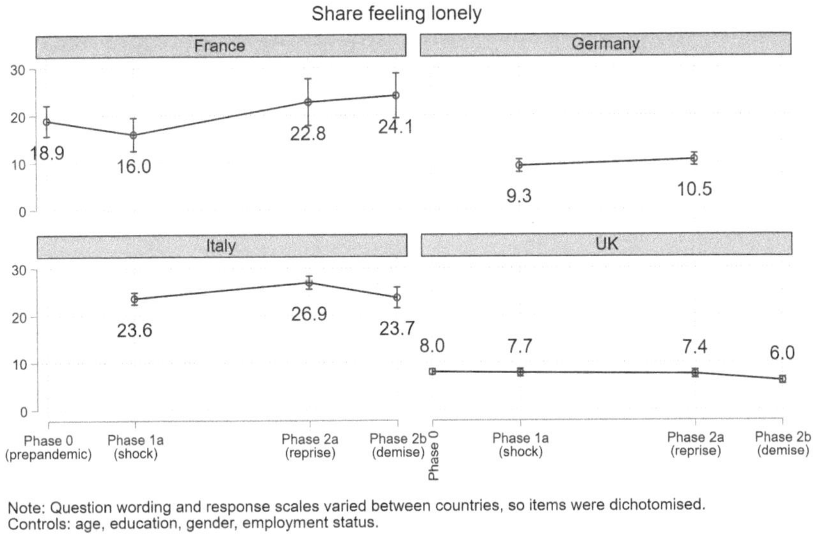

Fig. 4.6 The prevalence of feelings of loneliness before and during the pandemic: estimated proportion of people reporting feeling lonely. (Note: Questions wordings and response scales between countries, so items were dischotomised. Estimated values were adjusted for age, gender, education, and, employment status)

Cross-country Comparison: Identifying Vulnerable Groups

Results from the multivariate analysis into the chances of experiencing loneliness are reported in Table A4.9 in the Online Appendix. Consistent with earlier studies of loneliness during the pandemic, we see that reductions in loneliness over the course of the pandemic were greater for those older than 55 years old in the UK and France and from the age of 35 years in Italy. As in previous studies, women in the UK and Italy were more likely than men to report loneliness. This gender difference increased during the first year of the pandemic, but had lessened by September 2021 in both countries. Such gender differences were not apparent in France or Germany.

As expected, individuals living with partners were less likely to experience loneliness. Individuals living with older children in the UK were less likely to report feeling lonely, but that was not the case for parents of young children. In Italy, parents reported feeling higher effects of loneliness than non-parents. Higher income individuals in Italy and UK were also less likely to feel lonely. The protective effects of income on wellbeing have been observed in Italy and the UK, possibly highlighting more generalised, welfare-linked economic protections in Germany and France. Individuals who had contracted COVID-19 were also more likely to report loneliness during the pandemic. This was not observed in France, however.

Cross-country Comparison: Did the Pandemic Exacerbate Group-Level Differences?

As questions concerning loneliness were asked before the pandemic in both France and the UK, the multivariate analysis comparing the likelihood of feeling lonely before and during the pandemic is restricted to these two countries. The findings from this analysis are detailed in Table A4.10 in the Online Appendix.

In the UK, gender differences in the likelihood of loneliness were exacerbated during the pandemic but declined to negligible levels by the Demise phase. Before the pandemic, individuals over the age of 55 were less likely to feel lonely than the youngest age group, and these differences continued during the pandemic.

Reductions in loneliness over the pandemic in the UK were also concentrated among those in higher- and middle-income households compared with low-income households. Those in higher- and middle-income households in France were less likely than those in low-income households to be lonely before the pandemic. These differences reduced over the course of the pandemic but returned in the Demise phase.

Our findings do not indicate a dramatic increase in loneliness levels over the course of the pandemic in the observed countries. The proportions of people experiencing loneliness did not reach those figures shown in previous studies using SHARE data, except in Italy, where about a quarter of respondents reported feeling lonely. This regional difference aligns with earlier research showing higher levels of loneliness in southern European countries (Cohn-Schwartz et al., 2022). As in previous studies, we found that younger adults (Baarck et al., 2021; Varga et al., 2021; Buecker & Horstmann, 2021; Beutel et al., 2021), and those in low-income households (Bu et al., 2020; Cohen-Mansfield et al., 2016) were more affected by loneliness during the pandemic compared to older adults. The pattern is consistent with pre-pandemic trends. Many researchers have pointed out that the pandemic exacerbated existing social inequalities (Bambra et al., 2020; Recchi et al., 2020b). The increase in loneliness amongst younger people is particularly concerning, given the rising mental health challenges affecting this demographic in many countries (Gagne et al., 2021a, b). As in previous research (Varga et al., 2021; Bu et al., 2020; Baarck et al., 2021), we find inconsistent results in relation to gender differences. Men in the UK and Italy experienced lower levels of loneliness compared to women, whereas this trend was not observed in France or Germany. Germany stands out as the only country where there were very few predictors of loneliness during the pandemic. As seen in other regions, unemployment and living alone were associated with higher levels of loneliness, but changes over the course of the pandemic were minimal. This may be partly due to the fact that only two time points were available for Germany.

Conclusion

What did we learn about the impact of the pandemic on physical health and wellbeing? How can we use those lessons to prepare for future pandemics that epidemiologists are warning us of (Haileamlak, 2022)?

Using harmonised data collected during the pandemic in France, Germany, Italy, and the UK, we have examined how physical health, subjective wellbeing (life satisfaction and happiness), and several facets of mental health—such as depression, anxiety, and loneliness—varied across population sub-groups within these four countries during the pandemic. Numerous common patterns have emerged. Our findings are constrained by pre-pandemic data not being available in Italy, and a measure of anxiety not being available for UK.

First, we examined how physical and mental health evolved during the pandemic, and where possible compared that with pre-pandemic levels. In France, where this indicator was recorded in all time periods, general health improved during the Shock period, before it steadily declined, which could be attributed to the "eye of the hurricane" paradox. Meanwhile, in Italy, health was measured only during the pandemic and gradually declined after the Shock period. In the UK and Germany, general health was only measured before the pandemic and during Reprise, and demonstrated the greatest consistency with only a slight increase. This pattern for general health can be attributed to individuals being sheltered during the Shock and, and to a lesser extent, also in the Reprise period.

For most countries, loneliness decreased during the Shock and patterns of anxiety and depression mirrored this pattern. The pandemic resulted in families initially being 'forced' to spend time together, but less so in the later periods. As such, while those with families became less lonely, those without families were not lonelier than before. Family support networks provided a buffer against any increased levels of anxiety and depression resulting from the sudden disruption to normal life, fear, and anticipation of being infected with COVID-19. The concomitant economic anxiety was reduced to some extent owing to policies undertaken by most governments. While in Italy and the UK there was a decrease in anxiety, depression, and loneliness by the end of the pandemic, this was not the case in France and Germany.

We analysed cognitive measures of wellbeing, happiness and life satisfaction. Unlike physical and mental health measures, these are not concerned with how individuals feel in the moment, but rather reflect how people feel about their lives in general. In France, Germany, and the UK levels of happiness and life satisfaction fell during Shock before gradually increasing again. In Italy, happiness was constant during the pandemic, with only a slight upward trend. These findings are consistent with the pandemic suddenly plunging people's lives into chaos, and the possibility of returning to normal life improving during Reprise and Demise periods.

Next, we examined whether everyone's experiences within each country was the same. Some interesting differences emerged. In all four countries, we found that those who experienced COVID-19 reported not only worse physical health, but also worse mental health. We also found that physical and mental health varied by sub-groups (consistent with patterns established by existing pre-pandemic research). Those who are employed, have a partner, and higher incomes reported better physical and mental health in terms of depression and anxiety. One exception was that those who were retired, after controlling for age, reported lower levels of anxiety and depression in the UK.

During the pandemic, those who were below 35 years of age noted better physical health across all four countries. They had the highest chance of feeling anxious and depressed in Italy; in other countries, the pattern is not as clear. In France and Germany, there was no association of age with the likelihood of being depressed, while in UK individuals aged over 55 years were more likely to be depressed than younger age groups. In France, individuals aged over 55 years were more likely be anxious than younger age groups, while in Germany the likelihood of being anxious was the highest for the 35–54 years age group. Overall, we found poorer mental health but better physical health for younger age groups.

Women of all ages also reported better physical health but poorer mental health. This is consistent with existing research, demonstrating that the school closures during the pandemic encouraged parents to spend more time on childcare, but this increase was disproportionately higher for women. However, having children in the household was not associated with physical and mental health in most countries, aside from in Italy where there was a negative association. It is possible that being able to spend more time with children improved parents' mental health, but additional childcare responsibilities may have had the opposite association, nullifying each other.

While this descriptive analysis limits the ability to conclude causal relationships, overall findings in conjunction with existing research suggest the pandemic was something of a double-edged sword, with the experience varying by personal circumstances. The pandemic allowed people to spend more time with their family and afforded a better work–life balance, improving mental health, and following guidelines for better hygiene improving general health. However, the accompanying disruption to daily life, economic uncertainty, cessation or dramatic reduction in social interactions adversely affected population's health and wellbeing, particularly younger age groups. The greater burden of childcare responsibilities on women may have adversely affected their mental health. Further research is required to determine whether structural changes to people's lives—especially among groups most affected by the pandemic—can help safeguard their health and wellbeing against future pandemics or other adverse global crises.

References

Allas, T., Chinn, D., Sjatil, P. E., & Zimmerman, W. (2020). *Wellbeing in Europe: Addressing the high cost of Covid-19 on life satisfaction*. McKinsey & Company.

Ammar, A., Chtourou, H., Boukhris, O., Trabelsi, K., Masmoudi, L., Brach, M., Bouaziz, B., et al. on behalf of the ECLB-COVID19 Consortium COVID-19. (2022). Home confinement negatively impacts social participation and life satisfaction: A worldwide multicenter study. *International Journal of Environmental Research and Public Health, 19*(22), 14878. https://doi.org/10.3390/ijerph192214878

Arpino, B., Mair, C. A., Quashie, N. T., & Antczak, R. (2022). Loneliness before and during the COVID-19 pandemic—Are unpartnered and childless older adults at higher risk? *European Journal of Ageing*. https://doi.org/10.1007/s10433-022-00718-x

Atzendorf, J., & Gruber, S. (2021). Depression and loneliness of older adults in Europe and Israel after the first wave of COVID-19. *European Journal of Ageing*. https://doi.org/10.1007/s10433-021-00640-8

Baarck, J., Balahur-Dobrescu, A., Cassio, L. G., D'hombres, B., Pasztor, Z., & Tintori, G. (2021). *Loneliness in the EU: Insights from surveys and online media data* (EUR 30765 EN). Publications Office of the European Union. https://doi.org/10.2760/46553

Bachmann, R., Gonschor, M., Korfhage, T., & Wübker, A. (2021). COVID-19 and life satisfaction across Europe. *Applied Economics Letters*. https://doi.org/10.1080/13504851.2021.2005766

Bambra, C., Riordan, R., Ford, J., & Matthews, F. (2020). The COVID-19 pandemic and health inequalities. *Journal of Epidemiology and Community Health*. https://doi.org/10.1136/jech-2020-214401

Bartrés-Faz, D., Macià, D., Cattaneo, G., Borràs, R., Tarrero, C., Solana, J., Tormos, J. M., & Pascual-Leone, A. (2021). The paradoxical effect of COVID-19 outbreak on loneliness. *BJPsych Open, 7*(e30), 1–4. https://doi.org/10.1192/bjo.2020.163

Berkman, L. F., & Krishna, A. (2014). Social network epidemiology. In L. F. Berkman, I. Kawachi, & M. M. Glymour (Eds.), *Social Epidemiology* (2nd ed., pp. 234–289). Oxford University Press.

Beutel, M. E., Hettich, N., Ernst, M., Schmutzer, G., Tibubos, A. N., & Brähler, E. (2021). Mental health and loneliness in the German general population during the COVID-19 pandemic compared to a representative pre-pandemic assessment. *Scientific Reports, 11*, 14946. https://doi.org/10.1038/s41598-021-94434-8

Blom, A. G., Gathmann, C., & Krieger, U. (2015). Setting Up an Online Panel Representative of the General Population: The German Internet Panel. *Field Methods, 27*(4), 391–408. https://doi.org/10.1177/1525822X15574494

Blom, A. G., Cornesse, C., Friedel, S., Krieger, U., Fikel, M., Rettig, T.,... & Reifenscheid, M. (2020). High frequency and high quality survey data collection: the Mannheim Corona Study. *In Survey Research Methods, 14*(2), 171–178.

Bu, F., Steptoe, A., & Fancourt, D. (2020). Who is lonely in lockdown? Cross-cohort analyses of predictors of loneliness before and during the COVID-19 pandemic. *Public Health, 186*, 31–34.

Buecker, S., & Horstmann, K. T. (2021). Loneliness and social isolation during the COVID-19 pandemic: A systematic review enriched with empirical evidence from a large-scale diary study. *European Psychologist, 26*(4), 272–284. https://doi.org/10.1027/1016-9040/a000453

Cacioppo, J. T., Hughes, M. E., Waite, L. J., Hawkley, L. C., & Thisted, R. A. (2006). Loneliness as a specific risk factor for depressive symptoms: Cross-sectional and longitudinal analyses. *Psychology and Aging, 21*(1), 140–151. https://doi.org/10.1037/0882-7974.21.1.140

Carlsen, E. Ø., Caspersen, I. H., Ask, H., et al. (2022). Association between work situation and life satisfaction during the COVID-19 pandemic: Prospective cohort study in Norway. *BMJ Open, 12*, e049586. https://doi.org/10.1136/bmjopen-2021-049586

Chao, S.-Y., Berrington, A., & Perelli-Harris, B. (2021). *A troubled year: Life satisfaction during the pandemic.* Centre for Population Change, Southampton, UK.

Clark, A. E., & Lepinteur, A. (2021). Pandemic policy and life satisfaction in Europe. *The Review of Income and Wealth.* https://doi.org/10.1111/roiw.12554

Cohen-Mansfield, J., et al. (2016). Correlates and predictors of loneliness in older adults: A review of quantitative results informed by qualitative insights. *International Psychogeriatrics, 28*(4), 557–576. https://doi.org/10.1017/S1041610215001532

Cohn-Schwartz, E., Vitman-Schorr, A., & Khalaila, R. (2022). Physical distancing is related to fewer electronic and in-person contacts and to increased loneliness during the COVID-19 pandemic among older Europeans. *Quality of Life Research, 31*, 1033–1042. https://doi.org/10.1007/s11136-021-02949-4

Daly, M., Sutin, A. R., & Robinson, E. (2020). Longitudinal changes in mental health and the COVID-19 pandemic: Evidence from the UK Household Longitudinal Study. *Psychological Medicine, 13*, 1–10. https://doi.org/10.1017/S0033291720004432

de Pedraza, P., Guzi, M., & Tijdens, K. (2020). *Life dissatisfaction and anxiety in COVID-19 pandemic* (EUR 30243 EN). Publications Office of the European Union. https://doi.org/10.2760/755327

Dukhovnov, D., & Barbieri, M. (2022). County-level socio-economic disparities in COVID-19 mortality in the USA. *International Journal of Epidemiology, 51*(2), 418–428. https://doi.org/10.1093/ije/dyab267

Entringer, T. M., & Gosling, S. D. (2022). Loneliness during a nationwide lockdown and the moderating effect of extroversion. *Social Psychological & Personality Science, 13*(3), 769–780.

Ernst, M., Niederer, D., Werner, A. M., Czaja, S. J., Mikton, C., Ong, A. D., Rosen, T., Brähler, E., & Beutel, M. E. (2022). Loneliness before and during the COVID-19 pandemic: A systematic review with meta-analysis. *American Psychologist*. https://doi.org/10.1037/amp0001005

Eurofound. (2020). *Living, working and COVID-19 dataset*. http://eurofound.link/covid19data

Fancourt, D., Steptoe, A., & Bu, F. (2021). Trajectories of anxiety and depressive symptoms during enforced isolation due to COVID-19 in England: A longitudinal observational study. *The Lancet Psychiatry, 8*(2), 141–149. https://doi.org/10.1016/S2215-0366(20)30482-X

Feter, N., Caputo, E. L., Doring, I. R., Leite, J. S., Cassuriaga, J., Reichert, F. F., ... & Rombaldi, A. J. (2021). Sharp increase in depression and anxiety among Brazilian adults during the COVID-19 pandemic: findings from the PAMPA cohort. *Public Health, 190*, 101–107.

Gagné, T., Nandi, A., & Schoon, I. (2021a). Time trend analysis of social inequalities in psychological distress among young adults before and during the pandemic: Evidence from the UK Household Longitudinal Study COVID-19 waves. *Journal of Epidemiology & Community Health*. https://doi.org/10.1136/jech-2021-217266

Gagné, T., Schoon, I., & McMunn, A. (2021b). Mental distress among young adults in Great Britain: Long-term trends and early changes during the COVID-19 pandemic. *Social Psychiatry and Psychiatric Epidemiology*. https://doi.org/10.1007/s00127-021-02194-7

Gibson, L. Y., Lockyer, B., Dickerson, J., Endacott, C., Bridges, S., McEachan, R. R. C., Pickett, K. E., Whalan, S., Bear, N. L., Silva, D. T., Prescott, S. L., & Davis, J. A. (2021). Comparison of experiences in two birth cohorts comprising young families with children under four years during the initial COVID-19 lockdown in Australia and the UK: A qualitative study. *International Journal of Environmental Research and Public Health, 18*(17). https://doi.org/10.3390/ijerph18179119

Haileamlak, A. (2022). Pandemics will be more frequent. *Ethiopian Journal of Health Sciences, 32*(2), 228. https://doi.org/10.4314/ejhs.v32i2.1

Hajek, A., Neumann-Böhme, S., Sabat, I., Torbica, A., Schreyögg, J., Barros, P., Stargardt, T., & König, H. (2022). Depression and anxiety in later COVID-19 waves across Europe: New evidence from the European COvid Survey (ECOS). *Psychiatry Research, 317*, 114902. https://doi.org/10.1016/j.psychres.2022.114902

Hansen, T., & Slagsvold, B. (2015). Late-life loneliness in 11 European countries: Results from the Generations and Gender Survey. *Social Indicators Research, 124*(1), 1–20.

Hawkley, L. C., Thisted, R. A., Masi, C. M., & Cacioppo, J. T. (2010). Loneliness predicts increased blood pressure: 5-year cross-lagged analyses in middle-aged and older adults. *Psychology and Aging, 25*(1), 132–141. https://doi.org/10.1037/a0017805

HM Government. (2018). *A connected society: A strategy for tackling loneliness – laying the foundations for change*. Department for Digital, Culture, Media and Sport.

Holt-Lunstad, J., Smith, T. B., Baker, M., Harris, T., & Stephenson, D. (2015). Loneliness and social isolation as risk factors for mortality: A meta-analytic review. *Perspectives on Psychological Science, 10*(2), 227–237. https://doi.org/10.1177/1745691614568352

Holt-Lunstad, J., Smith, T. B., & Layton, J. B. (2010). Social relationships and mortality risk: A meta-analytic review. *PLOS Medicine, 7*(7), e1000316. https://doi.org/10.1371/journal.pmed.1000316

Institute of Global Health Innovation. (2020). Global insights on life satisfaction: COVID-19 behaviour tracker. Imperial College in collaboration with the World Happiness Report team.

Kawachi, I., & Berkman, L. F. (2014). Social capital, social cohesion, and health. In L. F. Berkman, I. Kawachi, & M. M. Glymour (Eds.), *Social Epidemiology* (2nd ed., pp. 290–319). Oxford University Press.

Khlat, M., Ghosn, W., Guillot, M., Vandentorren, S., Delpierre, C., Desgrées du Loû, A., Fouillet, A., Ghosn, W., Guillot, M., Lefèvre, T., Khlat, M., Rican, S., Vandentorren, S. (2022). Impact of the COVID-19 crisis on the mortality profiles of the foreign-born in France during the first pandemic wave. *Social Science & Medicine 313*, 115160. https://doi.org/10.1016/j.socscimed.2022.115160

Kivi, M., Hansson, I., & Bjälkebring, P. (2021). Up and about: Older adults' well-being during the COVID-19 pandemic in a Swedish longitudinal study. *The Journals of Gerontology: Series B, 76*(2), e4–e9. https://doi.org/10.1093/geronb/gbaa084

Kwong, A. S. F., Pearson, R. M., Smith, D. et al. (2020). Longitudinal evidence for persistent anxiety in young adults through COVID-19 restrictions. *Wellcome Open Research, 5*, 195. https://doi.org/10.12688/wellcomeopenres.16206.1

Kwong, A. S. F., Pearson, R. M., Adams, M. J., et al. (2021). Mental health during the COVID-19 pandemic in two longitudinal UK population cohorts. *The British Journal of Psychiatry, 218*(6), 334–343. https://doi.org/10.1192/bjp.2020.242

Lane, J., Therriault, D., & Dupuis, A. (2022). The impact of the COVID-19 pandemic on the anxiety of adolescents in Québec. *Child & Youth Care Forum, 51*, 811–833. https://doi.org/10.1007/s10566-021-09655-9

Lasgaard, M., Friis, K., & Shevlin, M. (2016). Where are all the lonely people? A population-based study of high-risk groups across the life span. *Social Psychiatry and Psychiatric Epidemiology, 53*, 1–31.

Lees, V., Hay, R., Bould, H., Kwong, A. S. F., Major-Smith, D., Kounali, D., & Pearson, R. M. (2022). The impact of routines on emotional and behavioural difficulties in children and on parental anxiety during COVID-19. *PsyArXiv Preprint.* https://doi.org/10.1101/2022.03.25.22272950

Lockyer, B., Endacott, C., Dickerson, J., & Sheard, L. (2022). Growing up during a public health crisis: A qualitative study of Born in Bradford early adolescents during COVID-19. *BMC. Psychology, 10*(1). https://doi.org/10.1186/s40359-022-00851-3

Lockyer, B., Sheard, L., Smith, H., Dickerson, J., Kelly, B., McEachan, R., Pickett, K. E., Sheldon, T., & Wright, J. (2020). *'Her whole little life has changed dramatically': Findings of a qualitative study into children's mental wellbeing in Bradford during COVID-19.* https://doi.org/10.1186/s40359-022-00851-3

Magnúsdóttir, I., Lovik, A., Unnarsdóttir, A. B., McCartney, D., Ask, H., Kõiv, K., Christoffersen, L. A. N., Johnson, S. U., Hauksdóttir, A., Fawns-Ritchie, C., Helenius, D., González-Hijón, J., Lu, L., Ebrahimi, O. V., Hoffart, A., Porteous, D. J., Fang, F., Jakobsdóttir, J., Lehto, K., et al. (2022). Acute COVID-19 severity and mental health morbidity trajectories in patient populations of six nations: An observational study. *The Lancet.* https://doi.org/10.1016/S2468-2667(22)00042-1

Mayer, L. H., Stolz, E., & Freidl, W. (2022). Trajectories of loneliness, depressive symptoms, and anxiety symptoms during the COVID-19 pandemic in Austria. *Public Health, 212*, 10–13. https://doi.org/10.1016/j.puhe.2022.08.004

Mishra, V., Seyedzenouzi, G., Almohtadi, A., Chowdhury, T., Khashkhusha, A., Axiaq, A., Wong, W. Y. E., & Harky, A. (2021). Health inequalities during COVID-19 and their effects on morbidity and mortality. *Journal of Healthcare Leadership, 13*, 19–26. https://doi.org/10.2147/JHL.S270175

Moreno-Agostino, D., Fisher, H. L., Goodman, A., Hatch, S. L., Morgan, C., Richards, M., Das-Munshi, J., & Ploubidis, G. B. (2022). Disruption of long-term psychological distress trajectories during the COVID-19 pandemic: Evidence from three British cohorts. *medRxiv.* https://doi.org/10.1101/2022.04.22.22274164

Nandi, A., & Platt, L. (2021). Ethnic differences in effect of COVID-19: Household and local context. *Understanding Society Working Paper Series, 2020-14.*

Nesterko, Y., Friedrich, M., Brähler, E., et al. (2019). Mental health among immigrants in Germany – The impact of self-attribution and attribution by others as an immigrant. *BMC Public Health, 19*, 1697. https://doi.org/10.1186/s12889-019-8060-y

Niedzwiedz, C. L., Green, M. J., Benzeval, M., Campbell, D., Craig, P., Demou, E., Leyland, A., Pearce, A., Thomson, R., Whitley, E., & Katikireddi, S. V. (2021). Mental health and health behaviours before and during the initial phase of the COVID-19 lockdown: Longitudinal analyses of the UK Household Longitudinal Study. *Journal of Epidemiology & Community Health, 75*(3), 224–231. https://doi.org/10.1136/jech-2020-215060

OECD (2021). COVID-19 and Well-being: Life in the Pandemic, OECD Publishing, Paris. https://doi.org/10.1787/1e1ecb53-en

Office for National Statistics (ONS). (2022). *Personal well-being in the UK: April 2021 to March 2022.*

Pan, K.-Y., Kok, A. A. L., Eikelenboom, M., Horsfall, M., Jörg, F., Luteijn, R. A., Rhebergen, D., van Oppen, P., Giltay, E. J., & Penninx, B. W. J. H. (2021). The mental health impact of the COVID-19 pandemic on people with and without depressive, anxiety, or obsessive-compulsive disorders: A longitudinal study of three Dutch case-control cohorts. *The Lancet Psychiatry, 8*(2), 121–129. https://doi.org/10.1016/S2215-0366(20)30491-0

Platt, L., & Warwick, R. (2020). COVID-19 and ethnic inequalities in England and Wales. *Fiscal Studies, 41*(2), 259–289. https://doi.org/10.1111/1475-5890.12228

Porter, C., Favara, M., Hittmeyer, A., et al. (2021). Impact of the COVID-19 pandemic on anxiety and depression symptoms of young people in the global south: Evidence from a four-country cohort study. *BMJ Open, 11*, e049653. https://doi.org/10.1136/bmjopen-2021-049653

Prati, G., & Mancini, A. D. (2021). The psychological impact of COVID-19 pandemic lockdowns: A review and meta-analysis of longitudinal studies and natural experiments. *Psychological Medicine, 51*(2), 201–211.

Proto, E., & Quintana-Domeque, C. (2021). COVID-19 and mental health deterioration by ethnicity and gender in the UK. *PLOS ONE, 16*(1), e0244419. https://doi.org/10.1371/journal.pone.0244419

Recchi, E., Ferragina, E., Godechot, O., Helmeid, E., Pauly, S., Safi, M., Sauger, N., Schradie, J., Tittel, K., & Zola, A. (2020b). *Living through lockdown: Social inequalities and transformations during the COVID-19 crisis in France.* OSC Working Paper. Sciences Po.

Recchi, E., Ferragina, E., Helmeid, E., Pauly, S., Safi, M., Sauger, N., & Schradie, J. (2020a). The 'eye of the hurricane' paradox: An unexpected and unequal rise of well-being during the COVID-19 lockdown in France. *Research in Social Stratification and Mobility, 68*, 100508.

Recchi, E., Safi, M., Ferragina, E., Schradie, J., Sauger, N., (2022). Sciences Po, Centre de données socio-politiques (CDSP), CNRS, Faire face au Covid-19 - vague 1 (ELIPSS 2020). https://doi.org/10.21410/7E4/PZT8SO

Salari, N., Hosseinian-Far, A., Jalali, R., et al. (2020). Prevalence of stress, anxiety, depression among the general population during the COVID-19 pandemic: A systematic review and meta-analysis. *Global Health, 16*, 57. https://doi.org/10.1186/s12992-020-00589-w

Sandu, V., Zolyomi, E., & Lieschsenring, K. (2021). *Addressing loneliness and social isolation among older people in Europe* (Policy Brief 2021/7). European Centre for Social Welfare Policy and Research.

Santini, Z., & Koyanagi, A. (2021). Loneliness and its association with depressed mood, anxiety symptoms, and sleep problems in Europe during the COVID-19 pandemic. *Acta Neuropsychiatrica, 33*(3), 160–163. https://doi.org/10.1017/neu.2020.48

Santomauro, D., et al. (2021). Global prevalence and burden of depressive and anxiety disorders in 204 countries and territories in 2020 due to the COVID-19 pandemic. *The Lancet, 398*, 1700–1712.

Shankar, A., McMunn, A., Banks, J., & Steptoe, A. (2011). Loneliness, social isolation, and behavioral and biological health indicators in older adults. *Health Psychology, 30*(4), 377–385. https://doi.org/10.1037/a0022826

Smith, M. L., Steinman, L. E., & Casey, E. A. (2020). Combatting social isolation among older adults in a time of physical distancing: The COVID-19 social connectivity paradox. *Frontiers in Public Health, 8*, 403. https://doi.org/10.3389/fpubh.2020.00403

Steptoe, A., Owen, N., Kunz-Ebrecht, S. R., Brydon, L. (2004). Loneliness and neuroendocrine, cardiovascular, and inflammatory stress responses in middle-aged men and women. *Psychoneuroendocrinology, 29*(5), 593–611.

The Independent Scientific Advisory Group for Emergencies (SAGE). (2020). *A closer look at Sweden's response to COVID-19.*

University of Essex, Institute for Social and Economic Research. (2023). Understanding Society: Waves 1–13, 2009–2022 and Harmonised BHPS: Waves 1–18, 1991–2009. [data collection]. 18th Edition. UK Data Service. SN: 6614, DOI: http://doi.org/10.5255/UKDA-SN-6614-19

van der Velden, P. G., Contino, C., Das, M., van Loon, P., & Bosmans, M. W. G. (2020). Anxiety and depression symptoms, and lack of emotional support among the general population before and during the COVID-19 pandemic: A prospective national study on prevalence and risk factors. *Journal of Affective Disorders, 277*, 540–548. https://doi.org/10.1016/j.jad.2020.08.026

van der Velden, P. G., Hyland, P., Contino, C., von Gaudecker, H.-M., Muffels, R., & Das, M. (2021). Anxiety and depression symptoms, the recovery from symptoms, and loneliness before and after the COVID-19 outbreak among the general population: Findings from a Dutch population-based longitudinal study. *PLOS ONE, 16*(1), e0245057. https://doi.org/10.1371/journal.pone.0245057

van Tilburg, T. G., Steinmetz, S., Stolte, E., van der Roest, H., & de Vries, D. H. (2021). Loneliness and mental health during the COVID-19 pandemic: A study among Dutch older adults. *The Journals of Gerontology: Series B, 76*(7), e249–e255. https://doi.org/10.1093/geronb/gbaa111

Van Winkle, Z., Ferragina, E., & Recchi, E. (2021). The unexpected decline in feelings of depression among adults ages 50 and older in 11 European countries amid the COVID-19 pandemic. *Socius, 7*, 23780231211032741.

Varga, T. V., Bu, F., Dissing, A. S., Elsenburg, L. K., Bustamante, J. J. H., Matta, J., van Zon, S. K. R., Brouwer, S., Bültmann, U., Fancourt, D., Hoeyer, K., Goldberg, M., Melchior, M., Strandberg-Larsen, K., Zins, M., Clotworthy, A., & Rod, N. H. (2021). Loneliness, worries, anxiety, and precautionary behaviours in response to the COVID-19 pandemic: A longitudinal analysis of 200,000 Western and Northern Europeans. *The Lancet Regional Health – Europe, 2*, 100020. https://doi.org/10.1016/j.lanepe.2020.100020

Vezzoni, C., Chiesi, A. M., Biolcati F., Dotti Sani, G. M., Guglielmi, S., Ladini, R., Maggini N., Maraffi M., Molteni F., Moroni M., Pedrazzani A., Piacentini F., Sarti S., Segatti, P., (2024). *ResPOnsE COVID-19. Cumulative file: Wave 1 to Wave 6 (English version)*, UNIMI Dataverse, V1. https://doi.org/10.13130/RD_UNIMI/IJDSVS

Walker, E., Ploubidis, G., & Fancourt, D. (2019). Social engagement and loneliness are differentially associated with neuro-immune markers in older age: Time-varying associations from the English Longitudinal Study of Ageing. *Brain, Behavior, and Immunity, 82*, 224–229.

Xue, B., & McMunn, A. (2021). Gender differences in unpaid care work and psychological distress in the UK COVID-19 lockdown. *PLOS ONE*. https://doi.org/10.1371/journal.pone.0247959

CHAPTER 5

Gender Inequality in Unpaid Care Work During the COVID-19 Pandemic. A Cross-Country Comparison of France, Germany, Italy, and the UK

Anne McMunn, Marija Bashevska, Marta Dominguez Folgueras, Giulia Dotti Sani, Thierry Gagne, and Bartholomew Konechni

Introduction

During the COVD-19 pandemic, the boundaries between work and family life were more intertwined than ever in recent history. The closure of schools and childcare facilities placed a significant burden on parents, who

A. McMunn (✉) • T. Gagne
Research Department of Epidemiology & Public Health, University College London, London, UK
e-mail: a.mcmunn@ucl.ac.uk; t.gagne@ucl.ac.uk

M. Bashevska
Department of Cultures, Politics and Society, University of Turin, Turin, Italy
e-mail: marija.bashevska@unito.it

E. Naumann et al. (eds.), *Social Life during COVID-19 in France, Germany, Italy and the UK*,
https://doi.org/10.1007/978-3-031-99349-7_5

had to balance childcare, homeschooling, and remote work. Early speculation suggested that these circumstances might encourage a more equitable division of unpaid care work—childcare and housework—between parents. This chapter examines whether such a shift occurred over the course of the pandemic in four European countries with different gender policy environments: France, Italy, Germany, and the UK. We use the term 'gender' in a binary fashion throughout this chapter to refer to roles and responsibilities that have traditionally been socially ascribed to men and women based on assumptions of binary biological sex. Our study therefore has an inherent heteronormative and cis-gendered bias, simply due to data availability. We use the term 'unpaid care work' to refer in a general way to all of the unpaid services that are provided within families for the health, wellbeing, development, and protection of family members (Moreira da Silva, 2019). Our empirical investigation focuses specifically on housework and childcare.

Pre-pandemic Gender Differences in Housework and Childcare in France, Germany, Italy, and the UK

In 2019, the European Institute for Gender Equality ranked France third in the EU for gender equality, while Germany was ranked eleventh equal with the EU average, and Italy thirteenth (European Institute for Gender Equality, 2019). Women's employment rates were similar in both Germany and the UK in 2018, at 76% of women aged 20–64 years employed in Germany and 74% in the UK (Eurostat, 2020). This figure was slightly lower in France at 68% although women's employment rates have been fairly equal across these three countries post-pandemic (71–72% in 2023) (Eurostat, 2020, 2024; ONS, 2024). These levels were slightly above the EU average of 67% in 2018 and compared with the equivalent 2018 figures for men at 84% in Germany and the UK, and 75% in France (Eurostat, 2020). However, part-time employment has long been a common way for

M. D. Folgueras • B. Konechni
Centre for Research on Social Inequalities, Sciences Po, Paris, France
e-mail: marta.dominguezfolgueras@sciencespo.fr;
bartholomew.konechni@sciencespo.fr

G. Dotti Sani
Department of Social and Political Sciences, University of Milan, Milano, Italy
e-mail: giulia.dottisani@unimi.it

mothers to combine employment with parenting in both the UK and especially Germany. In 2019, 47% of female workers in Germany and 38% in the UK were employed part-time, compared with 33% in Italy and 30% in France (European Institute for Gender Equality, 2019; Francis-Devine & Hutton, 2024). Women in both the UK and Germany are overrepresented in precarious and insecure employment (Bergmann et al., 2019; Florisson & Gable, 2022). Italian women have considerably lower employment rates than both Italian men and women in other European countries (OECD, 2023a). In 2018 only 53% of Italian women aged 20–64 were employed compared with 73% of Italian men in the same age group (Eurostat, 2020). The male 'breadwinner' work–family arrangement is still very common among Italian couples, especially those with young children (Dotti Sani & Scherer, 2018; Hook, 2015). Researchers partially attribute this pattern to the low welfare support offered to Italian families with children, particularly childcare for children under the age of three, which is comparatively less well established in Italy (OECD, 2023b). Conversely, France is above the OECD average regarding public investment in early childhood education and care. The nation has recently made education compulsory for all children from the age of three. In addition, the provision of formal childcare for children under the age of three is far greater in France than in either the UK, Germany, or Italy (OECD, 2023b). Most state-supported childcare provision for children under the age of three in the UK is part-time (fewer than 30 hours per week), while in Italy there is almost no provision at all (Mills et al., 2013; OECD, 2023b). Moreover, childcare costs in the UK are far higher than in any other European country, at 51% of median income for two-parent families compared with 16.7% in France and approximately 3% in Germany (Euronews, 2023).

The disadvantage women face in the labour market is often correlated to their disproportionate share of unpaid care work. This is consistently the case across countries but also varies across countries. For example, it is especially high in Italy (OECD, 2023c), in particular among parents of young children (Anxo et al., 2011; Dotti Sani, 2018), while the time that women in France spend on housework and childcare is nearer the EU average (Pailhé et al., 2021). Similarly, Italian mothers spend considerably more time than fathers on childcare. Time use surveys consistently demonstrate that women in Italy spend over five hours per day completing unpaid care work compared with just over two hours per day among men. In comparison, in France, Germany, and the UK, women spend approximately four hours per day on such work, whereas men in France spend nearly four hours and men in Germany and the UK only about two and a half hours (Champagne et al., 2015; Eurostat, 2016; OECD, 2015, 2023c). Even though women continue to complete the majority of unpaid domestic work, men have increased their participation in unpaid care work over the past 40 years, mainly in relation to childcare activities rather than housework (Altintas & Sullivan, 2016).

Gender imbalances in employment and unpaid care work are not necessarily predicted by the amount of parental leave offered to men and women in these countries. In the UK, mothers have access to a 39 weeks of maternity leave compared with 21.7 weeks in Italy, 16 weeks in France, and 14 weeks in Germany. However, rates of wage replacement are low at 30% in the UK, compared with up to 65% in Germany, 80% in Italy, and 100% for the majority of women in France (Boyer & Fagnani, 2023). Thus, a socio-economic imbalance is created in the UK where only women with access to independent or employer-provided resources can afford to take the entirety of the maternity leave that they are legally entitled to. Fathers in the UK are offered only two weeks of paternity leave, and again levels of wage replacement are much lower than in Germany, Italy, and France, at 30% in the UK compared with 100% in Italy and, as of 2024, Germany (where two weeks are also offered) and France (where fathers have access to five weeks' leave) (OECD, 2022).

Pandemic Responses in France, Germany, Italy, and the UK

France

In France, the first lockdown occurred between 17 March and 11 May 2020. The government officially recommended working from home where possible, and non-essential workplaces were temporarily closed (with access to unemployment benefits if working from home was impossible). Schools and childcare centres were closed too, and thus we observe the highest number of parents staying at home -either teleworking or unemployed- with their children during this first lockdown, although some schools and childcare centres were open for the children of essential workers. In theory, informal childcare was also possible, as it was one of the few reasons that French residents were permitted to leave their homes. However, there are no data on the number or frequency of these causal arrangements. It is important to note that the reopening of schools and childcare centres occurred after 11 May, with only small numbers of children rotating attendance to maintain social distancing. As many social distancing measures were still in place, many children had access to school before the summer holidays, but at a reduced number of hours.

The second lockdown in France took place between 30 October and 15 December 2020. The official guidance to work from home and the closure of all non-essential services were reminiscent of the first lockdown. However, there was a fundamental difference regarding work-family arrangements as schools and childcare centres remained open (only universities were required to move their teaching activities online). As such, parents relied on these institutions to take care of their children, and the additional childcare tasks were expected to be less significant than in the first lockdown.

Finally, France enforced a third and shorter lockdown in 2021, between 3 April and 3 May. This measure again entailed a closure of schools and childcare centres, but the closure took the form of an 'extended holiday', as schools in France typically close for two weeks in April. In 2021, the government decreed that all regions take the holidays simultaneously for three weeks instead of two. Some childcare options, such as camps, were still available to parents if certain hygiene measures were adhered to (for instance, sports camps were possible if the activities took place in the open air). As parents had already anticipated the spring holidays, the impact of this lockdown on work–family arrangements was expected to be minor, as it consisted only of an additional week of holiday.

Germany

Similar to most countries in Europe, Germany's curbing of the spread of the initial outbreak of COVID-19 was achieved through a nationwide lockdown introduced on 22 March 2020. The lockdown strategy required the closure of public spaces and events, limited physical contact, introduced stay at home requirements, restrictions on international travel, recommendations to work from home, and the closure of schools and childcare facilities which were limited to essential workers with children, such as those in the healthcare sector, or workers securing basic supply chains (Reimann et al., 2022). These restrictions were gradually relaxed from the end of April 2020. Schools and businesses reopened with strict hygiene standards in place and the first lockdown ended on 4 May 2020. Owing to rapidly growing numbers of new infections at the start of autumn, the German government reintroduced lockdown measures in

October 2020, marking the second lockdown. Social activities were gradually restricted throughout October, and stricter pandemic-containment measures were imposed in November 2020, re-introducing closure of retail stores, limiting physical contact, and advising work-from-home policies for businesses where feasible. Schools and day care facilities remained open, whereas most schools applied hybrid models as a combination of teachings at school and homeschooling (Reimann et al., 2022). Moreover, owing to the changing situation concerning infections, schools and childcare facilities had varying schedules and closures sometimes announced with only one day's notice, or even on the same day. This imposed unstable and challenging conditions for childcare routines and work–family arrangements for parents with young and school-aged children.

The third lockdown was introduced in January 2021, alongside a vaccination rollout. This led to a subsequent decrease of new cases towards the summer and gradual easing of lockdown measures. The increase in infections started again in July 2021, with the country entering the fourth wave of the pandemic which led to pandemic containment measures being applied on the basis of vaccination status. The increased infections continued throughout the autumn and winter of 2021 and 2022, with stabilisation appearing in the run up to March 2022. At this point, some restrictions on businesses and public events were revoked following the three-step, nationwide opening plan including measures for basic protection, such as wearing masks in public places and public transport. Despite further spikes in infections throughout 2022, the pandemic containment measures were gradually lifted throughout the country across the subsequent periods.

Italy

Italy was the first European country to be struck by COVID-19 and, as a result, the initial preventive measures were extremely strict. The virus first affected a small area in the north of the country which was quarantined on 23 February 2020. National lockdown was progressively imposed until the entire country was effectively shut down on 9 March. During this initial period, referred to by the press and government as 'Phase 1', schools and childcare services, non-essential economic and commercial activities were closed. Italians were strongly recommended not to leave the house and any form of public meeting was explicitly forbidden. Almost two months later, on 4 May, the restrictions were partially removed, and economic activities were permitted to re-open (named 'Phase 2'). However, travelling between regions was still not allowed and, critically, schools and childcare facilities remained closed, forcing working parents to engage in emergency strategies to combine work and care. With 'Phase 3' beginning on 3 June, restrictions were removed altogether, almost all commercial activities re-opened, and Italians could travel within and beyond the country. However, given that vaccines were still not available, citizens were requested to observe one-metre distancing, wear protective masks in closed spaces, and sanitise their hands wherever possible. While lockdown measures were removed altogether by the summer of 2020, schools and childcare services remained closed until the start following of the school year in September 2020. The virus peaked again in the autumn and winter of that year, and several preventive measures such as curfews or the restriction of movement between regions were enforced to curb the increase of COVID-19 infections. Schools and childcare facilities remained open during the period, but strict protective measures were enforced, such as distancing and the use of face masks for teachers and children above the age of six. Moreover, the high rates of COVID-19 cases in schools often required the closing of the specific class or even the entire school, with ensuing consequences for the work-family arrangements of working parents. In 2021, the vaccination campaign began, and other restrictions were gradually dropped although some remained in force until midway through 2022, such as the use of masks in closed spaces.

The UK

The initial cases of COVID-19 infection in the UK were confirmed in January 2020, with the first deaths being reported in March 2020 (UK Government, 2023). The UK government implemented the first national lockdown on 23 March 2020, in which all non-essential travel and contact were prohibited, and most public venues were closed, including schools and childcare facilities (with the exception of children of 'key' workers and vulnerable children). These restrictions were gradually lifted from late May 2020 in England and June 2020 in Wales. They were replaced with measures such as physical distancing, hygiene, wearing face coverings in public spaces, and isolation of symptomatic individuals. Students returned to school in Scotland in August 2020. Concerns of increasing transmission rates in autumn 2020 led the Welsh government to instate a two-week national 'firebreak' lockdown in late October, with similar restrictions to the first lockdown. The governments of England and Scotland subsequently introduced a similar month-long national lockdown in November 2020 (Baker et al., 2021; Senedd Cymru, 2022). Schools and childcare facilities were exempt from the November lockdown in England; however, they ran regimes of regular testing with widespread individual school closures in response to infections.

With the emergence of the Alpha variant in December 2020, national lockdown measures were implemented in both England and Wales from the end of the month, and from 5 January in Scotland, until March 2021, and April 2021 in Scotland. Schools were closed during this second lockdown, but infant care facilities remained open. Vaccination programmes started in December 2020 and by summer 2021 most restrictions were lifted. Limited restrictions—the use of face coverings in public spaces and recommendations to work from home where possible—were reintroduced in early 2022 as a response to the Omicron variant. All restrictions were lifted in England on 24 February 2022, on 30 April 2022 in Scotland, and 30 May 2022 in Wales (Cabinet Office, 2022; Prime Minister's Office, 2021; Senedd Cymru, 2022).

Previous Evidence on Gender Differences in Housework and Childcare During the Pandemic in Europe

Studies in Europe that investigate shifts in gender inequality in unpaid care work during the pandemic have generally found little change, at least at the aggregate level, with some variation for specific groups, such as Germany (Hank & Steinbach, 2021), Switzerland (Steinmetz et al., 2022), and Spain (Farré et al., 2021). In this section, we limit our review to studies deploying probability sampling and have excluded studies that use convenience sampling techniques.

Many studies have looked at gender differences in the UK. Early in the pandemic, a survey of approximately 5000 parents of children aged 4–15 found that mothers spent substantially longer than their partners on housework and childcare in April and May 2020, regardless of pre-pandemic occupation, in terms of sector or earnings (Andrew et al., 2022). Most UK studies have used data from the UKHLS to investigate changes in gender inequality in unpaid care work during the pandemic. One study found that, while the intensity of childcare and housework increased for both men and women, women continued to do more than men (Xue & McMunn, 2021). For example, women in partnerships completed approximately two-thirds of the housework and childcare, reflecting pre-pandemic data. Others found that this figure rose to nearly three-quarters where women had lost employment hours at the start of the pandemic (Zamberlan et al., 2021). Several studies built on these findings to examine periods after the initial lockdown and across the first year of the pandemic. Many studies found no change in gender differences in housework or childcare between April 2020 and March 2021 (Zhou & Kan, 2021). Others found that gender differences diminished compared with pre-pandemic for those with older school aged children, but not for those with younger children (Rodriguez Sanchez et al., 2021). Warren et al. (2021) found that working class mothers were less able to adjust their work hours to accommodate increases in childcare and homeschooling demands during the pandemic, as they had less access than middle class parents to flexible working. Finally, Zamberlan et al. (2022) demonstrated that men temporarily increased the time they spent in unpaid care work after the initial loss of working hours in the pandemic. However, this increase disappeared when they returned to pre-pandemic employment levels. Ultimately, gender inequality in unpaid care work returned to pre-pandemic levels or even higher for all couples under study.

Numerous studies of Germany have also examined the impact of the pandemic on gender divisions of unpaid care work, particularly with regard to childcare. An early study based on the German National Educational Panel Study found that mothers were the main caregivers during the initial months of the pandemic in spring 2020. Fathers also participated but were less involved, usually sharing the duties either with the mother or other caregivers (Zoch et al., 2020). Similarly, a comparison of mothers' and fathers' time spent in childcare between pre-pandemic period and Spring 2020 in the German Socioeconomic Panel Stud (SOEP) found that fathers increased their childcare hours, but so did mothers such that mothers continued to perform the bulk of childcare (Kreyenfeld & Zinn, 2021). A study based on the representative German Family Panel study (*pairfam*) found no significant changes in the distribution of unpaid care work between couples in March 2020 and pre-pandemic divisions (Hank & Steinbach, 2021). A more recent study that uses the same dataset suggests that the initial shock of the pandemic increased gender inequality in the division of care work in spring 2020. However, differences returned to the pre-pandemic level by the second lockdown nine months later in winter 2021 (Jessen et al., 2022). The authors conclude that the pandemic neither increased nor decreased inequality in the division of unpaid care work among parents in Germany.

Building on this, a study comparing gender differences in housework and childcare between April and November 2020 with pre-pandemic levels in Italy demonstrated a temporary increase in childcare and housework hours for both women and men in April 2020. However, the gender difference remained constant and women consistently undertook more hours than their male partners (del Boca et al., 2022).

In France, using data from the *CoCo* study, Pasqualini et al. (2022) found a marginal rebalancing in the gendered division of unpaid care work during the pandemic. However, on closer inspection, they found more gendered patterns in the specific tasks being completed with men more likely to go grocery shopping and women more likely to provide childcare.

Despite important country context differences in policy concerning gender and behaviour, previous investigations of the impact of the pandemic on gender inequality in unpaid care work have not yet deployed a comparative approach. This chapter brings together longitudinal survey data from France, Germany, Italy, and the UK to examine gender differences in housework and childcare over time. With the exception of France, where pre-pandemic measures are unavailable, we compare data collected before the pandemic with data from spring 2020 through summer 2020 in Germany, winter 2021 in the UK, and spring 2021 in France and Italy.

Data, Variables, and Methods

The data sets that are used have been described in Chap. 3. The waves at which information on housework and childcare were available for each study were:

- *UKHLS (UK)*: pre-pandemic main survey Wave 10 (2018–2020), COVID-19 survey waves in April, May, July, September 2020, and January 2021
- *CoCo (France)*: (no pre-pandemic wave available), 1–8 April 2020, 15–22 April 2020, May 2020, November 2020, and April 2021
- *ResPOnsE COVID-19 (Italy)*: pre-pandemic reported retrospectively in May 2020, April–May 2021
- *The German Panel Analysis of Intimate Relationships and Family Dynamics (pairfam) study (Germany)*: Wave 11 (2018/2019) (release 13.0) (Brüderl et al., 2022; Huinink et al., 2011) and COVID-19 survey data May–July 2020 (Walper et al., 2021a, 2021b)

In the UK and French datasets, all participants were asked how many hours they had spent completing housework in the past week. In the

Italian and German datasets, men and women who were living with a partner were asked who undertakes most housework using the following categories: 'I do all', 'I do most', 'We share equally', 'My partner does most', or 'My partner does all'. To compare the UK data with the Italian and German, we limited the sample to male-female couples and combined their reported housework hours. Where the split was 100–0%: each partner was allocated the 'I do all' or 'my partner does all' category respectively, where his or her share was 45–55% of what they were considered to share equally, and the remainder were allocated to 'I do most' or 'My partner does most' accordingly. This was not possible with the French data as partners were not interviewed. Owing to the low number of respondents in certain categories, we combined the extremes such that the variable takes three values: 'I do all/I do most', 'We share equally', or 'My partner does most/My partner does all'.

In the UK and French datasets, all participants were asked how many hours they had spent completing childcare or homeschooling in the past week. Information on childcare time was not available for Italy or Germany.

We demonstrate straightforward differences in means and percentages by gender and country over time. This approach is taken for the entire sample and then on a sub-sample of those who are cohabiting for France and the UK. Comparisons between Germany, Italy, and the UK are restricted to couples. We then deploy linear or multinomial multivariable regression models in a complete-case sample at a specific point in time to account for potential confounding of gender differences by adjusting for age, educational attainment, work status, cohabitation, and household income. Owing to the lack of available data, educational attainment and household income were not included for Germany. We also account for whether respondents are living with children at the time of the current wave when analysing housework as the outcome. We use cross-sectional sample weights to account for survey designs.

Trends in Unpaid Care Work over the Pandemic

Housework in France and the UK

Figure 5.1 shows the average hours of housework performed by women and men in France and the UK across the different time points. It also shows the Stringency Index, a composite indicator developed by the Oxford COVID-19 Government Response Tracker (OxCGRT) to

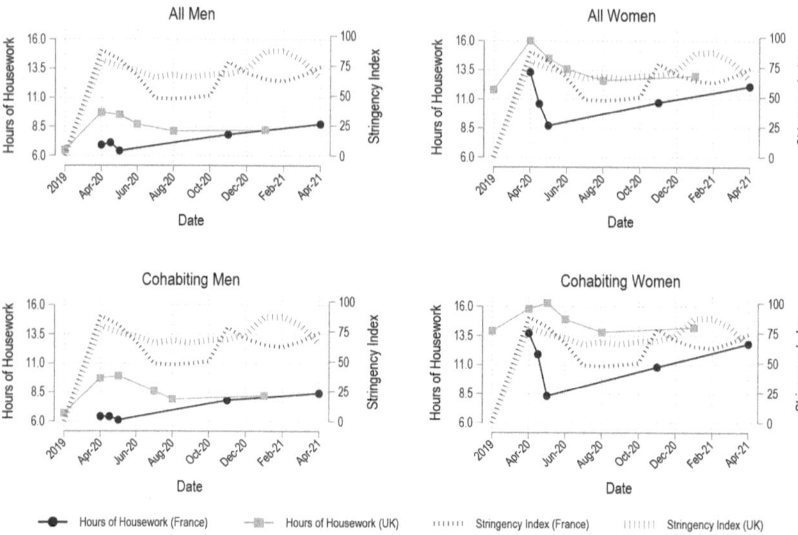

Fig. 5.1 Time trends in housework, general population of adults aged 16+ and cohabiting couples in UK & France. (All estimates differ between genders at the <0.001 level)

measure the strictness of government policies adopted in response to the COVID-19 pandemic. The higher panels report the estimates for the overall sample, whereas the lower panels show the values for cohabitating couples only. As is evident, women consistently report undertaking more housework than men in both countries across all the time points. The gender difference was greatest in both countries during the first lockdown in April 2020, when women's housework hours peaked at 16 hours per week in the UK and 13.3 in France. The gender difference decreased slightly in France, as men increased their housework hours from 6.4 hours per week in May 2020 to 8.7 in April 2021. In contrast to women in France, French men spent more time on housework in the third lockdown than in the first. This greater involvement during the second and third lockdown is challenging to decipher without data from the before COVID. Men might have decreased time spent in housework during the first lockdown, and in the second and third lockdown there may be a return to norms. Alternatively, men might have increased their housework participation in the second and third lockdowns as their partners were less available to take on the work. The increase in housework could be due also to specific activities. For example, there might not have been options for outsourcing work and households may have cooked their own meals more often.

Women in the UK reported completing more housework than women in France during the pandemic. After the initial spike in April, housework hours decreased in May and June as schools and other facilities re-opened in both countries. Housework hours then plateaued for women in the UK at around 13 hours per week, while they increased for women in France during the second lockdown in November. This continued to grow throughout the third lockdown in April 2021, but did not reach the high levels of early April 2020. There was also a minor increase in housework hours of men in April 2020. As with women, this was followed by a decline in May and June 2020, followed by a plateau in weekly housework hours for men in the UK, and an increase for men in France. Again, as with women, men in the UK reported completing more housework than men in France. This difference was smaller between men than women and gradually disappeared for men over time as French men increased their housework hours. These patterns were consistently observed across the overall population as well as among co-habiting couples.

Childcare in France and the UK

Figure 5.2 presents the average hours of childcare carried out by mothers and fathers in both the UK and France during different phases of the pandemic. As before, we distinguish between the sample of all parents and those who cohabit. As with housework, mothers report spending more time on childcare than fathers in both countries and at all time points. In this case, men and women follow similar trends in the two countries: parents report spending more time on childcare related activities in the first lockdown in April 2020, and less time as the pandemic progressed.

The reduction of childcare hours in France over April and May 2020 is difficult to explain by factors external to the household, as movement restrictions and distance measures were still in place. This trend might be explained by 'lockdown fatigue' and parents actively spending less time with children. Our childcare variables successfully capture some interactive activities, but might not cover 'supervision time', defined as moments when parents attend to children, but are not doing an activity with them. We hypothesise that the time spent with children was less interactive by the end of this period. The time in childcare increases again during the second and third lockdowns, reflecting the quantities of the first lockdown. The

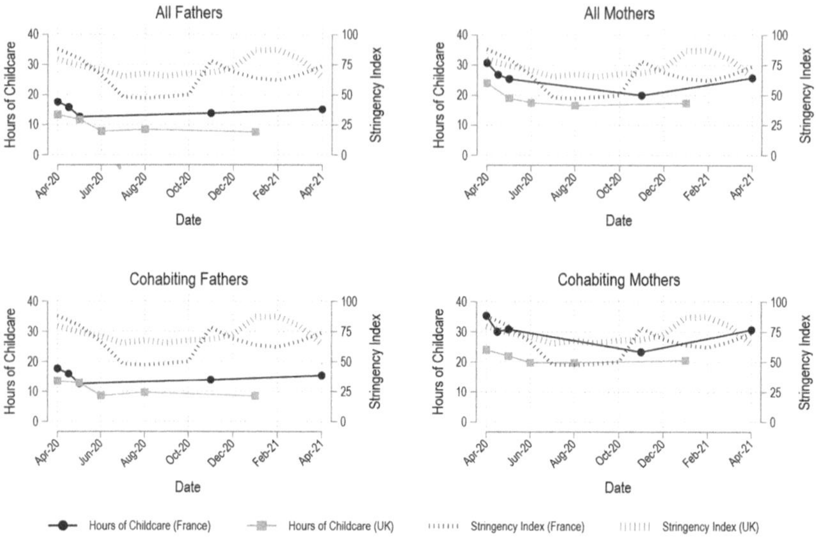

Fig. 5.2 Time trends in childcare, general population of adults aged 16+ and cohabiting couples in UK & France. (All estimates differ between genders at the <0.001 level)

similarities between the third and second points of the first lockdown can be accounted for by the school closures which occurred at both times.

Mothers in the UK also increased their childcare hours in January 2021 when the country experienced school closures again. However, these remained lower than during the initial lockdown. Childcare hours did not increase for fathers in January 2021 in the UK.

Overall, country differences in childcare hours were far smaller than for housework. Here, French parents reported more weekly childcare hours than parents in the UK. There is very little variation between cohabiting parents and parents overall.

Gender Differences in Housework and Childcare in France and the UK in April 2020

Table 5.1 reports the results for multivariable models of gender differences in housework and childcare in the UK and France at the start of the pandemic in April 2020. The table includes both the results from an unadjusted model alongside estimates after controlling for a set of co-variates. The results confirm that women completed far more housework and

Table 5.1 Multivariable models of gender differences in unpaid care work UK and France, April 2020

Dependent variable	*Housework hours*				*Childcare hours*			
Population	*Everyone*		*Cohabiting*		*Everyone*		*Cohabiting*	
UK	B	95% CI	B	95% CI	B	95% CI	B	95% CI
Sample size	$N = 15{,}918$		$N = 11{,}862$		$N = 5{,}299$		$N = 4{,}394$	
Female (ref. = male)								
Bivariate	4.85	[4.27, 5.42]	5.64	[5.03, 6.24]	9.69	[7.06, 12.33]	10.81	[7.78, 13.84]
Fully adjusted[a]	4.89	[4.33, 5.44]	5.59	[4.99, 6.20]	9.54	[7.11, 11.98]	7.28	[4.48, 10.08]
France	B	95% CI	B	95% CI	B	95% CI	B	95% CI
Sample size	$N = 1{,}071$		$N = 725$		$N = 1{,}062$		$N = 721$	
Female (ref. = male)								
Bivariate	6.40	[4.90, 7.89]	7.33	[5.55, 9.11]	7.73	[5.28, 10.18]	11.55	[8.40, 14.7]
Fully adjusted	5.91	[4.36, 7.46]	6.35	[4.48, 8.24]	5.07	[2.60, 7.54]	5.75	[2.72, 8.77]

[a]Adjusted for age, educational attainment, employment, cohabitation (amongst 'everyone' only), living with children (for housework only), household income

childcare—about five to nine times more—than men in both France and the UK. Gender differences were greater for childcare than for housework, except for the adjusted models in France. Indeed, adjusting for controls lessened the gender difference in childcare hours in France by about a third, and by half for cohabiting couples, although the gender differences remain statistically significant. Gender differences in childcare hours were marginally larger in the UK than in France. This is likely due to the greater availability of childcare in France.

Divisions of Housework in Germany, Italy, and the UK

The data for Germany, Italy, and the UK enable the exploration of the division of housework within couples during the pandemic. Figures 5.3 and 5.4 report time trends of the share of housework in the three countries between men and women. Two-thirds of partnered women report doing all or most of the housework in all three countries and at all time points. However, equal sharing of housework was much more common in

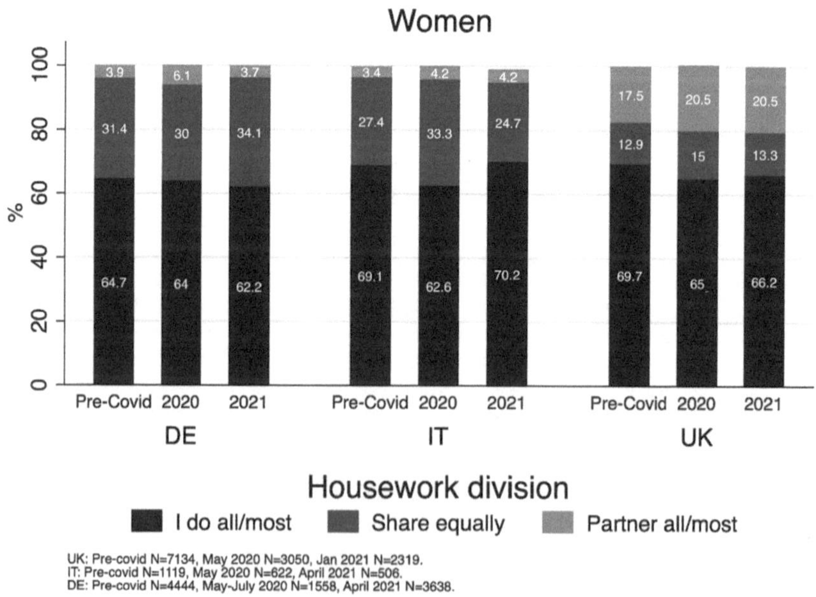

Fig. 5.3 Time trends in women's share of housework, Germany, Italy & the UK

Germany and Italy than in the UK. More than a third of German women reported equal sharing of housework after the peak of the pandemic in 2021 (34%), which is a minor increase compared with pre-pandemic data (31%), and during the midst of the pandemic in 2020 (30%). About a quarter of Italian women reported sharing housework equally before and after the height of the pandemic. This sharing rose to a third during the first lockdown. These figures compare to only 13% of UK women reporting sharing housework equally before and after the height of the pandemic, with a rise to only 15% during the first lockdown. As such, while women in Germany and Italy were more likely than women in the UK to report that they share the housework equally with their partners, they are less likely to state their partners do all or most of the housework. Approximately one-fifth of UK women reported that their partner completes all or most of the housework compared with only 4–6% in Germany and 3–4% in Italy. Comparisons with the UK should be treated with caution, however, as divisions of housework were created by categorising reported hours rather than reports of who does more (see Data section).

While about two-thirds of Italian women reported doing all or most of the housework, Figure 5.4 shows that only a slightly over half of men

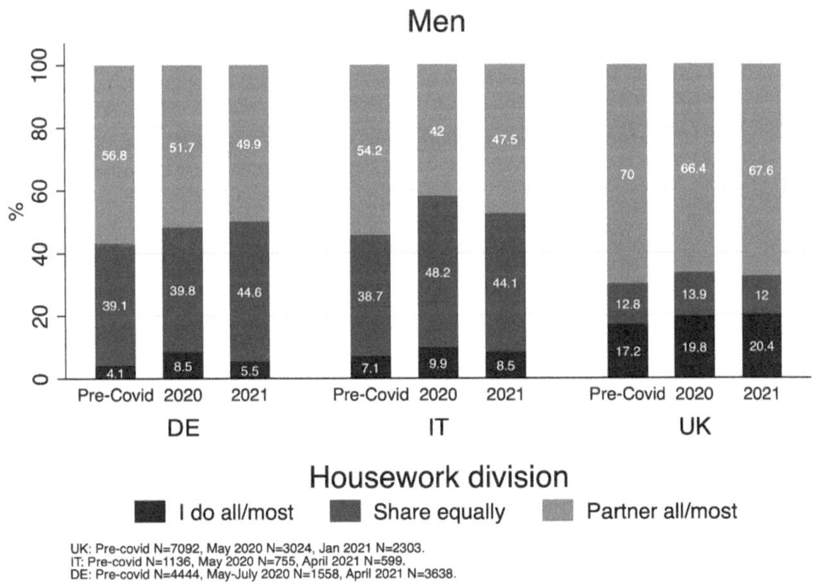

Fig. 5.4 Time trends in men's share of housework, Germany, Italy & the UK

reported that their partners did all or most of the housework before the pandemic. This declined to 42% during the first lockdown and rose to 48% by April 2021. In Germany, 57% of men reported that their partners did most or all of the housework before the pandemic. This declined to 52% during the pandemic period and 50% after lockdown. Figure 5.4 suggests that British men report more similarly to their partners than German and Italian men. However, this is by design as couples in the British data are allocated to groups based on share of hours rather than self-reports of share. Time trends suggest that during the first lockdown couples shared housework slightly more equally than both before and after that period, but slightly more so in Italy than in the UK. In Italy, the percentage of men who reported sharing housework equally went from about 38% in the pre-pandemic period to 48% during the first lockdown, and down to 44% a year later. The same trend is visible in the reports provided by women, from 27% in the pre-pandemic, 33% in May 2020, and 25% in April 2021. In Germany, men's reports of equal sharing of housework continued to rise into 2021 at 45%, compared with 39% and 40% pre-pandemic in 2020.

Gender Differences in Housework in Germany, Italy, and the UK

Table 5.2 reports the results for multivariable, multinomial models of gender differences in the division of housework within couples in Germany, Italy, and the UK at two time points: before the pandemic and once it has begun in May 2020. The models confirm that women were more likely than men to state they undertook most or all of the housework, and less likely than men to say that their partner does most or all of the housework. This gender difference is greater in Germany and Italy than in the UK (see the Data section to note differences in the way these measures were derived in the three countries). In Italy, despite reporting slightly greater equality, the gender difference in this reporting is greater during lockdown than previously. In May 2020, women had a higher chance of reporting that they did more housework than their partner (adjusted β = 2.56; 95% CI: 2.19, 2.93) and a lower chance of saying that their partner did more (adjusted β = −2.06; 95% CI: −2.57, −1.56). In the UK, the gender difference in reporting divisions of housework was weaker during the lockdown in May than pre-pandemic, and even more so in Germany, ('I do all/most housework' reducing to adjusted β = 2.26; 95% CI: 1.92,2.60 in May 2020 from adjusted β = 2.95; 95% CI: 2.70,3.21 pre-pandemic).

Table 5.2 Multinomial models of gender differences in housework amongst couples in the UK and Italy, Pre-covid and May 2020

Dependent Variable	*Pre- Covid Housework Share*				*May 2020 Housework Share*			
(ref. = share equal)	*I do more*		*Partner does more*		*I do more*		*Partner does more*	
	B	95% CI	B	95% CI	B	95% CI	B	95% CI
UK								
N	21,074				5980			
Coef. Women (ref. Men)								
Bivariate	1.39	[1.31, 1.47]	−1.40	[−1.48, −1.32]	1.12	[0.89, 1.36]	−1.25	[−1.49, −1.00]
Fully adjusted[a]	1.37	[1.29, 1.46]	−1.37	[−1.45, −1.29]	1.12	[0.90, 1.35]	−1.22	[−1.45, −0.99]
Italy								
N	1150				1142			
Coef. Women (ref. Men)								
Bivariate	2.32	[1.99; 2.65]	−1.78	[−2.25; −1.31]	2.57	[2.20; 2.93]	−2.22	[−2.71; −1.72]
Fully adjusted[a]	2.32	[1.98; 2.66]	−1.62	[−2.09; −1.14]	2.56	[2.19; 2.93]	−2.06	[−2.57; −1.56]
Germany								
N	4444				1558			
Coef. Women (ref. Men)								
Bivariate	2.99	[2.73; 3.24]	−2.45	[−2.68; −2.23]	2.31	[1.98; 2.64]	−1.85	[−2.18; −1.52]
Fully adjusted[a]	2.95	[2.70; 3.21]	−2.39	[−2.62; −2.15]	2.26	[1.92; 2.60]	−1.88	[−2.23; −1.54]

[a]Fully adjusted estimates control for age, education, current economic activity, currently living with children, and household income prior to the pandemic. For Germany, fully adjusted model for pandemic period excludes controls for education and household income due to data unavailability

Conclusions

This chapter investigated gender differences in housework and childcare over the course of the COVID-19 pandemic in France, Germany, Italy, and the UK. Pandemic-related lockdowns across these countries required parents to combine childcare and homeschooling, often alongside working from home. These changes suggested that having both parents working and parenting in a shared environment might increase fathers' involvement in unpaid care work and reduce gender inequality. There were policy differences between the countries: France provides universal childcare, Germany has been moving towards more egalitarian policies in childcare and parental leave, whereas the UK generally requires parents to purchase childcare on the market, and Italy relies on family support. There are reasons to hypothesise that any shifts in gender inequality in unpaid care work during the pandemic may have differed across European country contexts. Indeed, we found that women consistently completed more housework and childcare than men across all of the European countries under examination. Initial reports of fathers' increased participation in childcare during the first lockdown (Burgess & Goldman, 2021; Zamberlan et al., 2022) were also true for mothers. Rather than acting as a leveller, gender inequality in levels of unpaid care work remained constant across pre-pandemic and the first pandemic lockdown in spring 2020. Women reported completing about two-thirds of housework across countries, and this is in line with pre-pandemic estimates (Eurostat, 2016).

Despite this consistency, there were some country differences during the pandemic which follow country-specific policy environments. In the UK, gender differences were greater for childcare hours than for housework hours, though both were significant. This was not the case in France where gender differences were similar between housework and childcare. Additionally, gender differences in childcare hours were greater in the UK than in France in our adjusted models, but the opposite was the case for housework hours. This may reflect differing social norms and cultural contexts. Although childcare was not available during the pandemic, the fact of its availability for several decades in France may have contributed to a general shift towards more equality in parenting and childcare among French parents. It is, however, not possible to determine cause and effect between shifting policies and changing norms. In addition, while gender differences in housework remained strong during the first lockdown in spring 2020 in both Italy and Germany, the gender difference was stronger in Italy and weaker in Germany compared with pre-pandemic differences. Again, this may reflect differences in the normative environments of the two countries, with couples reverting to more traditional gendered behaviour within the Italian 'familialised' context compared with Germany, which is in the process of shifting towards a more 'defamilialised' gender regime context (Saraceno & Keck, 2010; SPLASH-db.eu, 2014).

Such country differences suggest that policy has a role to play in challenging the bias against women with regard to unpaid care work, which may go towards shifting gendered behaviours in housework and childcare as well as employment participation and occupational attainment. The persistent inequalities within unpaid care work that have been observed indicate that policies to encourage male participation in unpaid care work are needed in addition to accessible, high-quality childcare and early years education provision. This may include fairly compensated paternity and parental leave provision, and measures to tackle long work hours cultures, particularly in male-dominated sectors. Finally, in the future, it would be beneficial to monitor the impact of ongoing flexible and home working on gender inequality in childcare and housework.

References

Altintas, E., & Sullivan, O. (2016). Fifty years of change updated: Cross-national gender convergence in housework. *Demographic Research, 35*(16), 455–470. https://doi.org/10.4054/DemRes.2016.35.16

Andrew, A., Cattan, S., Costa Dias, M., Farquharson, C., Kraftman, L., Krutikova, S., Phimister, A., & Sevilla, A. (2022). The gendered division of paid and domestic work under lockdown. *Fiscal Studies, 43*, 325–340. https://doi.org/10.1111/1475-5890.12394

Anxo, D., Mencarini, L., Pailhé, A., Solaz, A., Tanturri, M. L., & Flood, L. (2011). Gender differences in time use over the life course in France, Italy, Sweden, and the US. *Feminist Economics, 17*(3), 159–195. https://doi.org/10.1080/13545701.2011.582822

Baker, C., Kirk-Wade, E., Brown, J., & Barber, S. (2021). *Coronavirus: A history of English lockdown laws.* House of Commons Library. https://commonslibrary.parliament.uk/research-briefings/cbp-9068/

Bergmann, N., Scheele, A., & Sorger, C. (2019). Variations of the same? A sectoral analysis of the gender pay gap in Germany and Austria. *Gender, Work & Organization, 26*(5), 668–687. https://doi.org/10.1111/gwao.12299

Boyer, D., & Fagnani, J. (2023). *Leave Network Report: France.* https://www.leavenetwork.org/fileadmin/user_upload/k_leavenetwork/annual_reviews/2023/France2023.pdf

Brüderl, J., et al. (2022). *The German Family Panel (pairfam).* GESIS Data Archive, Cologne. https://doi.org/10.4232/pairfam.5678.13.0.0

Burgess, A., & Goldman, R. (2021). *Lockdown Fathers: The untold story (Full Report)*. Contemporary Fathers in the UK series. : Fatherhood Institute.
Cabinet Office. (2022). *COVID-19 response: Living with COVID-19*. https://www.gov.uk/government/publications/covid-19-response-living-with-covid-19
Champagne, C., Pailhé, A., & Solaz, A. (2015). House-keeping and parenting time of men and women: What factors have driven change over the past 25 years? *Economie et Statistique, 478*, 209–242.
Del Boca, D., Oggero, N., Profeta, P., & Rossi, M. C. (2022). The impact of COVID-19 on the gender division of housework and childcare: Evidence from two waves of the pandemic in Italy. *IZA Journal of Labor Economics, 11*(1). https://doi.org/10.2478/izajole-2022-0003
Dotti Sani, G. M. (2018). *Time use in domestic settings throughout the life course: The Italian case*. Springer.
Dotti Sani, G. M., & Scherer, S. (2018). Maternal employment: Enabling factors in context. *Work, Employment and Society, 32*(1), 75–92. https://doi.org/10.1177/0950017016677942
Euronews. (2023). Differences in cost of childcare. https://www.euronews.com/next/2023/03/06/childcare-puzzle-which-countries-in-europe-have-the-highest-and-lowest-childcare-costs
European Institute for Gender Equality. (2019). *Gender Equality Index*. https://eige.europa.eu/gender-equality-index/2019/domain/work/
Eurostat. (2016). Eurostat Statistics Explained. [Accessed 7 Aug 2024]. https://ec.europa.eu/eurostat/statistics-explained/index.php?title=How_do_women_and_men_use_their_time_-_statistics&oldid=463738#Women_are_more_involved_in_household_and_family_care_activities
Eurostat. (2020). *Employment rate of women and men in the EU*. https://ec.europa.eu/eurostat/web/products-eurostat-news/-/edn-20200306-1
Eurostat. (2024). *Employment and activity by sex and age: Annual data*. https://ec.europa.eu/eurostat/databrowser/view/lfsi_emp_a__custom_12520473/default/table?lang=en
Farré, L., Fawaz, Y., González, L., & Graves, J. (2021). Gender inequality in paid and unpaid work during COVID-19 times. *Review of Income and Wealth, 68*(2), 323–347. https://doi.org/10.1111/roiw.12563
Florisson, R., & Gable, O. (2022). *The gender gap: Insecure work in the UK*. The Work Foundation, Lancaster University.
Francis-Devine, B., & Hutton, G. (2024). *Research briefing: Women and the UK economy*. House of Commons Library. https://researchbriefings.files.parliament.uk/documents/SN06838/SN06838.pdf
Hank, K., & Steinbach, A. (2021). The virus changed everything, didn't it? Couples' division of housework and childcare before and during the corona crisis. *Journal of Family Research, 33*(1), 99–114. https://doi.org/10.20377/jfr-488

Hook, J. L. (2015). Incorporating 'class' into work-family arrangements: Insights from and for Three Worlds. *Journal of European Social Policy, 25*(1), 14–31. https://doi.org/10.1177/0958928714556968

Huinink, J., et al. (2011). Panel analysis of intimate relationships and family dynamics (pairfam): Conceptual framework and design. *Zeitschrift für Familienforschung - Journal of Family Research, 23*(1), 77–101. https://nbn-resolving.org/urn:nbn:de:0168-ssoar-376463

Jessen, J., Spiess, C., Waights, S., & Wrohlich, K. (2022). The gender division of unpaid care work throughout the COVID-19 pandemic in Germany. *German Economic Review, 23*(4), 641–667. https://doi.org/10.1111/geer.12290

Kreyenfeld, M., & Zinn, S. (2021). Coronavirus and care: How the coronavirus crisis affected fathers' involvement in Germany. *Demographic Research, 44*(4). https://doi.org/10.4054/DemRes.2021.44.4

Mills, M., Prag, P., Tsang, F., Begall, K., Derbyshire, J., Kohle, L., Miani, C., & Hoorens, S. (2013). Use of childcare in EU Member States and progress towards the Barcelona targets. *RAND Europe.*

Moreira da Silva, J. (2019). Why you should care about unpaid care work. *OECD.* https://oecd-development-matters.org/2019/03/18/why-you-should-care-about-unpaid-care-work/

OECD. (2015). *Unpaid care work.* https://www.oecd.org/gender/balancing-paid-work-unpaid-work-and-leisure.htm

OECD. (2022). *Family data base maternity & paternity leave comparisons.* https://www.oecd.org/els/family/database.htm

OECD. (2023a). *OECD Data Explorer. Employment rate 15 to 64 years.* https://data-explorer.oecd.org/

OECD. (2023b). *OECD Family Database. PF3.2: Enrolment in childcare and pre-school.* https://www.oecd.org/els/family/database.htm

OECD. (2023c). *OECD Family Database. LMF2.5 Time used for work, care and daily household chores.* https://www.oecd.org/els/family/database.htm

Office for National Statistics. (2024). *Employment in the UK: April 2024.* https://www.ons.gov.uk/employmentandlabourmarket/peopleinwork/employmentandemployeetypes/bulletins/employmentintheuk/april2024

Pailhé, A., Solaz, A., & Stanfors, A. (2021). The great convergence: Gender and unpaid work in Europe and the United States. *Population and Development Review, 47*(1), 181–217. https://doi.org/10.1111/padr.12384

Pasqualini, M., Dominguez Folgueras, M., Ferragina, E., Godechot, O., Recchi, E., & Safi, M. (2022). Who took care of what? The gender division of unpaid work during the first year of the COVID-19 pandemic in France. *Demographic Research, 46*, 1007–1036. https://doi.org/10.4054/demres.2022.46.34

Prime Minister's Office. (2021). Prime Minister sets out new measures as Omicron variant identified in UK: 27 November 2021. https://www.gov.uk/government/news/prime-minister-sets-out-new-measures-as-omicron-variant-identified-in-uk-27-november-2021

Reimann, M., Peters, E., & Diewald, M. (2022). COVID-19 and work–family conflicts in Germany: Risks and chances across gender and parenthood. *Frontiers in Sociology, 6*. https://doi.org/10.3389/fsoc.2021.780740

Rodriguez Sanchez, A., Fasang, A., & Harkness, S. (2021). Gendered division of housework during the COVID-19 pandemic: Temporary shocks or durable change? *DIAL Working Paper Series, 06/*2021.

Saraceno, C., & Keck, W. (2010). Can we identify intergenerational policy regimes in Europe? *European Societies, 12*(5), 675–696. https://doi.org/10.1080/14616696.2010.483006

Senedd Cymru. (2022). *Coronavirus timeline: The response in Wales*. https://research.senedd.wales/research-articles/coronavirus-timeline-the-response-in-wales/

SPLASH-db.eu. (2014). *Policy: 'Family Policies: Germany'* (Information provided by Anke Radenacker). https://splash-db.eu

Steinmetz, S., Vandecasteele, L., Lebert, F., Voorpostel, M., & Lipps, O. (2022). The gendered consequences of the COVID-19 lockdown on unpaid work in Swiss dual-earner couples with children. *Gender, Work & Organization, 29*(6), 2034–2051. https://doi.org/10.1111/gwao.12875

UK Government. (2023). *Deaths in England | Coronavirus in the UK*. https://coronavirus.data.gov.uk/details/deaths

Walper, S., et al. (2021a). *The pairfam COVID-19 survey*. GESIS Data Archive, Cologne. https://doi.org/10.4232/pairfam.5959.1.1.0

Walper, S., et al. (2021b). The pairfam COVID-19 survey: Design and instruments. *Release 1.1. LMU Munich: pairfam Technical Paper, 15*.

Warren, T., Lyonette, C., & UK Women's Budget Group. (2021). *Carrying the work burden of the COVID-19 pandemic: Working-class women in the UK*. Final report, Nottingham: Nottingham University Business School.

Xue, B., & McMunn, A. (2021). Gender differences in unpaid care work and psychological distress in the UK COVID-19 lockdown. *PLOS ONE, 16*(3), e0247959. https://doi.org/10.1371/journal.pone.0247959

Zamberlan, A., Gioachin, F., & Gritti, D. (2021). Work less, help out more? The persistence of gender inequality in housework and childcare during UK COVID-19. *Research in Social Stratification and Mobility, 73*, 100583. https://doi.org/10.1016/j.rssm.2021.100583

Zamberlan, A., Gioachin, F., & Gritti, D. (2022). Gender inequality in domestic chores over ten months of the UK COVID-19 pandemic: Heterogeneous adjustments to partners' changes in working hours. *Demographic Research, 46*, 565–580. https://doi.org/10.4054/demres.2022.46.19

Zhou, M., & Kan, M.-Y. (2021). The varying impacts of COVID-19 and its related measures in the UK: A year in review. *PLOS ONE, 16*(9), e0257286. https://doi.org/10.1371/journal.pone.0257286

Zoch, G., Bächmann, A. C., & Vicari, B. (2020). Who cares when care closes? Care-arrangements and parental working conditions during the COVID-19 pandemic in Germany. *European Societies, 23*(51), 576–588.

CHAPTER 6

Labour Markets and Work During the COVID-19 Pandemic—Who Could and Who Did Work From Home?

Piotr Marzec, *Giulia Dotti Sani*, *Marco Maraffi*, *Marta Moroni*, *Elias Naumann*, *Marta Pasqualini*, *and Andrew Zola*

An earlier version of this chapter has been published as a research note: European Commission: Directorate-General for Employment, Social Affairs and Inclusion, Naumann, E., Dotti Sani, G., Marzec, P., & Pasqualini, M. (2024). Work and well-being during the COVID-19 pandemic: evidence from panel data in four countries, Publications Office of the European Union. https://data.europa.eu/doi/10.2767/363952. For this chapter, we have extended the empirical analysis to also cover more recent time periods and we have added a more detailed analysis of remote work based on British data (see study 2 in this chapter).

P. Marzec (✉)
Institute for Social and Economic Research, University of Essex, Colchester, UK
e-mail: p.marzec@essex.ac.uk

E. Naumann et al. (eds.), *Social Life during COVID-19 in France, Germany, Italy and the UK*,
https://doi.org/10.1007/978-3-031-99349-7_6

Introduction

The onset of the COVID-19 pandemic brought swift and profound transformations to the labour market. The closure of non-essential businesses, mandatory stay-at-home orders, and uncertainties surrounding job security became defining features of this unprecedented period. Amidst the economic upheaval, various European countries implemented furlough schemes as a strategy to mitigate mass redundancies and support struggling businesses. In this chapter, we explore these dynamics of the prevalent adoption of remote work and the increase of temporary work and unemployment during the first year of the pandemic.

Our approach focuses on the magnitude of these changes to explore variations across our chosen four countries and, more importantly, to investigate potential disparities between different social groups. To begin, we demonstrate that furlough schemes and unemployment emerge as temporary solutions that provided a rapid recovery. Remote work, on the other hand, endures as a lasting change to work practices. Its implications may reveal themselves to be significant, not only permanently transforming how people work but also affecting the socio-economic structures of cities and the spatial organisation of regional economies. Augmenting this comparative analysis, we provide a more detailed analysis of demographics who were and were not able to work from home in the second part of this chapter. Here, we focus on the UK because its labour market had the

G. Dotti Sani
Department of Social and Political Sciences, University of Milan, Milano, Italy

M. Maraffi
Università degli Studi di Milano, Milan, MI, Italy

M. Moroni
Johannes Kepler University Linz, Linz, Austria

E. Naumann
GESIS Leibniz Institute for the Social Sciences, Mannheim, Germany
e-mail: elias.naumann@gesis.org

M. Pasqualini
Fondazione Progetto Valtiberina, Sansepolcro AR, Italy

A. Zola
Centre for Research on Social Inequalities (CRIS), CNRS, Sciences Po, Paris, France
e-mail: andrew.zola@sciencespo.fr

largest proportion of teleworkable jobs (Dingel & Neiman, 2020), suggesting a higher prevalence of remote work among British workers compared with France, Germany, and Italy. Moreover, the UK Household Longitudinal Study data includes measures of job characteristics—occupation and industry—that are sufficiently detailed to allow for thorough analysis of patterns of remote work. We observe that the potential to work from home closely aligns with occupational characteristics, enabling the prediction of which jobs were able to utilise telework arrangements. We also examine how personal preference factors—such as the suitability of one's home workspace, household income, commuting time, and family circumstances—relate to these occupation- and industry-based constraints to influence who partakes in remote work.

The chapter concludes with a synthesis of our findings and their broader implications. We offer a nuanced perspective on the evolving intersection of work, health, society, and policy in the aftermath of the COVID-19 pandemic.

Labour Market-Related Inequalities During the COVID-19 Pandemic

The COVID-19 pandemic provoked a sharp macroeconomic downturn and non-pharmaceutical interventions such as strict lockdowns, which resulted in major changes in work patterns across Europe. The most substantial of these changes included a short period of significant job losses and the expansion or introduction of job retention schemes (Eurofound, 2021), alongside a mass shift to remote work to curb the spread of the virus. We begin by assessing these labour market changes in Europe during the COVID-19 pandemic and then review the sociodemographic inequalities which previous research has found these changes to provoke.

Job Loss and Temporary Work Patterns Across Countries

The economic downturn and lockdowns in the spring of 2020 put millions at risk of redundancy across Europe. Many countries expanded or introduced job retention schemes that allowed employers to hoard labour (Ebbinghaus & Lehner, 2022) and to legitimise lockdown measures among workers. While Germany, France, and Italy adapted and expanded their respective *Kurzarbeit*, *chômage partiel*, and *cassa integrazione* schemes, the UK introduced the Coronavirus Job Retention Scheme. The EU's Support to Mitigate Unemployment Risks in an Emergency (SURE) fund also supported numerous EU Member States such as Italy—but not Germany or France—to finance short-time work schemes, retain jobs, and support incomes, particularly for those who were self-employed.

An overview of employment protection for regular and temporary workers in these four countries is outlined below (Table 6.1). These data contextualise differences in how the pandemic affected the general employment. Given the impact of prolonged lockdown on the labour market, differences in employment protection legislation across countries might account for the ways in which the pandemic affected workers in different countries.

Chapter 2 demonstrates the rigour of these measures for each country over time. Italy and France had the strictest lockdowns during the first COVID-19 wave in spring 2020. While Italy left many of these lockdown measures in place over the following two years, France, Germany, and the UK experienced periods of eased lockdown measures, such as summer 2020.

Employment protection, such as job retention schemes, allowed substantial proportions of the four countries' labour forces to avoid job loss. Estimates suggest that 11.3 million French workers, 10.1 million German workers, 8.3 million Italian workers, and 6.3 million workers in the UK were supported by temporary work. Comparing these countries, it is clear that the employment protection index is weakest in the UK, and the job retention scheme covered the fewest number of workers, perhaps suggesting a relatively higher loss of jobs.

Protections offered by these schemes were comparable across all four countries. Over 60% of lost wages were reimbursed during the first year of

Table 6.1 Institutional differences between countries before the pandemic (2017–2019)

	FR	*DE*	*IT*	*UK*
Employment Protection Index—Temporary Worker	3.00	1.38	3.13	0.38
Employment protection regular worker	2.56	2.60	2.56	1.35

Notes: Employment Protection Index is from the Organisation for Economic Co-operation and Development (OECD) Employment Protection Legislation Database (2020). It captures the strictness of regulations on the dismissal of workers on regular contracts and the strictness of regulations of temporary contracts the pandemic, with the exception of individuals with very high incomes in Italy.[1] Short-term work benefits provided 60% of gross earnings. During the pandemic the benefits were raised, with a 10% increase beginning in the fourth month, followed by another 10% rise from the seventh month onward. The UK adopted a new Coronavirus Job Retention Scheme (CJRS), an earnings-related benefit of 80% for up to four months. Italy had an established short-term work scheme (CIG), with benefits for workers in industry at 80% of gross earnings. The CIG was extended to all sectors not yet included, although the duration varied between 6 and 12 months. France used 'partial' unemployment benefits (80% of gross wages for up to one year) to prevent mass unemployment.

Remote Work Patterns Across Countries

Remote working increased as a key policy measure both to prevent the spread of COVID-19 and to enable as many people as possible to continue working. Remote work was strongly encouraged, sometimes even made mandatory, with regulations usually applying to those jobs deemed teleworkable (i.e. jobs that could be performed from home even prior to the pandemic). As a consequence, other factors influencing the probability of remote work may have become, at least temporarily, of secondary importance.

The extent to which jobs are teleworkable is largely dependent on both their occupational characteristics and the industries in which they are performed (Dingel & Neiman, 2020; Dey et al., 2020; Yasenov, 2020). Occupations vary considerably in their potential for remote work, primarily owing to the nature of the tasks and duties involved. Those occupations that cannot be performed from home typically include activities requiring a specific location other than one's home, such as physical labour, handling and moving objects, operating machinery, maintaining and repairing vehicles and equipment, and working face-to-face with the public (Dingel & Neiman, 2020).

When analysing the degree of teleworkability, three main clusters of occupations emerge (Dingel & Neiman, 2020, Table 1). First are professional and managerial occupations, in which the vast majority—over two-thirds—of workers are able to work from home. Second are certain

[1] A thorough review and comparison of the job-retention policies in each country from the worker's perspective can be found in Chap. 9.

occupational groups, particularly those related to sales, community and social services, and personal care, where only about 25–35% of workers can telework. Finally, there is a broad category of occupations for which remote work is near impossible: this is an option for less than 6% of workers. This includes healthcare, transportation, farming, and various construction and maintenance trades, where physical labour is dominant. A similar pattern exists at the industry level (Dingel & Neiman, 2020, Table 3). Most jobs in industries such as educational services, professional, scientific, and technical services, management of companies and enterprises, finance and insurance, and information technology can be performed remotely. By contrast, manufacturing, transportation and warehousing, construction, retail trade, agriculture, forestry, fishing and hunting, accommodation, and food services generally offer far fewer telework opportunities.

The availability of teleworkable jobs in each country is an important factor to consider when examining cross-national differences in labour market outcomes during the pandemic. This figure differed across countries, with around 44% of jobs in the UK being teleworkable, followed by 38% in France, 37% in Germany, and 35% in Italy (Dingel & Neiman, 2020). These differences suggest that remote work might have consequentially been the most common in the UK, and that the massive shift to remote work could have resulted in fewer disruptions to the labour market.

Sociodemographic Consequences

This section presents a brief overview of the sociodemographic inequalities that these labour market changes influenced. Alon et al. (2020) argued that women would be more negatively affected by the economic downturn and the pandemic. In contrast to previous recessions which mainly affected male-dominated sectors of the economy, such as construction or manufacturing, the COVID-19 pandemic recession impacted sectors such as tourism or hospitality, which are dominated by female workers. In addition, most women are the main caregivers and tended to be more impacted by the closure of schools and childcare. Existing evidence largely supported this hypothesis: the recession caused by the pandemic had a disproportionately significant effect on working women across many countries, with an even greater impact on those with children (Andrew et al., 2020; Hipp & Bünning, 2021). In other words, women's childcare responsibilities increased during the pandemic, making them more likely to transition to remote work, reduce their working hours, and experience greater risk of losing their jobs (Stantcheva, 2022).

Workers with fewer educational qualifications faced two countervailing forces in relation to the possible consequences of the pandemic. While they were more likely to be employed in essential occupations, which reduced their risk of layoff or furlough, they were also overrepresented in jobs that faced greater exposure to adverse labour demand shocks and had limited remote work opportunities. Research on the short-term labour market effects found that low-income and lower-educated workers were more impacted by job loss and furlough schemes, and less likely to work remotely (Adams-Prassl et al., 2020; Eurofound, 2021; Stantcheva, 2022).

Finally, employment vulnerability is marginally higher among younger workers, who were more likely to be employed in 'non-essential' sectors, and to have atypical contracts that do not grant full access to social security measures (Quaranta et al., 2020). This trend was demonstrated by a Eurofound study (2021) which claims that young people experienced the sharpest decline in employment and a slower recovery than other age groups, while 'prime-aged' workers (25–54 years) and older male workers were the most likely to experience reductions in their working hours.

Study 1: Labour Market Changes in Employment Conditions and Place of Work

Employment Conditions During COVID-19 in France, Germany, Italy, and the UK

We begin by addressing whether changes occurred in labour market participation during the various stages of the pandemic in the four countries under consideration. Figure 6.1 shows the proportion of individuals in employment, furloughed, unemployed, retired, or in another work-related condition from before the onset of the pandemic until 2022 (Phase 2b—Demise).

The data reveal a clear reduction in the proportion of those in paid work between the pre-pandemic period and spring 2020 (Phase 1a) when the first lockdown occurred. This decline was particularly acute in France (from 50% to 29%) and the UK (68% to 50%), but less severe in Germany (62% to 54%). In all three countries, this led to the emergence of a category of workers in short-time work amounting to 7% of the population in

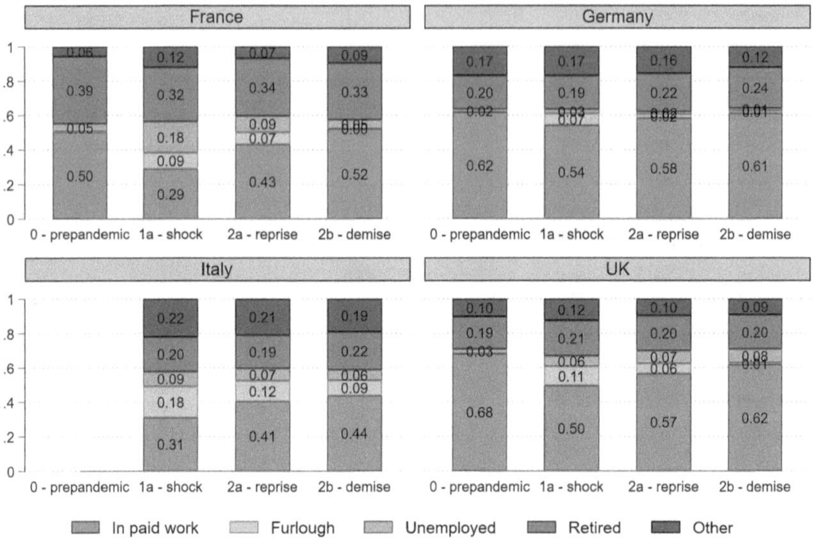

Fig. 6.1 Distribution of labour market activity, by country and point in time (proportions)

Germany and 18% in Italy. As a consequence, unemployment figures increased far less, with the largest increases observed in France and the UK. Moreover, we do not find that employees were pushed out of the labour market into retirement or other non-work-related tasks, such as housework or studying.

Crucially, as the pandemic unfolded, the proportion of respondents in paid work began to rise again in all four countries. Those proportions had not yet returned to pre-pandemic levels in Phase 2a (Reprise), but nearly rose to pre-pandemic levels in Phase 2b from autumn 2022 onwards.

These trends and numbers are comparable to official labour market statistics from Eurostat for France, Germany, and Italy, and from the Office for National Statistics for the UK. The employment rate—as a share of the total population aged 16 years and older—before the pandemic was 58% for France, 66% for Germany, 52% for Italy, and 62% for the UK. Therefore, respondents in paid work are slightly underrepresented in the surveys that are used here. Official labour market statistics also demonstrate that, after an initial drop in employment rates in Q2 2020 (France: 58% to 56%; Germany: 66% to 65%; Italy 52% to 49%; UK: 62% to 60%), employment rates recovered and reached pre-pandemic levels in France (57% in Q2 2022) and Germany (67% in Q2 2022), while remaining below pre-pandemic levels in Italy (50%) and the UK (60%). This trend was also captured by the surveys used in our analysis.

The same perspective is achieved even when focusing only on active labour market participation: respondents in paid work, furlough, and unemployed (Fig. 6.2). The proportion of respondents who were in paid work in the pre-pandemic period fell in spring 2020, and then increased although not to pre-pandemic levels. Germany suffered the fewest consequences in terms of paid work. In all four countries, furlough was most spread out in Phase 1a in spring 2020, then gradually decreased, and even entirely disappeared in France in Phase 2b. In contrast, the proportion of unemployment rates remained fairly stable during the pandemic in all four countries, with the exception of France during spring 2020, when there was a sudden surge in unemployment from 8% to 32%.

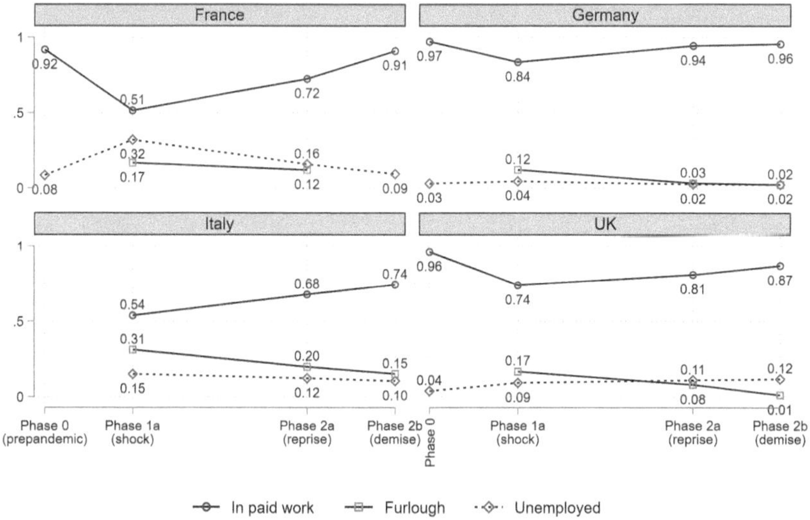

Fig. 6.2 Distribution of employment conditions, by country and point in time (proportions)

Location of Work During the COVID-19 Pandemic

One of the major changes brought about by the pandemic was the shift in workplace dynamics, particularly the need or possibility to work from home. As strict lockdowns aimed to contain the spread of the virus by limiting travel and daily life, public administrations and private companies began to implement remote working where possible. This was intended to maintain productivity, while allowing workers to keep their jobs and stay safe while in their homes.

Figure 6.3 shows the location of work by country and point in time. For information on how this was measured, we refer to the data chapter in this volume, Chap. 3. In France, the proportion of individuals who worked partly remotely rose from 33% to 49%, with a comparable increase in the UK of 29% to 47%. In Italy, about half of employed individuals worked remotely during Phase 1a in spring 2020, while the figure was somewhat lower for Germany at 34%.

Throughout the year, the proportion of respondents working remotely decreased in both France and Italy, following the easing of the pandemic

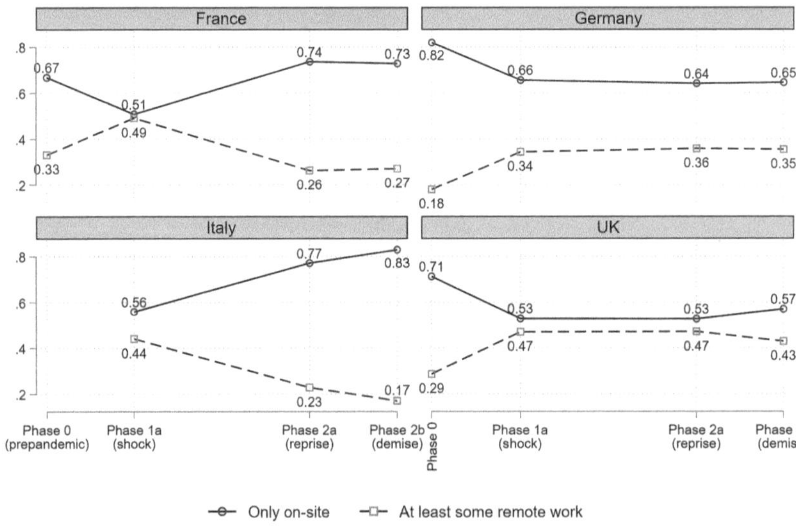

Fig. 6.3 Distribution of place of work, by country and point in time (proportions)

restrictions. In contrast, remote working remained stable and at a considerable higher level than before the pandemic in the UK and Germany. The share of workers doing at least some work from home stabilised at around 35% in Germany and at around 45% in the UK.

The question of how many workers—particularly *which* workers—worked from home during the pandemic pertains to various social inequalities. Only certain types of jobs could be done remotely (namely, 'white-collar' jobs), while other occupations were carried out 'on-site'. Therefore, during periods of strict lockdown, individuals in the latter group were at a greater risk of being dismissed or furloughed, or, if they were at work, exposed to a higher health risk.

Figure 6.4 displays the differences in the proportion of people working from home by gender of the respondents and the phase of the pandemic. In every country, gender differences regarding the location of work during the pandemic are moderate to non-significant. Overall, men tend to have worked from home more so than women, who were more likely to be employed in the care and service sectors, where working from home is often not feasible. In particular, in France the gender gap which existed

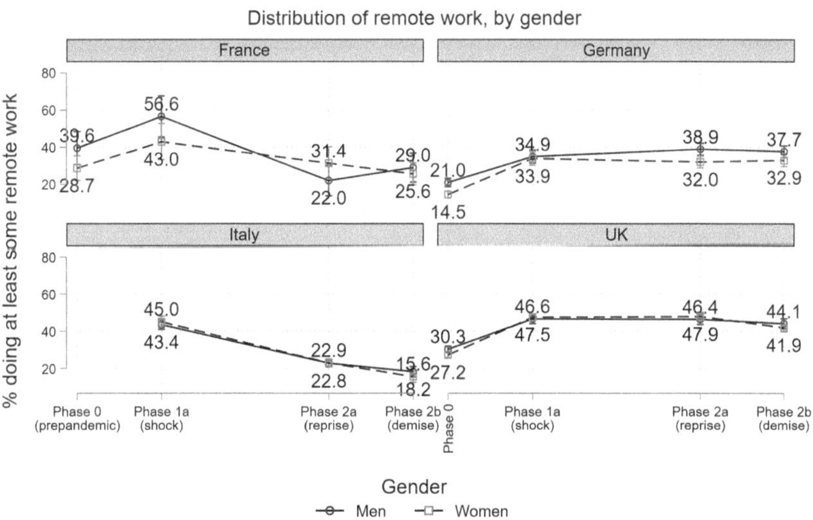

Fig. 6.4 Gender and remote work

before the pandemic started persisted during Phase 1a (Shock)—56.6% of men working remotely compared with 43% of women—to then decrease in the following phases. In Germany, however, the Shock phase of the pandemic resulted in the narrowing of the differences between men and women in working from home (from a 7.5 to 1 percentage point difference). As restrictions eased, the gap returned to around 7 and 5 percentage points, respectively, in the Reprise and Demise phase, similar to pre-pandemic levels. In the UK and Italy, the gender differences were minimal throughout the phases of the pandemic, but men still worked remotely more than women.

Figure 6.5 shows the distribution of remote working by country, point in time, and level of education. We distinguish lower-educated and higher-educated individuals through tertiary education qualifications. The graphs demonstrate that, in each country, the proportion of people working from home differs considerably by level of education in every phase of the pandemic: high-educated respondents were considerably more likely to work from home in comparison to low-educated ones. Throughout the pandemic, the proportion of people working from home decreased at the

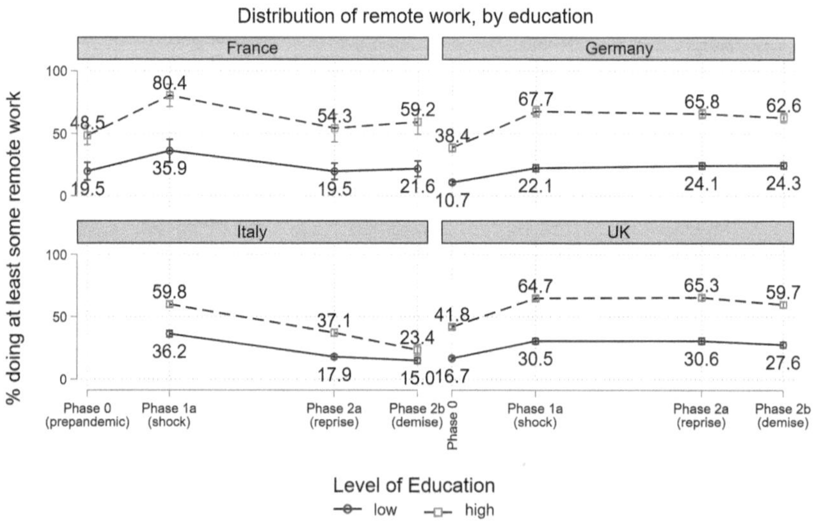

Fig. 6.5 Education and remote work

same rate among both highly educated and less educated individuals in France and Italy. It remained consistent for both low- and high-educated workers in both Germany and the UK.

Lastly, Fig. 6.6 depicts differences in proportions of workers according to family composition, by country and points in time. In particular, the results in France find that respondents with young children worked remotely much more than those living without children, particularly in the first Shock Phase (1a) of the pandemic. The differences remained noticeable though reduced in the following phases. On the contrary, in Germany, the differences between parents and non-parents working from home slightly decreased during the Shock period of the pandemic, before becoming significant again and stabilising from the Reprise phase onward. In the UK, parents were slightly more likely to work from home before and throughout the pandemic, except during the Demise phase when these differences became negligible. With regard to Italy, the differences between parents and non-parents are much less pronounced, with both groups similarly working from home throughout the pandemic.

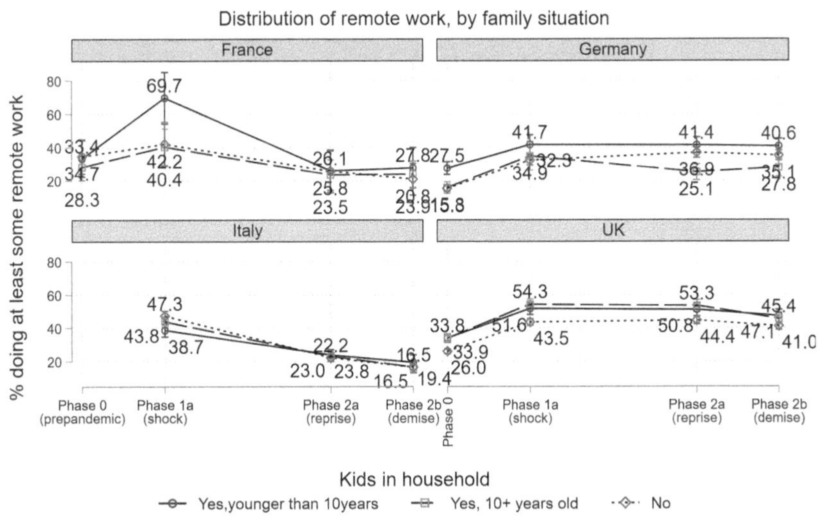

Fig. 6.6 Family situation and remote work

Study 2: Who Can and Who Actually Does Work From Home?

The determinants that might influence the probability of working from home form a hierarchical system in which occupation and industry are at the top, as these clearly distinguish between teleworkable and non-teleworkable jobs. However, they extend beyond the job characteristics already discussed (for an overview see: Bailey & Kurland, 2002; Mokhtarian et al., 1998; Laumer & Maier, 2021; Stephens & Szajna, 1998). Focusing on jobs that can be worked remotely, the likelihood of teleworking also depends on the employer's willingness to offer such arrangements (Morgan, 2004). From an employer's perspective, there are clear advantages, such as reducing operating costs through less office space and maintenance, and accessing a wider, better-matched talent pool than what is locally available. However, these benefits may be offset by the difficulty in monitoring and supervising off-site employees, leading managers, and supervisors to not support the expansion of remote work. Finally, when the nature of the job allows for remote work and it is offered by the employer, individual preferences also play a role in the decision to work remotely. Certain factors influence an employee's desire to work remotely, primarily those relating to the perceived benefits of not working on-site. For instance, working from home can reduce office distractions, such as disruptive colleagues, potentially increasing efficiency and productivity. It can also offer employees greater autonomy over how they complete their tasks and allow them to avoid potentially unpleasant workplace conditions. Moreover, teleworking can eliminate or shorten daily commutes, freeing up time which can be spent with family and thus improving work–life balance. There are, however, also factors that discourage telework. The success of working from home may depend on the home situation, as the presence of other family members—especially children—can create conflicts of responsibility that interfere with productivity. Additionally, some employees may fear social and professional isolation when working remotely. Finally, the feasibility of working from home depends on the availability of suitable workspace within the household.

Below, we further discuss the above-mentioned factors which can be empirically investigated. We begin by examining the objective characteristics of jobs, measured by occupation and industry. Next, we explore the relationship between teleworking and the length of the commute, the suitability of workspace at home, and the presence of children.

Factors Determining the Preference to Work from Home

There are many aspects of a home that might make it unsuitable for home-working, such as room size, office furniture, digital equipment, light quality, and noise insulation (Topi, 2004; Cuerdo-Vilches et al., 2021a, 2021b). Ample space at home allows people to create a dedicated work-space and has been found to be related to a positive attitude towards working from home (Iscan & Naktiyok, 2005; Wicks, 2002), which may increase the willingness to adopt remote work (Yen, 2000). Moreover, the quality of the Internet connection is also important (O'Keefe et al., 2016; Miao et al., 2012; McArthur & Hong, 2023). The importance of the characteristics listed above is attested by the fact that people whose on-site office was better equipped than their home office were less willing to work from home (Scott et al., 2012). The imposed and sudden switch to working from home resulting from the pandemic meant that many individuals struggled to organise a suitable working space at home and had to work in suboptimal conditions: for example, without a dedicated home office or even a desk, lacking equipment, and low internet speed (Cuerdo-Vilches et al., 2021a, 2021b). The proportion of people who reported problems was higher among those who had not worked from home prior to the pandemic, as they were less prepared to totally switch to remote working (Niu et al., 2021). Considering the above, it is reasonable to hypothesise that people who, due to seemingly objective shortcomings of their homes (such as lack of space and poor internet connection), would prefer working on-site rather than from home.

There is some evidence that women with children are more likely to work from home (Dockery & Bawa, 2014). However, the impact of having children on the willingness to work from home is more complex. On the one hand, working from home may provide additional flexibility needed to address children's needs (e.g. by facilitating working non-standard hours) improving work–life balance and thus making it a preferred solution by some employees, especially women considering that they often bear most of childcare responsibilities (Ammons & Markham, 2004; Johnson et al., 2007; Hill et al., 2010). On the other hand, working from home may increase the work-family conflict, particularly if the children are present at home during the working hours (Abendroth & Reimann, 2018; Bellmann & Hübler, 2021).

Although some earlier research (Olszewski & Mokhtarian, 1994) did not find a positive correlation between remote working and commute distance, more recent studies have established such a relationship (Wells et al., 2001; Zhu, 2013; de Abreu e Silva & Melo, 2018; Miao et al., 2012; Motte-Baumvol & Schwanen, 2024). Additionally, employees who are given the opportunity to work from home are more willing to accept longer commutes (de Vos et al., 2018). The question as to the causal direction of that relationship remains open. One might suggest that most people dislike long commutes and thus they would be disposed to avoid them through remote working. However, it may also be the case that people who were able to work remotely utilised this time to relocate to an area with a lower cost of living. The existing body of literature is not conclusive. Many studies suggest that commuting distance causes people to choose to telework (Wells et al., 2001; de Abreu e Silva & Melo, 2018), although some support a reversed causal path, in which remote working increased the commuting distance as individuals relocated (Zhu, 2013). Although our analysis cannot adjudicate between the causal direction of this relationship, it is clear that, at least for some workers, working from home could be a way to avoid undesirable commutes.

The Impact of the COVID-19 Pandemic on Working from Home

Lockdown measures resulted in a sudden and sharp increase in the number of people working from home within a very short period. This situation became an unplanned, large-scale experiment in implementing remote work, offering a unique opportunity to empirically test how many jobs in modern economies could be conducted remotely. The first objective of our analysis, therefore, is to compare hypothetical predictions of the proportion of jobs that could be done remotely in different occupations and industries—based on the distribution of tasks and responsibilities characteristic of them—with the percentage of individuals who worked from home during the pandemic. In doing so, we will identify the occupations and industries in which the share of home-workers increased, thereby revealing the potential for such remote conditions. Second, the new COVID-19 reality significantly constrained the freedom of employees to choose where they worked. As a result, some of the factors discussed above may have been muted or vanished entirely. At the same time, for those who still retained some degree of choice, the pandemic may have reinforced the importance of particular lifestyle factors. Moreover, the impact was not limited only to strength, as the nature of these effects may also have changed.

Consider first the suitability of one's home as an office. A sizeable portion of workers who were thrust into working from home did not already have dedicated workspaces at home. Under these circumstances, their motivation to return to the office whenever possible might have been even stronger (Cuerdo-Vilches et al., 2021a, 2021b). Similarly, parents faced prolonged closures of nurseries and schools, forcing them to manage work and childcare simultaneously (Ipsen et al., 2021). Thus, one might expect that, given the opportunity, many parents would have chosen to avoid such an environment and instead return to in-person work. As most parents were relatively young and the risk profile of the SARS-CoV-2 virus was understood early in the pandemic, some may have considered going to the office a reasonable option.

The pandemic may have also influenced the commute time in relation to the preference of working from home, though this relationship is not straightforward. On the one hand, given challenging home setups, many workers may have found long commutes more tolerable than staying at home. On the other, those who had homes better suited for remote work and who did not have to manage children's needs may have still preferred to avoid commuting, especially as public transport was significantly reduced. In addition, fear of contracting the virus probably resulted in many avoiding high-risk activities such as commuting, potentially strengthening the relationship between working from home and commuting distance.

Data Analysis—Strategy

The analysis consists of two parts. First, we consider the number of individuals working from home in different occupations and industries before the pandemic. We then investigate how the share of home-workers changed, identifying occupations and industries with the largest increases, focusing on three times: May 2020, September 2020, and March 2021. In the second half, we examine additional factors influencing the probability of working from home. Three key factors are noted. First, we assess the impact of having children. Second, we analyse the suitability of the workspace represented by two variables: the amount of space available measured by the number of rooms per person, and household income which serves as a proxy for important housing characteristics that may influence the quality of the work-from-home experience but cannot be directly measured. Last, we investigate the relationship between the time spent on commuting to work and the probability of working from home.

The periods before and during the pandemic are analysed separately. Four logistic regression models were run: the first on retrospective data reflecting the situation in January and February 2020 (as collected in April 2020), the second on data from the first wave of the pandemic in April 2020, the third on data from September 2020, and the fourth on data from March 2021. All reported effects are presented as predicted probabilities. The following variables were included as controls: gender, education, managerial or supervisory duties, occupation, and industry.

Working from home is measured using two similar questions. Eligible respondents—those in paid work or self-employment in January and February 2020—were asked in their initial interview how frequently they worked at home during that period: 'During January and February, how often did you work at home?'. The response options were: 'Always', 'Often', 'Sometimes', and 'Never'. A similar question concerning working at home during the pandemic was asked to the same group and was included in every wave of the Understanding Society COVID-19 Study, though used slightly different wording: 'During the last four weeks, how often did you work at home?'. The same four response options were used.

Although the reference periods differ, the questions are broadly comparable and provide a reasonably accurate representation of working-from-home patterns. A potential concern is the imprecision of the terms relating to frequency within the response options ('often' and 'sometimes' may be interpreted differently by different respondents, for example). However, this is mitigated by recoding the responses into a binary format: 'Yes, worked at home' against 'No, didn't work at home'.

While this binary approach reduces the granularity of the data and risks grouping diverse types of home-workers—such as those occasionally working at home and those working exclusively at home—it is justified in this context. The aim is to analyse general trends, and the binary categorisation provides the clarity and simplicity required by such an analysis.

Data Analysis—Results

The survey data closely aligns with our predictions, revealing three groups of occupations differentiated by the share of home-workers (Table 6.2). Pre-pandemic, the highest rate of working from home, at least occasionally—ranging from 40 to 50%—was observed among professional,

Table 6.2 Share of teleworks among different occupations

	Jan/Feb 2020	*Apr 2020*	*Sep 2020*	*Mar 2021*
Occupation SOC2000 major groups				
Managers and Senior Officials	0.48	0.66	0.68	0.66
Professional Occupations	0.54	0.84	0.70	0.76
Associate Professional and Technical Occupations	0.39	0.62	0.62	0.67
Administrative and Secretarial Occupations	0.22	0.56	0.51	0.60
Skilled Trades Occupations	0.19	0.20	0.17	0.19
Personal Service Occupations	0.12	0.34	0.18	0.24
Sales and Customer Service Occupations	0.08	0.22	0.21	0.23
Process, Plant, and Machine Operatives	0.11	0.14	0.16	0.13
Elementary Occupations	0.05	0.10	0.08	0.11
Number of observations	9924	7456	6200	6070

managerial, associate professional, and technical occupations. These were followed by administrative and secretarial roles, alongside skilled trades occupations, in which approximately 20% of workers engaged in remote working. The lowest likelihood of working from home—around 10% or less—was found among low-skilled personnel, sales and customer service workers, skilled workers, and those in elementary occupations.

The pandemic resulted in a sharp increase in the share of home-workers across most occupational groups, though the general hierarchy between them remained largely unchanged, with a handful of exceptions. Overall, the rate of remote work remained elevated throughout the pandemic. However, a notable decline occurred around September 2020, which was probably linked to the relaxation of COVID-19 measures during the summer of that year. This was followed by another increase in March 2021, coinciding with the third national lockdown in the UK.

The proportion of individuals working from home was highest among professional occupations, reaching 84% in April 2020, dropping to 70% in September 2020, and rising again to 76% in March 2021. Similarly, remote working exceeded 60% among managerial, associate professional, and technical occupations, at approximately 62% in April and September 2020, increasing to 67% in March 2021. For administrative and secretarial occupations, the share exceeded 50% in April and September 2020 and rose to 60% in March 2021.

Associate professionals, technical, administrative, and secretarial occupations experienced the largest increase in remote working. This trend follows with their high potential for remote work, as noted by Dingel and Neiman (2020).

Among low-skilled service occupations, the share of home-workers increased to levels largely dictated by the degree to which the tasks and duties associated with these roles could be done remotely. A significant increase was observed at the beginning of the pandemic among personal service occupations, with the share of teleworkers reaching 34% in April 2020. However, this figure dropped sharply to 18% in summer 2020, before rising again to 24% in spring 2021. Interestingly, a contrasting pattern emerged among sales and customer service occupations, where the share of teleworkers remained stable at around 22% across all three time points.

Finally, consistent with theoretical predictions, there was a minimal increase in teleworking among traditional working-class occupations. Only around 20% of skilled trades workers and 14–15% of process, plant, and machine operatives worked from home. While elementary occupations nearly doubled, the overall share of teleworkers in this group remained the lowest among all nine occupational categories, ranging from roughly 9% to 11%, even at the peak of pandemic restrictions.

The UK data reveals that industries varied in their potential for teleworking, as predicted by Dingel and Neiman (2020). Overall, there was less fluctuation in teleworking rates across industries over the pandemic compared with the occupational groups discussed previously, though some exceptions were noted. Broadly, three distinct groups of industries can be identified as shown in Table 6.3.

The first group includes industries in which most jobs do not require on-site presence or physical interaction with others. For some of these industries—such as information and communication, and professional, scientific, and technical activities—the proportion of individuals working from home was already relatively high before the pandemic, exceeding 50%. During the pandemic, this figure rose to around 75–80% and remained relatively stable. In other similar industries, where the pre-pandemic share was moderate, teleworking increased notably, reaching over 70% in sectors such as financial and insurance activities, public administration and defence, compulsory social security, and education. For most of these industries, the proportion of remote workers varied only slightly, except for public administration and defence, and education. In

Table 6.3 Share of teleworks among different industries

	Jan/Feb 2020	*Apr 2020*	*Sep 2020*	*Mar 2021*
Industry SIC07				
Agriculture, Forestry, and Fishing	0.33	0.46	0.48	0.34
Mining and Quarrying	0.23	0.60	0.58	0.63
Manufacturing	0.23	0.34	0.34	0.38
Electricity, gas, steam, and air conditioning supply	0.53	0.53	0.61	0.64
Water supply, sewerage, waste management, and remediation activities	0.34	0.51	0.52	0.59
Construction	0.25	0.35	0.36	0.43
Wholesale and retail trade; repair of motor vehicles and motorcycles	0.15	0.22	0.20	0.24
Transportation and storage	0.13	0.19	0.24	0.25
Accommodation and food service activities	0.10	0.18	0.22	0.24
Information and communication	0.64	0.80	0.80	0.81
Financial and insurance activities	0.47	0.87	0.84	0.84
Real estate activities	0.41	0.64	0.63	0.77
Professional, scientific, and technical activities	0.55	0.73	0.76	0.78
Administrative and support service activities	0.22	0.32	0.41	0.32
Public administration and defence; compulsory social security	0.38	0.71	0.65	0.73
Education	0.33	0.78	0.45	0.56
Human health and social work activities	0.24	0.40	0.40	0.44
Arts, entertainment, and recreation	0.30	0.46	0.40	0.53
Other service activities	0.41	0.40	0.55	0.57
Number of observations	10,031	7528	6262	6120

education, the share of home-workers dropped significantly in summer 2020, from almost 80% to just 45%. This reflected the relaxation of COVID-19 restrictions, as educational institutions reopened for students during this period. However, with schools gradually reopening from early March 2021 and the survey fieldwork occurring later that month, the share of home-workers in education saw only a slight increase at the final observed time point.

The second group consists of industries with a moderate share of remote workers pre- pandemic, ranging from 25% to 40%. During the pandemic, this share slightly increased, surpassing 40% in human health and social work activities and construction, and exceeding 50% in arts, entertainment, and recreation, as well as other service activities.

Finally, the third group comprises large and essential industries in which on-site presence is unavoidable. These industries comprised the lowest proportion of remote working before the pandemic, and their share could not significantly increase owing to inherent limitations. At its peak, teleworking in these industries reached a maximum of around 25%. This group includes transportation and storage, wholesale and retail trade, and accommodation and food service activities.

Our analysis confirms the relationship between home characteristics and the likelihood of working from home (Table 6.4). Before the pandemic, the amount of space available per person was positively associated with teleworking. Individuals living in spacious homes (defined as 2.1 rooms per person or more) were five percentage points more likely to work from home than those in the smallest homes or flats (fewer than 1.3 rooms per person).

Household income also influenced the likelihood of remote working. Respondents from the wealthiest households (top quintile, with household incomes over £4800 per month) had a probability of working from home that was eight percentage points higher than those in the least affluent households (bottom quintile, household income below £1731 per month). This suggests that, although the pandemic somewhat 'democratised' working from home—in that it extended such conditions to workers in mid- and low-level service occupations—household financial status remained an important factor in determining who worked remotely in practice.

Interestingly, having children under the age of ten reduced the probability of working from home by around five percentage points. However, people with older children had the same chance of remote working as those without children. This supports the hypothesis that the potential conflict between parenting and professional roles may discourage working from home.

Finally, commuting time was also positively associated with the likelihood of teleworking. Workers with longer commutes (over 35 minutes) were five percentage points more likely to work remotely compared to those with shorter commutes (10 minutes or less).

During the pandemic, the pattern of relationships shifted somewhat. As previously stated, this is to be expected, as having limited options of working on-site or from home might have reduced the significance of certain factors. For instance, the coefficient for the top quintile of household

Table 6.4 Predicted probabilities of working from home at least sometimes (logit models for different time periods)

	Jan/Feb 2020	*Apr 2020*	*Sep 2020*	*Mar 2021*
Number of rooms per person available (Ref.: below 1.3 rooms per person)				
1.3–2 rooms per person	0.02	0.05*	0.03	0.03
	(0.017)	(0.025)	(0.028)	(0.031)
2.1–2.6 rooms per person	0.05*	0.03	0.06	0.03
	(0.021)	(0.029)	(0.032)	(0.035)
Children in household (Ref.: No children)				
Yes (youngest is below 10 years old)	−0.05**	−0.07**	−0.04	−0.04
	(0.019)	(0.022)	(0.023)	(0.028)
Yes (youngest is 10 or older)	0.00	−0.03	0.03	−0.00
	(0.020)	(0.024)	(0.026)	(0.027)
Household net income quintiles (Ref.: below 1731)				
1731–2574	0.04	0.01	0.04	0.06
	(0.030)	(0.037)	(0.047)	(0.042)
2575–3513	0.03	0.00	0.06	0.06
	(0.030)	(0.035)	(0.042)	(0.039)
3514–4820	0.04	0.02	0.05	0.08
	(0.028)	(0.034)	(0.041)	(0.042)
Over 4820	0.08**	0.07	0.09*	0.13**
	(0.028)	(0.039)	(0.042)	(0.043)
Time travelling to work quartiles (Ref.: 0–10 minutes)				
11–20 minutes	−0.03	0.02	0.02	0.01
	(0.018)	(0.024)	(0.027)	(0.030)
21–35 minutes	0.02	0.05	0.05	0.07
	(0.020)	(0.029)	(0.031)	(0.034)
Over 35 minutes	0.05**	0.10**	0.10**	0.11**
	(0.019)	(0.026)	(0.029)	(0.029)
Gender (Ref.: male)				
Female	−0.00	0.01	0.01	0.03
	(0.014)	(0.021)	(0.021)	(0.023)
Education (Ref.: no degree)				
High (university degree)	0.08**	0.09**	0.11**	0.11**
	(0.017)	(0.022)	(0.026)	(0.027)
Managerial duties: current job (Ref.: not a manager or a supervisor)				
Manager	0.08**	0.06*	0.04	0.03
	(0.019)	(0.026)	(0.026)	(0.028)
Foreman/supervisor	0.03	−0.04	−0.05	−0.05
	(0.021)	(0.027)	(0.033)	(0.033)
Number of observations	6616	5427	4584	4521

Note: Industry and occupation have been used as controls but are not displayed in the table for clarity

** $p < 0.01$; * $p < 0.05$

income was no longer statistically significant in May 2020, although it regained significance in the models for September 2020 and March 2021.

The relationship between the amount of space available for working at home also became less clear. In spring 2020, the coefficient for the largest homes lost significance, while the one for medium-sized homes became significant. However, by September 2020 and March 2021, none of the coefficients for space availability were significant.

The association with commute time, however, strengthened slightly compared to the pre-pandemic period and remained constant throughout. A long commute (over 35 minutes) consistently increased the probability of working from home by 10–11 percentage points.

Having children younger than ten years old had a marginally stronger impact in May 2020 than pre-pandemic, reducing the likelihood of working from home by about seven percentage points compared to those without children. However, this effect was no longer significant in the models for September 2020 and March 2021. This supports the hypothesis that some parents chose to work on-site to avoid the dual burden of childcare during school closures and remote work. This pressure probably relaxed when schools reopened in summer 2020 and again in early March 2021.

Conclusion

Overall, the findings highlight significant but gradually diminishing disruptions to employment patterns, working arrangements, and participation in the labour market during the COVID-19 pandemic. Initially, there was a significant decline in paid work, most pronounced in France and the UK, while Germany and Italy experienced more moderate falloffs. During the early Shock phase of spring 2020, furlough schemes served as a critical buffer, particularly in Italy and the UK, mitigating steep increases in unemployment. Over time, employment rates recovered in all four countries, returning close to pre-pandemic levels by autumn 2022, although not always fully. These trends are largely consistent with official labour market data from Eurostat and national statistical offices.

A key development during the pandemic was the adoption and implementation of remote work. As lockdowns restricted movement, many employers adopted telework as a practical solution. This transition was particularly notable in France and the UK, although its impact varied across countries. By the later stages of the pandemic, remote work had stabilised at levels higher than pre-pandemic in Germany and the UK, while France and Italy experienced declines as restrictions eased. It would therefore appear likely that remote work will become a permanent feature of the post-COVID-19 employment landscape in both the UK and Germany.

Differences in the probability of working from home emerged along several demographic lines. Highly educated workers were consistently more likely to work remotely than those with lower levels of education. Gender gaps were minimal, although men tended to work remotely slightly more than women. Overall, parents were also more likely to telework than adults with no children, aside from in Italy.

The level of working from home by occupation and industry, as observed in the analysed UK survey data, closely followed the probability predicted by the distribution of the type of tasks and duties across different occupations and industries. This relationship was strong before the pandemic, allowing predictions of which occupations might have the highest shares of teleworkers. However, the lockdowns imposed a sudden shift to remote work, acting as something of a 'natural experiment'. This allowed for the more detailed assessment of the potential for adoption of telework across different occupations and industries, effectively settling long-standing debates about who is and is not able to work from home.

As shown, before the pandemic, in high-income developed Western economies, working from home was most prevalent among professional and managerial occupations. This arrangement was beneficial for these workers, as many enjoyed higher wages than their on-site counterparts (ILO, 2021). However, the pandemic resulted in an increase in the rate of remote work also among mid- and low- level services and administrative occupations, raising questions about how working from home affected working conditions, career prospects, and pay. Research on low- and middle-income countries finds that working from home is more common among mid- and low-skilled workers, whose overall working conditions are generally worse than those of on-site counterparts (ILO, 2021). While a thorough examination of remote work's effects extends beyond the scope of this chapter, research from low- and middle-income countries suggests that some undesirable outcomes may arise for mid- and low-skilled workers (ILO, 2021). Future research might therefore investigate whether similar challenges appear in high-income countries.

Our analysis demonstrates how numerous factors influenced working from home both before and during the pandemic. Household income and home size were important factors. Before the pandemic, individuals in wealthier households and those living in larger homes were more likely to work from home. However, during the early months of the pandemic, these relationships became less consistent, probably as a result of government and employer mandates which enforced remote work, limiting personal preference. By the later stages of the pandemic, the influence of income re-emerged, while home size remained less significant.

Commuting time also was a notable factor both before and throughout the pandemic. Workers with longer commutes consistently showed a higher likelihood of remote working before and during the pandemic. This relationship strengthened slightly during the early phases of the pandemic, suggesting that avoiding lengthy commutes was a strong driver for remote work.

Overall, the combination of a preference for improving home office space and the incentive to avoid commutes may have wider implications. As shown by our results, the overall quality of the home workspace, indirectly measured by household income and home size, is an important factor in determining the decision to work from home. This aligns with existing evidence to suggest that individuals planning to work from home may seek larger, more suitable homes, potentially causing property prices to rise, a trend observed throughout the pandemic (Guglielminetti et al., 2021; Mondragon & Wieland, 2022). Moreover, this could reflect a tendency among workers to invest in improving their workspaces while employers cut office costs by outsourcing them to employees (Behrens et al., 2024; Stanton & Tiwari, 2021). If these additional costs incurred by employees are not fully compensated, and assuming the popularity of homeworking remains higher after the pandemic, it could become a significant new aspect of the capital versus labour conflict.

Furthermore, changes in telework behaviour have the potential to influence urban structures and regional economies. As Gokan et al. (2022) note, many high-income professionals who regularly choose to work from home and no longer are required to commute frequently are likely to relocate to more affordable areas, often in the suburbs or less economically productive regions. This shift could transform the socio-economic geography of regions and cities, supporting trends such as hyper-urbanisation and contributing to the emergence of 'doughnut cities', where city centres experience neglect and a decline in economic activities like local consumption services such as cafes and restaurants. These changes may also trigger second-order effects, potentially exacerbating existing social inequalities. For example, unskilled workers who are disproportionately employed in local consumption services may face job losses or be forced to transition to lower-paying sectors with poorer working conditions. This underscores the complex, widespread consequences of changes in commuting behaviours on economic and social structures.

Finally, family situations also impacted remote work patterns in the UK. Before the pandemic, parents with younger children were less likely to work from home, possibly owing to potential conflicts between childcare and professional responsibilities. This effect intensified during school closures, but subsided as schools reopened and caregiving pressures were relaxed. This highlights the risk of distractions in a home office, which can reduce the willingness to work remotely, and underscores the importance of organising home offices to minimise such disruptions. This effect also suggests a broader need for supportive childcare policies and family-friendly work arrangements to help parents balance their professional and caregiving responsibilities effectively.

References

Abendroth, A.-K., & Reimann, M. (2018). Telework and work–family conflict across workplaces: Investigating the implications of work–family supportive and high-demand workplace cultures. In S. L. Blair & J. Obradović (Eds.), *The work–family interface: Spillover, complications, and challenges* (pp. 323–348). Emerald Publishing.

Adams-Prassl, A., Boneva, T., Golin, M., & Rauh, C. (2020). Inequality in the impact of the coronavirus shock: Evidence from real-time surveys. *Journal of Public Economics, 189*, 104245. https://doi.org/10.1016/j.jpubeco.2020.104245

Alon, T., Doepke, M., Olmstead-Rumsey, J., & Tertilt, M. (2020). The impact of COVID-19 on gender equality. *National Bureau of Economic Research*. Advance online publication. https://doi.org/10.3386/w26947.

Ammons, S. K., & Markham, W. T. (2004). Working at home: Experiences of skilled white-collar workers. *Sociological Spectrum, 24*(2), 191–238. https://doi.org/10.1080/02732170490271744

Andrew, A., Cattan, S., Costa Dias, M., Farquharson, C., Kraftman, L., Krutikova, S., Phimister, A., & Sevilla, A. (2020). Inequalities in children's experiences of home learning during the COVID-19 lockdown in England. *Fiscal Studies, 41*(3), 653–683. https://doi.org/10.1111/1475-5890.12240

Bailey, D. E., & Kurland, N. B. (2002). A review of telework research: Findings, new directions, and lessons for the study of modern work. *Journal of Organizational Behavior, 23*, 383–400. https://doi.org/10.1002/job.144

Behrens, K., Kichko, S., & Thisse, J.-F. (2024). Working from home: Too much of a good thing? *Regional Science and Urban Economics, 105*, 103990. https://doi.org/10.1016/j.regsciurbeco.2024.103990
Bellmann, L., & Hübler, O. (2021). Working from home, job satisfaction and work–life balance—Robust or heterogeneous links? *International Journal of Manpower, 42*(3), 424–441. https://doi.org/10.1108/IJM-10-2019-0458
Cuerdo-Vilches, T., Navas-Martín, M. Á., March, S., & Oteiza, I. (2021a). Adequacy of telework spaces in homes during the lockdown in Madrid, according to socioeconomic factors and home features. *Sustainable Cities and Society, 75*, 103262. https://doi.org/10.1016/j.scs.2021.103262
Cuerdo-Vilches, T., Navas-Martín, M. Á., & Oteiza, I. (2021b). Working from home: Is our housing ready? *International Journal of Environmental Research and Public Health, 18*(14). https://doi.org/10.3390/ijerph18147329
de Abreu e Silva, J., & Melo, P. C. (2018). Home telework, travel behavior, and land-use patterns: A path analysis of British single-worker households. *Journal of Transport and Land Use, 11*(1). https://doi.org/10.5198/jtlu.2018.1134
de Vos, D., Meijers, E., & van Ham, M. (2018). Working from home and the willingness to accept a longer commute. *The Annals of Regional Science, 61*, 375–398. https://doi.org/10.1007/s00168-018-0873-6
Dey, M., Frazis, H., Loewenstein, M. A., & Sun, H. (2020). Ability to work from home: Evidence from two surveys and implications for the labor market in the COVID-19 pandemic. *Monthly Labor Review*, 1–19. https://doi.org/10.21916/mlr.2020.14
Dingel, J., & Neiman, B. (2020). *How many jobs can be done at home?* No. w26948. National Bureau of Economic Research. https://doi.org/10.3386/w26948
Dockery, A., & Bawa, S. (2014). Is working from home good work or bad work? Evidence from Australian employees. *Australian Journal of Labour Economics, 17*(2), 163–190. https://doi.org/10.3316/informit.746092618289790
Ebbinghaus, B., & Lehner, L. (2022). Cui bono – Business or labour? Job retention policies during the COVID-19 pandemic in Europe. *Transfer: European Review of Labour and Research, 28*(1), 47–64.
Eurofound. (2021). *COVID-19: Implications for employment and working life.* Publications Office of the European Union.
Gokan, T., Kichko, S., Matheson, J. A., & Thisse, J.-F. (2022). *How the rise of teleworking will reshape labor markets and cities.* Sheffield Economic Research Paper Series, 2022013. University of Sheffield.
Guglielminetti, E., Loberto, M., Zevi, G., & Zizza, R. (2021). *Living on my own: The impact of the COVID-19 pandemic on housing preferences.* Occasional Paper No. 627. Bank of Italy.
Hill, E. J., Erickson, J. J., Holmes, E. K., & Ferris, M. (2010). Workplace flexibility, work hours, and work–life conflict: Finding an extra day or two. *Journal of Family Psychology, 24*(3), 349–358.

Hipp, L., & Bünning, M. (2021). Parenthood as a driver of increased gender inequality during COVID-19? Exploratory evidence from Germany. *European Societies, 23*(sup1), S658–S673. https://doi.org/10.1080/14616696.2020.1833229

International Labour Organization. (2021). *Working from home: From invisibility to decent work.* International Labour Office. https://www.ilo.org

Ipsen, C., van Veldhoven, M., Kirchner, K., & Hansen, J. P. (2021). Six key advantages and disadvantages of working from home in Europe during COVID-19. *International Journal of Environmental Research and Public Health, 18*(4). https://doi.org/10.3390/ijerph18041826

Iscan, O. F., & Naktiyok, A. (2005). Attitudes towards telecommuting: The Turkish case. *Journal of Information Technology, 20*(1), 52–63.

Johnson, L. C., Andrey, J., & Shaw, S. M. (2007). Mr. dithers comes to dinner: Telework and the merging of women's work and home domains in Canada. *Gender, Place & Culture, 14*(2), 141–161. https://doi.org/10.1080/09663690701213701

Laumer, S., & Maier, C. (2021). Why do people (not) want to work from home? An individual-focused literature review on telework. In *Proceedings of the 2021 computers and people research conference (SIGMISCPR '21)* (pp. 41–47). ACM. https://doi.org/10.1145/3458026.3462155

McArthur, D. P., & Hong, J. (2023). Are slow internet connections limiting home working opportunities? *Travel Behaviour and Society, 23.* https://doi.org/10.1016/j.tbs.2023.100629

Miao, F., Kelly, J. A., Clinch, J. P., & King, F. (2012). Environmental policy implications of working from home: Modelling the impacts of land-use, infrastructure, and socio-demographics. *Energy Policy, 47*, 416–423. https://doi.org/10.1016/j.enpol.2012.05.014

Mokhtarian, P. L., Bagley, M. N., & Salomon, I. (1998). The impact of gender, occupation, and presence of children on telecommuting motivations and constraints. *Journal of the Association for Information Science and Technology, 49*, 1115–1134. https://doi.org/10.1002/(SICI)1097-4571(1998)49:12<1115::AID-ASI7>3.0.CO;2-Y

Mondragon, J. A., & Wieland, J. (2022). *Housing demand and remote work.* NBER Working Paper No. 30041. National Bureau of Economic Research. https://doi.org/10.3386/w30041

Morgan, R. E. (2004). Teleworking: An assessment of the benefits and challenges. *European Business Review, 16*(4), 344–357. https://doi.org/10.1108/09555340410699613

Motte-Baumvol, B., & Schwanen, T. (2024). Telework, travel times, and peak hour avoidance in England: An overview using travel times across five weekdays. *Travel Behaviour and Society.* https://doi.org/10.1016/j.tbs.2023.100668

Niu, Q., Nagata, T., Fukutani, N., Tezuka, M., Shimoura, K., Nagai-Tanima, M., & Aoyama, T. (2021). Health effects of immediate telework introduction during the COVID-19 era in Japan: A cross-sectional study. *PLoS One, 16*(10), e0256530. https://doi.org/10.1371/journal.pone.0256530

O'Keefe, P., Caulfield, B., Brazil, W., & White, P. (2016). The impacts of telecommuting in Dublin. *Research in Transportation Economics, 57*, 13–20. https://doi.org/10.1016/j.retrec.2016.06.010

Olszewski, P., & Mokhtarian, P. L. (1994). Telecommuting frequency and impacts for state of California employees. *Technological Forecasting and Social Change, 45*, 275–286.

Quaranta, R., Trentini, F., & Villosio, C. (2020). First estimates of the effects of COVID-19 on young workers in Italy. *Youth Employment PartnerSHIP*. https://youthemploymentmag.net/2020/10/20/first-estimates-of-the-effects-of-covid-19-onyoung-workers-in-italy/

Scott, D. M., Dam, I., Paéz, A., & Wilton, R. D. (2012). Investigating the effects of social influence on the choice to telework. *Environment and Planning, 44*(5), 1016–1031.

Stantcheva, S. (2022). *Inequalities in the times of a pandemic*. NBER Working Paper. https://doi.org/10.3386/w29657

Stanton, C. T., & Tiwari, P. (2021). *Housing consumption and the cost of remote work*. NBER Working Paper No. 28483. National Bureau of Economic Research. https://doi.org/10.3386/w28483

Stephens, G. K., & Szajna, B. (1998). Perceptions and expectations: Why people choose a telecommuting work style. *International Journal of Electronic Commerce, 3*(1), 70–85. https://doi.org/10.1080/10864415.1998.11518328

Topi, H. (2004). Supporting telework: Obstacles and solutions. *Information Systems Management, 21*(3), 79–85. https://doi.org/10.1201/1078/44432.21.3.20040601/82481.12

Wells, K., Douma, F., Loimer, H., Olson, L., & Pansing, C. (2001). Telecommuting implications for travel behavior: Case studies from Minnesota. *Transportation Research Record, 1752*(1), 148–156. https://doi.org/10.3141/1752-20

Wicks, D. (2002). Successfully increasing technological control through minimizing workplace resistance: Understanding the willingness to telework. *Management Decision, 40*(7), 672–681. https://doi.org/10.1108/00251740210438508

Yasenov, V. (2020). *Who can work from home?* IZA Discussion Paper, No. 13197. https://doi.org/10.2139/ssrn.3590895

Yen, J. R. (2000). Interpreting employee telecommuting adoption: An economics perspective. *Transportation, 27*, 149–164. https://doi.org/10.1023/A:1005200513201

Zhu, P. (2013). Telecommuting, household commute, and location choice. *Urban Studies, 50*(12), 2441–2459. https://doi.org/10.1177/0042098012474520

CHAPTER 7

The Consequences of Working from Home on Health and Wellbeing

Elias Naumann, Piotr Marzec, and Andrew Zola

Introduction

The advent of the digital age coupled with unprecedented global events has transformed the possibilities of professional lives. In recent years, remote work or telecommuting has steadily increased, with a growing number of individuals choosing to work from home. The COVID-19

E. Naumann (✉)
GESIS Leibniz Institute for the Social Sciences, Mannheim, Germany
e-mail: elias.naumann@gesis.org

P. Marzec
Institute for Social and Economic Research, University of Essex, Colchester, UK
e-mail: p.marzec@essex.ac.uk

A. Zola
Centre for Research on Social Inequalities (CRIS), CNRS, Sciences Po, Paris, France
e-mail: andrew.zola@sciencespo.fr

E. Naumann et al. (eds.), *Social Life during COVID-19 in France, Germany, Italy and the UK*,
https://doi.org/10.1007/978-3-031-99349-7_7

pandemic accelerated this shift, pushing organisations and employees to adapt quickly to new ways of working (Barrero et al., 2021; see also Chap. 6).

The transition to working from home (WFH) is associated with a transformation in work–life dynamics. This may offer several potential benefits, such as increased flexibility and autonomy, reduced commuting time, and an improved work–life balance. Moreover, studies have shown that work from home increases the intensity of tasks and subsequent productivity (Bloom et al., 2015). However, the departure from the conventional office environment may also result in negative consequences. WFH may blur the boundaries between work and personal life (van der Lippe & Lippényi, 2020). The confusion between the two can lead to longer work hours, difficulty from separating work-related tasks, and increased stress. Moreover, the changing frequency, quality, and nature of interactions led to concerns that society at large may lack communication skills and be less trusting (Knight et al., 2022). Understanding the complex impacts of remote work on individuals will benefit employees, employers, policymakers, and sociologists, as it can influence the future work policies and strategies.

This chapter aims to explore the consequences of WFH on different health and wellbeing outcomes (Gajendran & Harrison, 2007). We focus on how the transition to remote work during the COVID-19 pandemic affected both general and psychological health, using indicators such as depressive feelings and loneliness, as well as subjective wellbeing. Through analysing individual-level panel data (including the pre-pandemic period) from three countries, we provide a robust understanding of the individual-level implications of remote work on health and wellbeing.

Our empirical analysis provides three key contributions to the existing literature surrounding remote work. First, the COVID-19 pandemic was an external shock to labour markets, forcing many to adopt remote working arrangements. This allows for robust and comparatively unbiased results in relation to previous research, which faced issues with self-selection. Bloom (2023) estimates that work from home days in the United States doubled every 15 years before the pandemic and reached approximately 5% in 2020, and then substantially increased to 60% in spring 2020, stabilising to around 30% in 2023. While the shift to remote work was related to the type of work (see Chap. 6 for details on occupation, industry, or job duties), the shock was probably not related to individual preferences, personal or the family situation, which reduced the number of possible confounders. Second, we analyse related studies that examine the huge uptake in work from home in spring 2020 (Adams-Prassl et al., 2020; Brynjolfsson et al., 2020; Eurofound, 2020) as our multi-wave panel data span until spring 2022, which facilitates the analysis of medium-term effects, such as adaptation or accumulation dynamics (Hudde et al., 2023). Third, WFH can have both positive and negative impacts on individuals. Previous research suggests that these effects vary in relation to gender, parenthood, home environment, and available social support (Yucel & Chung, 2023; Hudde et al., 2023). Relying on high-quality, probability samples of the general population, we explore these varied effects. Recognising and addressing such heterogeneities can help individuals and organisations to optimise the benefits of remote work while reducing potential negative impacts.

Theory

WFH can have a variety of effects on health and wellbeing. Theoretical mechanisms are not exclusive but may work alongside such practicalities (Gajendran & Harrison, 2007). Understanding the impact of these effects is crucial for individuals and organisations to create a supportive and healthy work environment. In the following, we begin with summarising the existing literature on how work from home influences wellbeing, outlining both positive and negative effects. We then elaborate on how these immediate effects may develop over time, and whether dynamics of adaptation or accumulation may be expected. In the final section, we address the most likely individual-level heterogeneities in such effects.

The Main Effect

One of the main advantages of WFH is increased flexibility. Remote work allows individuals to have more control over their schedules, enabling a better balance between work and personal life (Bakker & Geurts, 2004). For example, WFH usually increases the capacity to complete both professional work and housework, as well as care for children and other family members (Kelly et al., 2014). Reduced commuting time further saves time and energy. This setup can reduce stress, improve sleep quality, and provide more time for self-care, exercise, or leisure activities (Norgate et al., 2020). WFH also often grants individuals a greater sense of independence and control over their work, another factor contributing towards job satisfaction and overall wellbeing (Wheatley, 2017). Remote work can also provide a less disruptive work environment compared with traditional office settings. Minimising distractions can enhance focus, productivity, and satisfaction with work tasks, all of which contribute to improved wellbeing.

While remote work offers benefits, it can also have negative effects. The lack of face-to-face interactions and limited opportunities for informal social interactions can negatively affect wellbeing and result in social isolation and loneliness. Such distancing can also negatively affect the career development for those at the start of their professional lives, as they are presented with fewer opportunities to network and informally learn about their workplace. WFH can blur the boundaries between work and personal life, resulting in challenges in distinguishing the two (Kossek et al., 2006). This leads to longer work hours, difficulty disconnecting from work-related tasks, and increased stress (Lott, 2020). On the whole, empirical evidence suggests that WFH leads to more work–family conflict—extrapolated from the idea that family satisfaction suffers if one works at home—but does not have an effect on family-to-work conflicts, understood from the notion that work satisfaction or performance is reduced if an individual works from home in close proximity to their families (Allen et al., 2015). Moreover, reliance on digital tools and communication platforms for remote work can lead to digital fatigue. Constant connectivity, information overload, and increased time spent looking at screens can contribute to stress and exhaustion, and ultimately decrease wellbeing.

The Dynamic Effect

As previously argued, the COVID-19 pandemic and subsequent lockdown and social distancing policies led to an increase in remote work, particularly across the first months of the pandemic in spring 2020 (see Chap. 6). While remote work remained one of the key policy measures to reduce social contact in subsequent lockdowns, the prevalence of remote work did not return to the rates of the first lockdown. However, the proportion of employees WFH remained significantly above pre-pandemic levels (Bloom, 2023). Such a development with an initial shock facilitates the possibility of different dynamics of wellbeing and mental health after the change to work from home: adaptation, habituation, or accumulation.

After the unexpected, potentially shocking transition to remote work (von der Lippe & Lippényi, 2020; Yucel & Chung, 2023), employees were able to recover and adjust to this new reality. Research has demonstrated a notable degree of resilience during times of crisis, highlighting individuals' ability to adapt to adversity (Cummins & Wooden, 2014). It is reasonable to anticipate a swift adaptation to daily life in the pandemic, including being used to new communication methods and the development of work routines that addressed emerging work–family conflicts. Studies have observed patterns of habituation (Mata et al., 2021) and adaptation to unusual circumstances (Myrskylä & Margolis, 2014). Furthermore, previous research demonstrates a difference between voluntary and enforced work from home. A voluntary choice supports perceptions of independence and provides control over the integration between work and family domains (Ashforth et al., 2000). Conversely, mandatory work from home, as occurred throughout the first lockdown, increases stress and may even decrease job satisfaction and performance (Gajendran & Harrison, 2007).

Rather than observing a recovery or adaptation, we may observe the emergence of lasting negative effects of COVID-19's work from home routine. In later phases of the pandemic, individuals may have experienced deeper and sustained periods of hardship compared to the initial wave (Simona-Moussa & Ravazzini, 2019). For example, the absence of social interaction, loneliness, and work-to-family tensions may only gradually emerge and affect wellbeing in the so-called medium term. The negative experience and exhaustion from the first lockdown may also have reduced resilience in later lockdowns and periods of work from home. This suggests that the accumulated stress of multiple pandemic waves may result in prolonged and intensified negative impacts on wellbeing more generally (Hudde et al., 2023).

Heterogeneous Effects

Working remotely was a key strategy in many stay-at-home lockdown policies (Felstead & Reuschke, 2020). Our study examines how the sudden proliferation in remote work impacted health and subjective wellbeing. However, we may expect heterogeneous effects to be moderated by factors such as gender and the individual family situation. For example, Wheatley (2017) and Reuschke (2019) found a positive correlation between remote work and subjective wellbeing, but only for employees and not for the self-employed. They also found positive effects more strongly effecting men compared to women (Binder, 2016). In contrast, Song and Gao (2020) found that remote work is associated with lower happiness and more stress and that 'parents, especially fathers, report a lower level of subjective wellbeing when working at home [...]. Non-parents' subjective wellbeing does not vary much by where they work on weekdays' (p. 2649). One limitation of these studies is institutional and workplace barriers to remote working: remote work is not possible everywhere, nor for everyone (Beham et al., 2019).

The lockdowns in response to COVID-19 provide some influence in this respect, but must also be understood as a specific circumstance that may not be comparable to remote working under 'normal' conditions. For example, combining working from home with childcare and homeschooling constituted an additional burden for working parents when schools and childcare facilities closed. Current studies on the subjective wellbeing of parents during lockdown have resulted in mixed findings. Benzeval et al. (2020) demonstrate that parents reported an improvement in their relationship with their children during the lockdown, an effect that was even stronger for those who were WFH. In Germany, by contrast, satisfaction with family life decreased throughout the lockdown, especially among mothers with young children, who were disproportionately responsible for care tasks (Huebener et al., 2021). In the Netherlands, there was a reduction in the satisfaction of work–life balance among couples with children (Yerkes et al., 2020). In France, parents' increased stress resulted in lower family satisfaction. Meanwhile, those without children were impacted by their reduced social life. Each of these had negative effects on subjective wellbeing, especially among those who worked from home (Recchi et al., 2020).

The theoretical and empirical literature does not provide a clear expectation as to whether the presence of children might moderate the relationship between work from home and subjective wellbeing. As such, our study remains hypothetical in this respect. In regards to gender differences, we assume that women are still the primary caregivers in the majority households, particularly those with younger children. We expect that mothers will experience much more family-to-work conflicts if they work from home, especially when childcare and support from others—such as grandparents and friends—are not available. Overall, we hypothesise that remote work will lead to lower levels of health and wellbeing for mothers than fathers.

Estimation Method

The optimal design to research the effect of WFH on wellbeing and related outcomes would involve observing individuals who switch to WFH before and after the transition (a treatment group) and comparing this change with people who continue to work on-site (a control group). In such an ideal design, assignment to treatment and control groups would be random, such that there are no systematic variations between the two groups, and neither any anticipation of the switch to WFH. With observational, non-experimental data, we attempt to design our analysis in a way that resembles such an optimal research project as closely as possible.

Compared to pre-pandemic studies on work from home, the pandemic provides two empirical advantages. First, the prevalence of remote work provides sufficient case numbers of 'treated' persons. Second, while not totally randomised, there is much less self-selection into WFH compared with a pre-pandemic context, in which long commuting times, a suitable work environment at home, and individual preferences might have strongly affected who selected to work from home (see Chap. 6). Accordingly, WFH before the pandemic could be seen as the most likely situation in which to find a positive effect of work from home on wellbeing. Conversely, the pandemic context is a much less likely case to find these positive effects.

To determine the causal effect of WFH on wellbeing, the shift in wellbeing among those who switch to WFH is compared to the change among those who consistently work on-site throughout the pandemic. This research design excludes respondents who were not at risk of experiencing the shift in working arrangements, such as those not working at the first time point or already working remotely. This empirical strategy accounts for pre-existing differences in wellbeing levels, for time trends, and unobserved time-constant heterogeneity (Imai and Kim, 2020).

Multi-wave panel studies offer the opportunity to analyse both immediate and longer-term post-treatment effects and explore variations in the impacts of altered workplaces. For example, the study is able to examine whether the effect of WFH differs during the initial lockdown compared to later phases of the pandemic (Goodman-Bacon, 2021).

The Data

We use individual-level panel data from three countries. The *Coping with Covid-19* survey together with the *Étude Longitudinale par Internet pour les Sciences Sociales* (*ELIPSS*) for France, the *German Internet Panel* (*GIP*) for Germany and *Understanding Society*, also known as the *UK Household Longitudinal Survey* (*UKHLS*). Following the framework of this book, we rely on data from four different pandemic periods. For our FE panel data analysis and our identification strategy, it is vital to use pre-treatment information on the dependent and independent variables. As such, we exclude all item–country combinations without pre-pandemic information: Italy is excluded from the analyses as the *ResPOnsE* survey did not include the pre-pandemic period.

Table 7.1 shows all dependent variables used throughout this chapter, including a measure of subjective health status, an indicator of depressive feelings and of loneliness (which aim to capture mental health), and two

Table 7.1 List of dependent variables and availability

		0 – Pre-pandemic	*1a - shock*	*2a - reprise*	*2b - demise*
Health					
Subjective Health	**France**	X	X	X	X
	Germany	X	–	X	–
	UK	X	–	X	–
Depressive Feelings	**France**	X	X	X	X
	Germany	–	X	X	X
	UK	X	X	X	X
Loneliness	**France**	X	X	X	X
	Germany	–	X	X	–
	UK	X	X	X	X
Wellbeing					
Happiness	**France**	X	X	X	X
	Germany	–	–	–	–
	UK	X	X	X	X
Life Satisfaction	*France*	–	–	–	–
	Germany	X	X	X	X
	UK	X	X	X	X

* Item–Country combinations in italics are not included in the analysis, but only those in bold

– item not available for this time period in this country

X item is available for this time period in this country

indicators of wellbeing as happiness and life satisfaction (see also Chaps. 3 and 5).

We chose this broad set of indicators to provide a detailed and overarching account of the potential consequences of WFH on health and wellbeing. The choice was only restricted by data availability. As discussed in the Theory section, there is no underlying expectation concerning the strength and direction of WFH on these different indicators.

As the deployment of such concepts in the surveys differs between countries, we estimate our models separately for each country and indicator.

Results

The Main Effect

The estimated effect of a switch from work on-site to doing at least some remote work is related to a change in health indicators as shown in Tables 7.2 (health, depressive feelings, and loneliness) and 7.3 (happiness and life satisfaction). The results for each country–item combination are provided in a separate column, with the header indicating the country and the item.

Our results suggest that a switch to work from home did not affect the subjective health status of residents of any country. The estimates are nearly zero and therefore not significant (Table 7.2, Models 1–3). There is some evidence that WFH increased feelings of loneliness (Models 4 and 5) and this effect is statistically significant for the UK. Our analysis does not show any clear evidence that work from home necessarily results in a change to depressive feelings. Table 7.3 demonstrates that the predicted coefficients for life satisfaction are positive, but these are not statistically significant. Consequently, we conclude that work from home does not have an effect on life satisfaction nor happiness.

This result, or lack thereof, of a main effect for most indicators reflects the inconclusive findings of pre-pandemic times. There are two main reasons for this. First, work from home and health and wellbeing may have a more dynamic relationship. Instead of an immediate, single effect, there might be a process of recovery and adaptation, such that potential positive effects on wellbeing and satisfaction are only revealed after a certain amount of time. However, the negative consequences may also accumulate over time. Resilience might fade and negative effects on (mental) health might emerge over a longer period. Second, a null effect might also

Table 7.2 Work from home and health—Average treatment effects of FE models

	(1)	*(2)*	*(3)*	*(4)*	*(5)*	*(6)*	*(7)*	*(8)*
	Health FR	Health DE	Health UK	Loneliness FR	Loneliness UK	Depressive Feelings FR	Depressive Feelings DE	Depressive Feelings UK
Switch to WFH	-0.10	0.00	0.00	0.02	0.05***	−0.08	−0.05	0.02
	(0.18)	(0.99)	(0.89)	(0.74)	(0.00)	(0.49)	(0.22)	(0.19)
0 – pre-pandemic	Ref.	Ref.	Ref.	Ref.	Ref.	Ref.	Ref.	Ref.
1a - shock	0.42***			−0.16**	−0.04***	−0.09	0.00	0.09***
	(0.00)			(0.00)	(0.00)	(0.22)	(.)	(0.00)
2a - reprise	0.20***	0.03	0.12***	−0.02	−0.03**	−0.04	0.11***	0.08***
	(0.00)	(0.06)	(0.00)	(0.56)	(0.01)	(0.57)	(0.00)	(0.00)
2b - demise	−0.07			0.01	−0.09***	0.05	0.20***	0.03*
	(0.12)			(0.68)	(0.00)	(0.37)	(0.00)	(0.01)
Constant	3.71***	3.83***	3.43***	2.08***	1.46***	2.26***	1.47***	1.91***
	(0.00)	(0.00)	(0.00)	(0.00)	(0.00)	(0.00)	(0.00)	(0.00)
Observations	964	3944	12,475	962	22,463	952	4369	22,498

p-values in parentheses

* $p < 0.05$, ** $p < 0.01$, *** $p < 0.001$

Table 7.3 Work from home and wellbeing—Average treatment effects of FE models

	(1)	*(2)*	*(3)*	*(4)*
	Happiness FR	Happiness UK	Life Satisfaction DE	Life Satisfaction UK
Switch to WFH	−0.05	0.02	0.12	0.02
	(0.69)	(0.49)	(0.16)	(0.45)
0 – pre-pandemic	Ref.	Ref.	Ref.	Ref.
1a - shock	−0.30**	0.09***	−0.29***	−0.28***
	(0.00)	(0.00)	(0.00)	(0.00)
2a - reprise	0.02	0.13***	−0.12	−0.20***
	(0.79)	(0.00)	(0.09)	(0.00)
2b - demise	0.01	0.06**	0.02	−0.16***
	(0.84)	(0.00)	(0.74)	(0.00)
Constant	−0.04	−0.04***	6.68***	5.09***
	(0.22)	(0.00)	(0.00)	(0.00)
Observations	958	22,498	6729	22,493

p-values in parentheses

* $p < 0.05$, ** $p < 0.01$, *** $p < 0.001$

conceal potential variations if some groups benefit from a switch to remote work, while others are impacted negatively. We explore both perspectives in the following.

Dynamic Effects

To evaluate whether a switch to remote work has lasting effects on individuals' health and wellbeing, we examine how such indicators developed after a switch to remote work occurred, examining the pre-pandemic period against period 1a (Shock). Do initial effects accumulate over time? Or do we observe dynamics which suggest a recovery or adaptation to new work circumstances? In Tables 7.4 and 7.5, we show how the overall effect evolves over time, but this is available only for country–item combinations with more than two waves.

Most of the analyses (Table 7.4, models 1, 4, and 5) find that the estimates increase in strength over time. This suggests that the positive effect of WFH on an improved subjective health and fewer depressive feelings may only be revealed after some time, although these differences never

Table 7.4 Work from home and health—Average treatment effects over time

	(1)	*(2)*	*(3)*	*(4)*	*(5)*	*(6)*
	Health FR	Loneliness FR	Loneliness UK	Depressive Feelings FR	Depressive Feelings DE	Depressive Feelings UK
Effect of switch to WFH…						
…at time 1a	−0.04	0.09	0.05^{***}	0.02	−0.01	0.04
	(0.64)	(0.29)	(0.00)	(0.90)	(0.80)	(0.07)
…at time 2a	−0.12	0.15	0.05^{**}	−0.17	−0.07	0.03
	(0.26)	(0.09)	(0.00)	(0.29)	(0.16)	(0.20)
…at time 2b	−0.16	−0.14	0.04^{*}	−0.14	−0.07	−0.01
	(0.17)	(0.14)	(0.02)	(0.33)	(0.20)	(0.54)
Observations	964	962	22,463	952	4369	22,498
Subpop. no. obs*	(166)	(166)	(4086)	(165)	(629)	(4083)

* *only those respondents who switched to remote between pre-pandemic and 1a*

p-values in parentheses

* $p < 0.05$, ** $p < 0.01$, *** $p < 0.001$

Table 7.5 Work from home and wellbeing—Average treatment effects over time

	(1)	*(2)*	*(3)*	*(4)*
	Happiness FR	Happiness UK	Life Satisfaction DE	Life Satisfaction UK
Effect of switch to WFH…				
…at time 1a	−0.14	0.04	0.11	0.00
	(0.40)	(0.16)	(0.42)	(0.97)
…at time 2a	−0.17	−0.00	0.09	−0.03
	(0.26)	(0.89)	(0.48)	(0.51)
…at time 2b	0.15	−0.01	0.15	0.11^{*}
	(0.33)	(0.86)	(0.15)	(0.02)
Observations	958	22,498	6729	22,493
	(164)	(4082)	(961)	(4079)

* *only those respondents who switched to remote between pre-pandemic and 1a*

p-values in parentheses

* $p < 0.05$, ** $p < 0.01$, *** $p < 0.001$

reached statistical significance. In the UK, the estimates for depressive feelings are too insignificant to allow for meaningful interpretation (Table 7.4, model 6). The manifestations of loneliness in France demonstrate a pattern which could support adaptive processes (Table 7.4, model 2). In the earlier periods of Shock (1a) and Reprise (2a), work from home led to higher levels of loneliness. Later, during Demise (2b), individuals had the possibility to adapt to new working conditions, and working from home reduced feelings of loneliness. As none of these estimates reach our standards of statistical significance, caution must be taken when interpreting these results. The estimate for loneliness in the UK is the only figure significantly different from zero. This shows that there is an initial increase in loneliness among those who switch to remote work, and this difference remains constant over the pandemic periods.

Our analyses of subjective wellbeing, presented in Table 7.5, support the hypothesis that work from home has positive effects on wellbeing over a longer timeframe. However, these results are statistically significant only for life satisfaction in the UK. For example, a switch to remote work leads to no change or even lower happiness in periods 1a and 2a, but has positive effects on life satisfaction in Germany and the UK (Table 7.5, models 3 and 4).

Heterogeneous Effects

Utilising existing research, we argued that the consequences of WFH might be moderated by the individual social context. In particular, family dynamics and gender differences may play a crucial role. In our analysis, we examine whether the impact of WFH varies according to whether parents' children still live in the household. Moreover, we explore whether mothers and fathers are affected differently by WFH arrangements. In Tables 7.6 and 7.7, we estimate the impact of WFH on the health and wellbeing for women and men without co-resident children and for parents who live with their children. We estimated models separately for each group and did not test for differences between groups.

We observe limited differences between men and women without co-resident children. For health and depressive feelings in France (Table 7.6, models 1 and 6) and for loneliness in the UK (Table 7.6, model 5), we find that women without co-resident children benefit less from switching to remote work, as this coincides with a decrease in health, noted by increased feelings of loneliness and depression. The estimates for mothers

Table 7.6 Work from home and health—Average treatment effects for different groups (based on FE models)

Switch to WFH	*(1)*	*(2)*	*(3)*	*(4)*	*(5)*	*(6)*	*(7)*	*(8)*
	Health FR	Health DE	Health UK	Loneliness FR	Loneliness UK	Depressive Feelings FR	Depressive Feelings DE	Depressive Feelings UK
Women without co-resident children	−0.32	−0.01	0.01	0.19	0.05**	0.57	−0.11	0.02
	(0.25)	(0.87)	(0.89)	(0.07)	(0.01)	(0.06)	(0.15)	(0.38)
Men without co-resident children	−0.13	0.03	−0.03	0.24	0.03	−0.13	−0.10	−0.00
	(0.52)	(0.65)	(0.50)	(0.19)	(0.15)	(0.75)	(0.19)	(0.98)
Mothers with co-resident children	−0.05	0.11	0.01	0.08	0.03	−0.06	0.12	0.02
	(0.69)	(0.30)	(0.81)	(0.44)	(0.18)	(0.71)	(0.24)	(0.58)
Fathers with co-resident children	−0.05	−0.02	−0.01	−0.20	0.08**	−0.38	−0.01	0.05
	(0.67)	(0.77)	(0.87)	(0.10)	(0.00)	(0.10)	(0.91)	(0.17)
Observations	964	3944	12,475	962	22,463	952	4369	22,438

p-values in parentheses

* $p < 0.05$, ** $p < 0.01$, *** $p < 0.001$

Table 7.7 Work from home and wellbeing—Average treatment effects for different groups (based on FE models)

	(1)	*(2)*	*(3)*	*(4)*
	Happiness FR	Happiness UK	Life Satisfaction DE	Life Satisfaction UK
Women without co-resident children	−0.69	0.07	0.16	−0.02
	(0.05)	(0.07)	(0.33)	(0.70)
Men without co-resident children	0.36	−0.05	0.21	0.09
	(0.35)	(0.26)	(0.17)	(0.13)
Mothers with co-resident children	−0.18	−0.01	−0.20	0.03
	(0.23)	(0.90)	(0.33)	(0.63)
Fathers with co-resident children	0.37	0.02	0.17	0.00
	(0.05)	(0.68)	(0.34)	(0.98)
Observations	958	22,498	6729	22,493

p-values in parentheses

* $p < 0.05$, ** $p < 0.01$, *** $p < 0.001$

and fathers with co-resident children do not lead to straightforward conclusions. We find no differences between the two in health in France, and for neither health nor depressive feelings in the UK. WFH reduces fathers' feelings of loneliness in France, and depressive feelings in both France and Germany. Mothers with co-resident children experience an increase in depression when working from home is adopted. Loneliness in the UK is the only evidence (Model 5) that could suggest that mothers with co-resident children may benefit more from a switch to WFH than fathers with co-resident children.

Our evidence that relies on indicators of happiness and life satisfaction (Table 7.7) demonstrates that men without co-resident children tend to benefit more from WFH than women, with the only exception of happiness in the UK (model 2). The gender difference is even stronger for mothers and fathers with co-resident children. While WFH results in a decrease of mothers' happiness in France (model 1) and a lower life satisfaction of mothers in Germany (model 3), fathers' happiness in France and life satisfaction in Germany increases if they work remotely. This suggests that gender roles and care responsibilities are significant in determining whether remote work has positive or negative effects on wellbeing.

Conclusion

The study examines the transition to remote work during the COVID-19 pandemic and its effects on health and wellbeing. The findings highlight both the advantages and challenges of working from home. As positives, WFH provided increased flexibility, autonomy, and reduced commuting stress, which were largely associated with improved work–life balance. However, such benefits were unevenly distributed: outcomes varied based on gender, family status, and the stage of the pandemic. The study also underscores the dynamic nature of the impacts of WFH, suggesting adaptation over time, where initial negative effects such as loneliness gradually diminished.

Despite these insights, our study comprises some significant limitations. First, sample sizes for some countries and measures of health and wellbeing were relatively small. These analyses may lack the statistical authority to detect differences between groups and over time. Second, despite careful design, the reliance on observational data limits the possibility to fully establish causal relationships between WFH and health outcomes. External confounders may have influenced results, particularly those unaccounted for in each study. Furthermore, our analysis relies on subjective evaluations of health and wellbeing and does not observe physical changes in health statuses or stress levels. Related to this, while we capture a variety of different dimensions of health, there are some aspects of health that we do not cover, such as stress or eating behaviours. Third, the study focuses on pandemic-induced WFH, a unique context that included lockdowns, limited opportunities of social contact beyond the household, and closed childcare facilities. As such, this context does not accurately reflect a typical remote work experience. Even the latest time point in our period of observation is likely to still be affected by these circumstances. Fourth, although problems of biased selection of remote work during the pandemic were reduced compared to the pre-pandemic context, WFH was not assigned randomly among workers. As a result, those whose work shifted to work from home were limited to professions that could be completed remotely.

As Chap. 6 suggests, higher levels of remote work will probably remain as a way of working. Our findings suggest that these changes are not a significant risk to health and wellbeing. However, the normalisation of remote work may have serious societal implications. Through reshaping social interactions and limiting casual, in-person workplace exchanges, remote work may challenge the development of trust and social cohesion in both professional and casual settings. This shift may also influence political attitudes and polarisation, as reduced face-to-face contact with diverse social groups may limit exposure to differing viewpoints, which is a different experience to encountering such views online. Future studies into the consequences of work from home would do well to extend their focus to other indicators of health and wellbeing, including also indicators of social conflict and social cohesion. Moreover, these shifts may amplify digital fatigue, reshape social interaction norms, and widen inequities between those who can and cannot work remotely. As work practices adapt to this evolving landscape, it will be crucial to proactively address these challenges to ensure equitable and sustainable outcomes.

References

Adams-Prassl, A., Boneva, T., Golin, M., & Rauh, C. (2020). Inequality in the impact of the coronavirus shock: Evidence from real-time surveys. *Journal of Public Economics, 189*, 104245.

Allen, T. D., Johnson, R. C., Kiburz, K. M., & Shockley, K. M. (2015). Work–family conflict and flexible work arrangements: Deconstructing flexibility. *Personnel Psychology, 68*(2), 345–376.

Ashforth, B. E., Kreiner, G. E., & Fugate, M. (2000). All in a day's work: Boundaries and micro role transitions. *Academy of Management Review, 25*(3), 472–491.

Bakker, A. B., & Geurts, S. A. (2004). Toward a dual-process model of work–home interference. *Work and Occupations, 31*(3), 345–366.

Barrero, J. M., Bloom, N., & Davis, S. J. (2021). Why working from home will stick. *NBER Working Paper Series, No. 28731.*

Beham, B., Drobnič, S., Präg, P., Baierl, A., & Eckner, J. (2019). Part-time work and gender inequality in Europe: A comparative analysis of satisfaction with work–life balance. *European Societies, 21*(3), 378–402.

Benzeval, M., Borkowska, M., Burton, J., Crossley, T., Fumagalli, L., Jäckle, A., & Read, B. (2020). *Understanding Society COVID-19 Survey, April 2020: Wave 1.* Institute for Social and Economic Research, University of Essex.

Binder, M. (2016). Revisiting Cheerful Jane and Miserable John: The impact of income, good health, social contacts and education declines with increasing subjective well-being. *Applied Economics Letters, 23*(8), 544–553.

Bloom, N. (2023). *The bright future of remote work.* The Stanford Institute for Economic Policy Research.

Bloom, N., Liang, J., Roberts, J., & Ying, Z. J. (2015). Does working from home work? Evidence from a Chinese experiment. *The Quarterly Journal of Economics, 130*(1), 165–218.

Brynjolfsson, E., Horton, J. J., Ozimek, A., Rock, D., Sharma, G., & TuYe, H. Y. (2020). COVID-19 and remote work: An early look at US data. *NBER Working Paper Series, No. 27344.*

Cummins, R. A., & Wooden, M. (2014). Personal resilience in times of crisis: The implications of SWB homeostasis and set-points. *Journal of Happiness Studies, 15*, 223–235.

Eurofound. (2020). Living, working, and COVID-19. *European Foundation for the Improvement of Living and Working Conditions.*

Felstead, A., & Reuschke, D. (2020). Homeworking in the UK: Before and during the 2020 lockdown. *WISERD Report, Cardiff: Wales Institute of Social and Economic Research.*

Gajendran, R. S., & Harrison, D. A. (2007). The good, the bad, and the unknown about telecommuting: Meta-analysis of psychological mediators and individual consequences. *Journal of Applied Psychology, 92*(6), 1524–1541.

Goodman-Bacon, A. (2021). Difference-in-differences with variation in treatment timing. *Journal of Econometrics, 225*(2), 254–277.

Hudde, A., Hank, K., & Jacob, M. (2023). Parenthood and dynamics of life satisfaction in times of COVID-19. *The British Journal of Sociology, 74*(3), 419–432.

Huebener, M., Waights, S., Spiess, C. K., Siegel, N. A., & Wagner, G. G. (2021). Parental well-being in times of Covid-19 in Germany. *Review of Economics of the Household, 19*(1), 91–122.

Imai, K., & Kim, I. S. (2020). On the use of two-way fixed effects regression models for causal inference with panel data. *Political Analysis, 29*(4), 405–415.

Kelly, E. L., Moen, P., Oakes, J. M., Fan, W., Okechukwu, C., Davis, K. D., & Casper, L. M. (2014). Changing work and work-family conflict: Evidence from the work, family, and health network. *American Sociological Review, 79*(3), 485–516.

Knight, C., Patterson, M., & Dawson, J. (2022). The impact of COVID-19 on organizational trust and social capital. *Group & Organization Management, 47*(1), 121–151.

Kossek, E. E., Lautsch, B. A., & Eaton, S. C. (2006). Telecommuting, control, and boundary management: Correlates of policy use and practice, job control, and work–family effectiveness. *Journal of Vocational Behavior, 68*(2), 347–367.

Lott, Y. (2020). Does flexibility help employees switch off from work? Flexible working-time arrangements and cognitive work-to-home spillover for women and men in Germany. *Social Indicators Research, 151*(2), 471–494.

Mata, J., Wenz, A., Rettig, T., Reifenscheid, M., Möhring, K., Krieger, U., & Naumann, E. (2021). Health behaviors and mental health during the COVID-19 pandemic: A longitudinal population-based survey in Germany. *Social Science & Medicine, 287*, 114333.

Myrskylä, M., & Margolis, R. (2014). Happiness: Before and after the birth of children. *Demography, 51*(5), 1841–1866.

Norgate, S. H., Cooper-Ryan, A. M., Lavin, S., Stonier, C., & Cooper, C. L. (2020). The impact of public transport on the health of work commuters: A systematic review. *Health Psychology Review, 14*(2), 325–344.

Recchi, E., Ferragina, E., Helmeid, E., Pauly, S., Safi, M., Sauger, N., & Schradie, J. (2020). The "eye of the hurricane" paradox: An unexpected and unequal rise of well-being during the Covid-19 lockdown in France. *Research in Social Stratification and Mobility, 68*, 100508.

Reuschke, D. (2019). The subjective well-being of homeworkers across life domains. *Environment and Planning A: Economy and Space, 51*(6), 1326–1349.

Simona-Moussa, J., & Ravazzini, L. (2019). From one recession to another: Longitudinal impacts on the quality of life of vulnerable groups. *Social Indicators Research, 142*, 1129–1152.

Song, Y., & Gao, J. (2020). Does telework stress employees out? A study on working at home and subjective well-being for wage/salary workers. *Journal of Happiness Studies, 21*(7), 2649–2668.

Van der Lippe, T., & Lippényi, Z. (2020). Beyond formal access: Organizational context, working from home, and work–family conflict of men and women in European workplaces. *Social Indicators Research, 151*(2), 383–402.

Wheatley, D. (2017). Employee satisfaction and use of flexible working arrangements. *Work, Employment and Society, 31*(4), 567–585.

Yerkes, M. A., André, S. C., Besamusca, J. W., Kruyen, P. M., Remery, C. L., van der Zwan, R., & Geurts, S. A. (2020). 'Intelligent' lockdown, intelligent effects? Results from a survey on gender (in)equality in paid work, the division of childcare and household work, and quality of life among parents in the Netherlands during the Covid 19 lockdown. *PLOS ONE, 15*(11), e0242249.

Yucel, D., & Chung, H. (2023). Working from home, work–family conflict, and the role of gender and gender role attitudes. *Community, Work & Family, 26*(2), 190–221.

CHAPTER 8

Political Support and Anti-Liberal Orientations in the Pandemic Period

Riccardo Ladini, Nicola Maggini, Ferruccio Biolcati Rinaldi, Emanuele Ferragina, Simona Guglielmi, Andrea Turković, and Andrew Zola

Introduction

The COVID-19 pandemic triggered an unprecedented and challenging crisis, profoundly impacting societies, economies, and political systems. From early 2020, the pandemic exposed vulnerabilities within democratic societies and tested the resilience of societal values and attitudes towards political institutions. Throughout this period, politicians, scholars, and civil society leaders appealed to safeguard democracy. Their primary concern was the impact of the pandemic on democratic governance, rights, freedoms, and

Supplementary Information The online version contains supplementary material available at https://doi.org/10.1007/978-3-031-99349-7_8.

R. Ladini • A. Turković
University of Milan, Milan, Italy
e-mail: riccardo.ladini@unimi.it; andrea.turkovic@unimi.it

E. Naumann et al. (eds.), *Social Life during COVID-19 in France, Germany, Italy and the UK*,
https://doi.org/10.1007/978-3-031-99349-7_8

the intensification of anti-system politics. One example is 'A Call to Defend Democracy', an open letter initiated by the Stockholm-based International Institute for Democracy and Electoral Assistance (International IDEA) and the National Endowment for Democracy, based in Washington D.C., in June 2020, supported by 73 pro-democracy institutions, political figures, and civic leaders worldwide. The message was unequivocal:

> The COVID-19 pandemic threatens more than the lives and livelihoods of people throughout the world. It is also a political crisis that threatens the future of liberal democracy. [...] Democracies that perform poorly further weaken society and create openings for authoritarians.

There is a substantial body of research that has examined the changes in public attitudes towards decision-makers, institutions, and political systems throughout different phases of the pandemic. In this chapter, we rely on the conceptualisation proposed by Reeskens et al. (2021) to rank values, attitudes, and preferences along the stability-volatility continuum. Such a framework departs from then field-leading insights on the stability and volatility of public opinion (Converse, 1964; Inglehart, 1977; Uslaner, 2002). These argue that values are socialised at a young age and become stable within individuals over time. In contrast, attitudes are expected to be more volatile as they are reflective of current conditions. Values are enduring beliefs about desirable behaviours and outcomes (Schwartz & Bilsky, 1987) and are central to one's general worldview, ensuring that they are resistant to change (Converse, 1964). Attitudes, however, are

F. Biolcati Rinaldi • S. Guglielmi
Department of Social and Political Sciences, University of Milan, Milano, Italy
e-mail: ferruccio.biolcati@unimi.it; simona.guglielmi@unimi.it

N. Maggini (✉)
University of Bologna, Bologna, Italy
e-mail: nicola.maggini2@unibo.it

E. Ferragina
Sciences Po, Paris, France
e-mail: emanuele.ferragina@sciencespo.fr

A. Zola
Centre for Research on Social Inequalities (CRIS), CNRS, Sciences Po, Paris, France
e-mail: andrew.zola@sciencespo.fr

defined as dispositions to respond to objects, people, or events (Ajzen, 2005). Preferences derived from attitudes are influenced by current conditions and assessments rather than ingrained norms (Converse, 1964; Uslaner, 2002). Unlike core values, attitudes and preferences are easily altered through information, policy changes, or external circumstances. Notably, government approval is volatile as it depends on government performance (Mishler & Rose, 2001) and populations might 'rally' around incumbent governments when faced with an existential threat (Mueller, 1973). Developing the ideas of Easton (1965, 1975), several scholars have identified the multidimensional nature of political support (Booth & Seligson, 2009; Norris, 2017; Katz & Levin, 2018). This involves both general trust in representative institutions and the satisfaction or approval of the performances of governments, with the latter being expected to be more volatile than the former. The importance of analysing the dynamics of political support during the pandemic is also emphasised by the number of studies that have investigated the consequences of political support regarding risk perception, compliance, vaccination, and other COVID-related outcomes (for a review on political trust, see Devine et al., 2021, 2024). During crises, political trust functions as a heuristic, serving to simplify complexity and reduce uncertainty (Siegrist & Zingg, 2014; Hooghe & Zmerli, 2011; van der Meer, 2017; Citrin & Stoker, 2018).

As stated, values tend to persist over time when compared with attitudes. Nonetheless, the stability of values may be impacted by exceptional circumstances, such as the COVID-19 pandemic. Economic declines or physical insecurities can lead to temporary changes of values, even in typically stable values, such as (post-)materialism (Inglehart, 1985). During the pandemic, citizens of several Western countries witnessed restrictions on their freedoms and rights not experienced since World War II, resulting, too, in a concentration of power in executive systems (Goetz & Martinsen, 2021). This erosion of liberal democratic norms and structures may have affected citizens' opinions towards liberal democracy. Furthermore, the high uncertainty of the pandemic period and the adoption of policies emphasising the collective interest over the individual ones may have boosted collectivistic orientations (Biolcati, 2021).

Through deploying the comparative perspective that characterises this book, the chapter aims to answer the following research questions: How did the pandemic impact the dynamics of political support and anti-liberal/collectivistic orientations? How did political contexts of individual countries impact this relationship? Is there a common pattern among Western European countries?

The chapter adopts the following structure. Section "Mechanisms of Attitude and Value Change During the COVID-19 Pandemic" introduces the theories used to explain the dynamics of political support and collectivistic orientations during the pandemic. Section "Data and Variables" outlines the survey measures that have been analysed through highlighting possible limitations as a result of the harmonisation process. Section "Satisfaction with Governments Across Pandemic Phases" analyses the trends in political support across different pandemic phases in each of the four countries. Section "The Role of Party Preferences in Political Support During the COVID-19 Pandemic: The Italian Case" focuses on Italy as a case study, exploring the relationship between party preference and political support, highlighting the interplay between the unfolding pandemic and evolving political context. Section "Anti-Liberal and Collectivist Orientations at the Onset of the COVID-19 Pandemic" examines the dynamics of anti-liberal and collectivist orientations at the onset of the COVID-19 pandemic in France, Germany, and Italy. Section "Conclusions" provides a conclusion to our study.

Mechanisms of Attitude and Value Change During the COVID-19 Pandemic

Through the lens of Easton's (1975) conceptualisation of political support, citizens may demonstrate differing degrees of diffuse support for the core values and procedures that define the political regime. They may also exhibit varying levels of specific support for public officials and institutions, such as trust in institutions and government approval. The former is rooted in citizens' loyalty to political systems and the legitimacy they find within it, whereas the latter relates to satisfaction or approval of specific policies, political authorities, government actions, or perceived overall performance.

Specific political support prospered during the pandemic, particularly during the first phase of the outbreak (on institutional trust, see Bol et al., 2020; Sibley et al., 2020; Bækgaard et al., 2020; Yam et al., 2020; Jennings et al., 2021; Wang & Cheng, 2021; Kudrnáč & Klusáček, 2022). This boost in political support has been explained as a 'rally round the flag' effect, a concept developed in the 1970s (Mueller, 1973) to describe the growing support for national leaders in times of international crises as a response to the understanding that the nation as whole was under threat. However, this mechanism only partly accounts for such situations. Several researchers, for example, stressed that the effects of crises on political support are mainly temporary. A sort of 'bounce-back' effect occurs, after which opinions largely tend to return to how they were before the crisis (de Wilde, 2021; Kritzinger et al., 2021). The findings presented in this chapter support this perspective through drawing on repeated survey observations that reinforce this pattern, further illustrating the tendency for public opinion to revert to their pre-crisis states.

Regarding the COVID-19 crisis, the 'rally round the flag' effect did not manifest consistently across contexts. For example, despite the COVID-19 outbreak representing a 'rare moment of cross-partisan consensus' (Merkley et al., 2020), at least initially, studies revealed that party preferences were key to forming trust in governments and their stabilities, with supporters of governing parties generally displaying higher trust, while opposition voters and populist-leaning individuals exhibited more variation (Satherley et al., 2022; Dietz et al., 2023; Roccato et al., 2024). For example, Dietz et al. (2023) found increased trust in governments across all partisan groups in Germany, but the scope of this effect was dependent on interactions between individuals' level of anxiety regarding COVID-19 and party affiliation. In Italy, Roccato et al. (2024) observed that populist-leaning individuals exhibited more volatile levels of trust than non-populists during the pandemic, highlighting the influence of political ideology on trust in government during crises. Similarly, beyond Europe, Satherley et al. (2022) found that government satisfaction and trust in institutions increased and remained at this level for five months in New Zealand. Centre-right opposition voters, however, returned to baseline levels more quickly than centre-left government supporters.

The evolution of political support during the pandemic was influenced by context. This was particularly the case for the significant 'rally round the flag' effect, which was gradually moderated by political partisanship. Comparative studies, for example, show that the magnitude of political support varied across countries and was influenced by external factors, such as the severity of the pandemic and the strictness of lockdown measures. These, too, were governed by factors such as pre-existing levels of political trust and political polarisation (Bol et al., 2020; Jørgensen et al., 2021; Cardenal et al., 2021). For instance, Bol et al. (2020) suggest that countries with higher infection and mortality rates (such as in Italy and Spain) displayed an initially stronger public support for government actions. This effect was driven by the perceived urgency of intervention but diminished over time. Conversely, Jørgensen et al. (2021) showed that countries with lower case numbers and deaths (e.g., Denmark and

Germany) maintained stable political support, as governments were seen to manage the crisis effectively without resorting to strict or extreme measures. Notably, Cardenal et al. (2021) highlighted that in highly politically polarised societies, the perceived severity of the pandemic was often filtered through partisan lenses, shaping the trust that citizens placed in their governments' responses. The severity of the pandemic moulded perceptions not only across countries but also within them. In Italy, one of the most severely impacted countries, a positive evaluation of the regional health system increased the sense of safety from the virus, but only in the harshly affected North-West regions (Guglielmi et al., 2020).

Moving from specific support for the government to a broader confidence in the political system, the literature emphasises some particularities of the COVID-19 pandemic. As stressed in the introduction, governments adopted extensive powers, including the suspension of civil liberties and democratic norms. In such a context, citizens increased their support for authoritarian leaders who promised swift and decisive action, with a preference for strong leadership over democratic deliberation (Filsinger & Freitag, 2022). Citizens accepted the introduction of surveillance measures, such as contact tracing apps or tracking of their movements, despite potential infringements on privacy rights (Ioannou & Tussyadiah, 2021; Kokkoris & Kamleitner, 2020).

Overall, some scholars have pointed out that the short-term 'rally round the flag' effect might conceal the erosion of support for democratic institutions in favour of authoritarian decisions during the pandemic (Roccato et al., 2020; Pedrazzani et al., 2021). The COVID-19 pandemic could have served as fertile ground for the resurgence of authoritarian and intolerant attitudes within European liberal democracies. It is notable that such a shift occurred when Europeans have increasingly supported both the demand for state regulation and equality over the last few decades (Gonthier, 2017). We provide empirical evidence to such claims in the remainder of this chapter.

Moreover, as combatting COVID-19 required a collective effort—from restrictions on freedom of movement, to the call for mass vaccination—it is relevant to understand whether the crisis caused a shift in collectivistic orientations in societies characterised by rising individualism (Beck & Beck-Gernsheim, 2002), and whether this trend reflects respective political support. Collectivistic societies, such as those in East Asia, often prioritise group interests and obedience to authority, founded in Confucian traditions (Shi, 2015; Zhai, 2018, 2019), which foster political trust and compliance with government measures (Yang & Tsai, 2020). While values are generally more stable than attitudes (Converse, 1964; Uslaner, 2002) and individualistic values are more prevalent in Western societies (Welzel, 2013, reporting a lower prevalence of emancipative values in Italy, compared to France, Germany, and Great Britain), periods of existential insecurity can lead to a rise in collectivistic tendencies (Inglehart & Welzel, 2005). This shift may also have been observed during the COVID-19 crisis.

Data and Variables

In this section, we discuss the data, variables, and methods used in the analyses presented in sections "Satisfaction with Governments Across Pandemic Phases", "The Role of Party Preferences in Political Support During the COVID-19 Pandemic: The Italian Case", and "Anti-Liberal and Collectivist Orientations at the Onset of the COVID-19 Pandemic". We outline the variables specific to each section, the time of their administration, and how they were harmonised to enable comparative analysis. We offer detailed discussions of each section below.

We draw on data from *ELIPSS* (France), *MCS* (Germany), and *ResPOnsE* (Italy), in addition to the *British Social Attitudes* (*BSA*) survey to examine political attitudes in the UK. The *BSA* is an annual cross-sectional survey of a probability sample of the British population which has been administered since 1983. The analyses presented here use the 2019 and 2020 datasets. The 2019 survey was administered using face-to-face, computer-assisted interviews between July and October 2019 and has a sample of 3224 respondents. The 2020 survey was administered using web and telephone interviews between October and December 2020 and has a sample of 3964 respondents.

In sections "Satisfaction with Governments Across Pandemic Phases" and "The Role of Party Preferences in Political Support During the COVID-19 Pandemic: The Italian Case", we explore the political attitudes of respondents. In section "Satisfaction with Governments Across Pandemic Phases", we analyse opinions concerning the performance of national governments by using four outcome variables. Although these measurements are not perfectly harmonised, they present two distinctive groups. The German and British surveys include general questions that do not explicitly refer to COVID-19, which enables the assessment of the rallying effect of the pandemic through comparison with pre-COVID measurements. In contrast, the French and Italian surveys ask respondents to evaluate their respective governments' management of the COVID-19 pandemic. The presentation of our results follows this grouping, providing insight into both the rallying effect at the onset of the pandemic and individuals' evaluations of the governments' performances in managing the pandemic.

In Germany, respondents were asked to state 'how dissatisfied or satisfied [they are] with the federal government's performance', with responses ranging from 0 to 10, corresponding to fully dissatisfied to fully satisfied, respectively. In the UK, the survey asks 'Which of these statements best describes your opinion on the present system of governing Britain?'. The response options are: (1) Needs a great deal of improvement, (2) Could be improved quite a lot, (3) Could be improved in small ways but mainly works well, and (4) Works extremely well and could not be improved. We rescaled the UK measure to 0 to 10 for consistency with the German scale. In France, the question is phrased as: 'Generally speaking, are you satisfied with the way in which the French government is handling the COVID-19 pandemic?' Responses are on a four-point satisfaction scale, also rescaled to a 0 to 10 scale for consistency. Finally, in Italy, respondents were asked to 'rate the measures imposed by the government to stop the spread of the Coronavirus' on a scale from 0 to 10, completely negative to completely positive, respectively.

Table 8.1 displays when each of these questions was administered in each country based on our harmonised periodisation (see Chap. 2). This timing captures pre-pandemic trends in Germany and the UK. All countries except the UK have multiple measures through the pandemic period, providing insight into attitudinal developments through different phases of the COVID-19 crisis.

To examine how trends change over time, we employ descriptive analyses of mean response levels across the pandemic phases as defined by our periodisation, alongside pooled Ordinary Least Squares (OLS) regression models to provide a control for time. Though focusing on dynamics, we also include cross-sectional OLS regression models to analyse socio-political divisions within the rallying effect.

We use a harmonised list of predictor variables to compare socio-political divisions between countries. These include gender (limited to male and female), age category (18–34, 35–54, 55+ years), education level (less than a university degree, a university degree and higher), and political stance (left, centre, right).

Table 8.1 Wording and availability over time of the outcome variables of interest in each country

	Pre-COVID	*Shock*	*Adjustment*	*Reprise*	*Demise*
DE: How dissatisfied or satisfied are you with the federal government's performance?	✓	✓	✓		
FR: Generally speaking, are you satisfied with the way in which the French government is handling the COVID-19 pandemic?		✓	✓	✓	
IT: How would you rate the measures imposed by the government to stop the spread of the Coronavirus?		✓	✓	✓	✓
UK: Which of these statements best describes your opinion on the present system of governing Britain?	✓		✓		

In section "The Role of Party Preferences in Political Support During the COVID-19 Pandemic: The Italian Case", we employ Italian survey data from four waves of the *ResPOnsE* COVID-19 project to analyse the role of party preferences in explaining the different measures of political support during the phases of the COVID-19 pandemic. This analysis estimates the predicted means of the evaluation of the Italian government in handling the COVID-19 crisis, trust in the parliament, and the European Union, all of which are measured on a 0 to 10 scale by party preference and period of data collection. The measure of party preference is constructed from the propensities to vote (PTV) measured on a 0 to 10 scale for the five main Italian parties: Democratic Party (Partito Democratico - PD), Five Star Movement (Movimento 5 Stelle - M5S), Go Italy (Forza Italia - FI), the League (Lega), and Brothers of Italy (Fratelli D'Italia - FDI). Specifically, when a respondent reported at least one PTV equal to or higher than six, and assigned the highest value of the PTVs to a single party, we assigned the party preference accordingly. A residual category included all the respondents whose propensity to vote for each party was lower than six. We do not include the results for those respondents who reported at least two PTVs equal to or higher than six and provided the highest PTV to two parties or more. Predicted means of the measures of political support are estimated by linear regression models, with interaction terms between party preference and the wave of the survey. This approach controls for socio-demographic variables and applies socio-demographic weights.

Finally, in section "Anti-Liberal and Collectivist Orientations at the Onset of the COVID-19 Pandemic", we explore changes to anti-liberal and collectivistic orientations in Germany, France, and Italy. In Germany, we use the following question which was asked every week during the MCS: 'In order to contain the negative impact of the COVID-19 pandemic on society, the federal government should adopt far-reaching measures even without the approval of the Bundestag or the states'. Responses were collected on a 1 to 7 scale in which responses ranged from 'Fully disagree' to 'Fully agree'. In France, we use two questions asked in April 2020 and again in October 2020: 'The spread of the COVID-19 virus teaches us that the State must be able to (1) more easily requisition private property for the collective good, and (2) ensure the collective good without worrying about the balance of public finances'. Both questions took responses on a 1–4 scale from 'Fully disagree' to 'Fully agree'. Finally, Italy asked two questions for 14 weeks in the spring of 2020 that read: 'In a group, we should sacrifice our individual interests for the sake of the group's collective interest' and 'If necessary for the interest of the country, the interest of the individual can be sacrificed'. For both questions, responses ranged from 0 to 10, 'Fully disagree' to 'Fully agree', respectively. These questions capture different aspects of anti-liberal and collectivistic orientations, allowing the illustration of an overarching perspective of value change at the onset of the pandemic. We analyse average response levels to these measures and across the same socio-political groups used in section "Satisfaction with Governments Across Pandemic Phases".

Satisfaction with Governments Across Pandemic Phases

Numerous studies have demonstrated that trust in government substantially increased during the initial outbreak of the COVID-19 pandemic, as citizens across Western Europe 'rallied around the flag' (Bol et al., 2020; Bækgaard et al., 2020; Jennings et al., 2021; Roccato et al., 2021; Sibley et al., 2020; Yam et al., 2020). However, there is not a consensus on the duration of such a rallying effect, and studies suggest that this considerably varied across social groups (Bol et al., 2020; Esaiasson et al., 2021;

Guglielmi et al., 2020; Hegewald & Schraff, 2024; Jørgensen et al., 2021; Kritzinger et al., 2021). We contribute to this debate by investigating temporal trends in satisfaction with the performance of the government in Germany, France, Italy, and the UK.

The descriptive analyses of mean response levels (see Fig. 8.1) demonstrate higher satisfaction with the government and its handling of the crisis at the onset of the pandemic. This reached a peak during the period of Shock in all four countries. However, the data also show that this change may have been temporary, peaking during the initial Shock period in the spring of 2020 (for the UK, we observe a straightforward increase in satisfaction with the government between the pre-COVID-19 and the adjustment phase). In Germany, there was a substantial increase between the pre-COVID-19 and the Shock period, with a slight decrease in the following phase. In Italy and France, where data concerning the pre-COVID-19 phase are not available, we note a significant decrease in governments' approval between the Shock and the Adjustment phase. In Italy, where data is available for the period marking the decline of the COVID-19 pandemic in winter 2021, there is evidence of a renewed boost in the

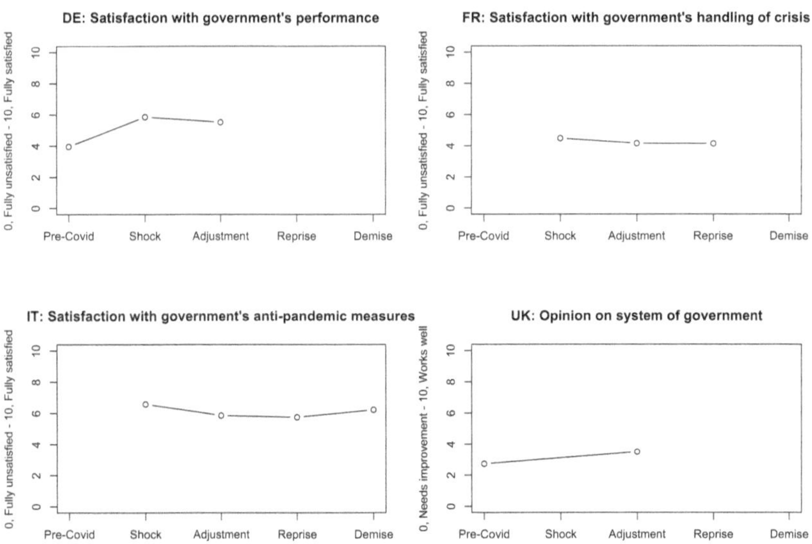

Fig. 8.1 Average satisfaction with the performance of the government throughout the pandemic in Germany, France, Italy, and the UK

government approval. However, it is challenging to speculate about the relationship between this increased satisfaction and the decline of the pandemic. Moreover, Italy was characterised by a change in the government at the beginning of 2021. As such, distinguishing between the effect of the unfolding of the pandemic and the effect of the change in the political context is problematic (see section "The Role of Party Preferences in Political Support During the COVID-19 Pandemic: The Italian Case"). Furthermore, it is difficult to discern whether this increase signifies a rebound attributed to the relaxation of pandemic-related restrictions, as there are no comparable data from the pre-pandemic period in the case of Italy.

To ensure the robustness of the data, we predicted the satisfaction with government based on different waves, controlling for socio-demographics and political stances. Results confirm a rallying effect at the beginning of the pandemic in all four countries. Satisfaction with the governments and their handling of the crisis increased, peaking during the Shock period in the spring of 2020, when uncertainty was at its highest. Satisfaction with government was also impacted by socio-demographic characteristics and self-placement on the left-right political scale (see Tables A8.1 and A8.2 in the Online Appendix). The effect of the latter is dependent on context. In both France and the UK, individuals with both centre and right-leaning affiliations expressed higher satisfaction with the government's crisis management than those with left-leaning political alignment. Meanwhile, in Germany and Italy, this relationship was reversed, and individuals who tended towards the centre or right demonstrated lower satisfaction levels in comparison to their left-leaning counterparts. We understand these differences as reflecting the national governments' political positions. Whereas France and UK had centre-right party majorities in their legislative bodies in 2020 (La République en Marche and the Conservative Party, respectively), the German government had a left-right coalition government in power, consisting of the CDU/CSU and the SPD. The Italian government comprised a coalition government formed between the Five Star Movement and various left-wing parties. This interpretation suggests that the rallying effect's intensity probably varied among individuals with different political views and was influenced by the initial composition of national governments at the pandemic's onset. As such, while satisfaction with governments overall increased during the start of the pandemic, individuals who were already politically aligned with the government may have viewed actions taken to combat the virus disproportionately favourably. Section "The Role of Party Preferences in Political Support During the COVID-19 Pandemic: The Italian Case" examines this relationship in detail, with a focus on the Italian case. Previous studies also suggest that the rallying effect was not uniform across individuals, with satisfaction often being polarised across social groups and political stances in particular (Kritzinger et al., 2021).

To further explore how these divisions developed throughout the onset of the pandemic, we also draw on cross-sectional regression results in Germany and the UK (Tables A8.3 and A8.4 in the Online Appendix). In both countries, women and older respondents showed increased satisfaction with the government from the period before the pandemic to after its onset. We suggest that this reflects citizens' considerations of the ways in which respective governments managed COVID-19. As older individuals were at greater epidemiological risk, and women probably had greater care obligations for vulnerable groups such as children and the elderly, lockdown measures and other non-pharmaceutical interventions may have increased their satisfaction.

The BSA data further enable additional contextualisation of trends throughout the onset of the pandemic in a broader perspective, as the outcome variable of interest has been administered regularly since the mid-1990s. Cross-sectional regression results by year (see Table A8.5 in the Online Appendix) reveal that the patterns observed between 2019 and 2020 are statistically divergent: they are the only years in which women were more satisfied with the government than men, and 2020 marks the year with the highest divisions in political satisfaction.

In summary, these results offer evidence for a rallying effect at the onset of the pandemic across all four countries. Satisfaction levels towards respective governments and their management of the COVID-19 peaked in the initial phase of Shock when uncertainty was at its highest. This surge in satisfaction, however, was neither long-lasting nor uniform across societies. Instead, the shift was varied between contexts, with satisfaction levels often becoming more polarised across social groups, further contributing to the discourse of context-dependency of such phenomena. This was particularly evident in differing political stances. Further implications and manifestations of the rallying effect are discussed in the following sections.

The Role of Party Preferences in Political Support During the COVID-19 Pandemic: The Italian Case

As argued in section "Mechanisms of Attitude and Value Change During the COVID-19 Pandemic", it is important to understand whether the trends of political support correlate to citizens' party preferences. As such, we present a single-country analysis of Italy, where a previous study (Ladini & Maggini, 2023) highlighted the role of party preferences in explaining the acceptance of restrictions of liberties during the pandemic. Italy is a paradigmatic case of these issues, as the nation was the first Western country to be hit by COVID-19 and also to adopt harsh non-medical containment measures against the virus. The Italian case is particular, however, given the change in the Italian government in February 2021. The (almost) national unity cabinet, led by Mario Draghi, replaced the previous government led by Giuseppe Conte, which was supported by the populist Five Star Movement and the centre-left Democratic Party (plus minor centrist and left-wing allies). As two centre-right parties (Go Italy and the League) happened to come into power, it is possible to assess whether, in 2021, the political support among citizens backing those parties converged towards the attitudes of citizens supporting other government parties. Furthermore, Italy is a remarkable case as populist parties were both in government (Five Star Movement, the League in the cabinet led by Mario Draghi) and in opposition (Brothers of Italy, the League during the first cabinet led by Giuseppe Conte).

An increase at the aggregate level of specific support was expected throughout the first phase of the pandemic, characterised by high emergency and marginal politicisation of the COVID-19 issue (Bertero & Seddone, 2021). This would occur to such an extent as to cross-cut party preferences, resulting in several supporters of parties of different types (left-wing or right-wing, government or opposition) trusting institutions and approving governmental action. Accordingly, was the association between party preferences and political support weaker during this phase? And how did this association develop in the subsequent phases of the pandemic? In this section, we examine whether the association between party preferences and political support shifted throughout the pandemic in Italy.

The analysis focuses on specific political support by considering measures of institutional trust and government approval. Specifically, we measure government support through satisfaction with the national government's management of the crisis, and trust in political institutions through confidence in parliament and the EU. Compared to government approval, we anticipate that trust in parliament will be less influenced by party preferences and less affected by a rally around the flag effect as it had a marginal role in managing the crisis, especially during the first wave of the pandemic. Institutional trust, however, is a multidimensional concept (Rothstein & Stolle, 2008; Ladini, 2021a) and confidence in parliament only captures political trust at a national level. Therefore, it is also worthwhile investigating the supra-national dimension of institutional confidence (Anderson, 1998), considering that EU Member States are embodied in a system of multilevel governance (Hooghe & Marks, 2010). The latter is particularly important for a context characterised by a global pandemic, with EU institutions playing key roles in managing both health and the economy, especially regarding procurement of the vaccine and subsequent Recovery Plan. In this regard, we hypothesise that trust in the EU during the pandemic emergency benefited from a 'rally round the flag' effect. Previous studies, indeed, have demonstrated that trust in the EU increased after the outbreak of COVID-19 emergency (for the Italian case, see Guglielmi, 2021). However, the level of trust in the EU should be associated with a long-lasting, overall orientation towards the EU political conglomerate and is thus less 'sensitive', at least in the short term, to the judgement of how European institutions manage unexpected situations. At the same time, since the 2010 sovereign debt crisis, the EU became politically contested in Italy (Conti & Memoli, 2015), with partisan orientations influencing attitudes towards the EU (Ladini, 2021b).

In Figure 8.2a and b, we show that party preferences significantly contributed to the predication of political support during the COVID-19 pandemic. When considering at the first phase of the pandemic in Italy (Shock period), individuals supporting the main government parties (Democratic Party and Five Star Movement) reported substantially higher satisfaction with the government's management of the crisis and trust in parliament when compared with supporters of the opposition parties (especially, populist right-wing parties, Brothers of Italy and the League). As hypothesised, the position of party preference was more significant in predicting satisfaction with the government than trust in parliament. Indeed, the split between supporters of government and opposition parties was larger in the satisfaction with government. The predicted gap in average satisfaction with the government between citizens who preferred the Democratic Party and those who supported the League or Brothers of Italy was 3.5 and 3.4, respectively (this was even greater between

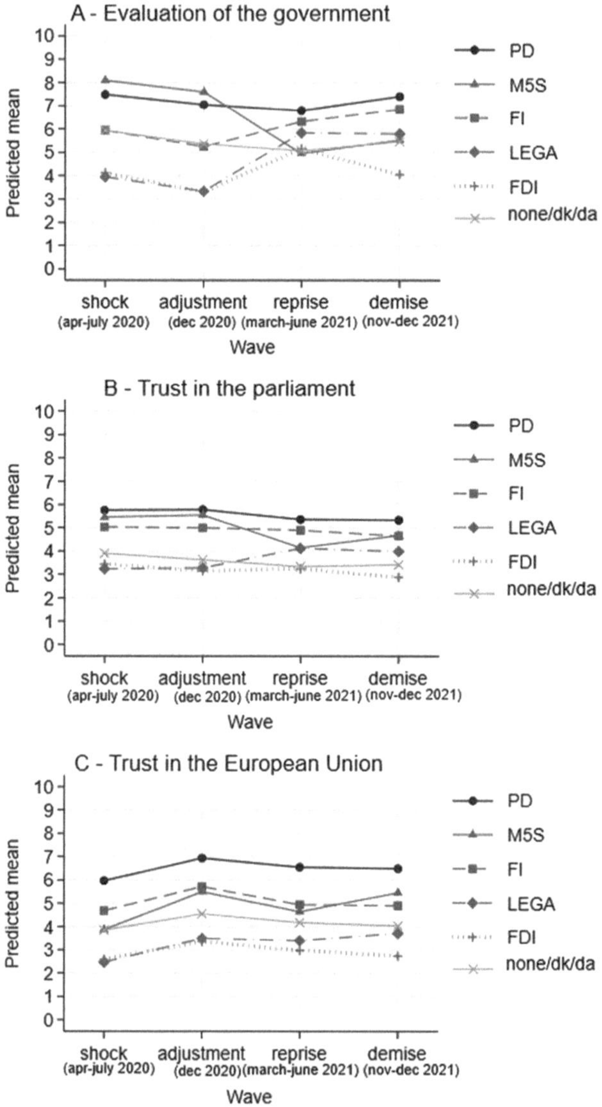

Fig. 8.2 Predicted means of evaluation of the Italian government in handling the COVID-19 pandemic (**a**) trust in the Italian parliament (**b**) and in the European Union (**c**) by party preference. ResPOnsE COVID-19 Italian data (N = 20,997, N = 20,703 for a)

supporters of the Five Star Movement and League or Brothers of Italy). The same gap was equal to 2.5 and 2.3 in the average trust in parliament. Considering the dynamics of political support, the trend in political support between Shock and Adjustment phases of the pandemic was similar across party preferences, with an overall decrease in satisfaction with government, and an overall stability of trust in parliament.

We notice substantially contrasting patterns by party preference after the settlement of the national unity government led by Mario Draghi (Reprise and later Demise). In particular, we observed opposite patterns for supporters of the two populist parties, Five Star Movement and the League. The former reported a significant decrease in trust of the national parliament and satisfaction with the government after the Five Star Movement lost its presidency. By contrast, individuals who supported the League, which came into power, display an increase in both indicators of political support. Furthermore, citizens who supported the other centre-right party, Go Italy, which moved from the opposition to the government, increased their overall satisfaction with the government, while trust in parliament remained constant. We also report an increase in satisfaction with the government among individuals supporting the only party that remained in the opposition, Brothers of Italy. Nonetheless, unlike individuals preferring the other centre-right parties, their satisfaction with the government decreased in the latter part of 2021, the Demise phase. Finally, the dynamics of both measures of political support are more constant among supporters of the Democratic Party, which securely remained in the government coalition for both cabinets.

Figure 8.2c allows further detection of the multidimensional traits of institutional trust. The role of party preference in predicting trust in the EU is different compared with the prediction of trust in the Italian parliament. Throughout the first phase of the pandemic, trust in the EU was substantially higher among supporters of the Democratic Party than supporters of the Five Star Movement. The same does not apply to trust in parliament. Following the suggestions of previous literature, supporters of non-populist parties (Democratic Party and Go Italy) display a higher level of trust in the EU compared to supporters of populist parties (Five Star Movement, and in particular Brothers of Italy and the League). Furthermore, unlike the satisfaction with the government and trust in parliament, trends of average trust in the EU do not significantly vary across party preferences (coherently with previous results on the Italian case, Colloca et al., 2024).

Overall, our results find that COVID-19 did not represent a decontextualised event in which political support was unrelated to party preference. As the first wave of the COVID-19 survey was collected during the Shock phase, there is no data to measure political support before the beginning of the pandemic by party preference. Nonetheless, analysis of the German context demonstrates that the increase in satisfaction with the government at the start of the pandemic was similar across party preferences, irrespective of starting level (Dietz et al., 2023). Although a 'rally round the flag' effect characterised the initial phase of the pandemic, it did not diminish the differences in the level of political support. Contextual factors related to the unfolding of the pandemic influenced the overall dynamics of political support, such as the beginning of the vaccination campaign. Regardless, these did not have a significant impact on the relationship between party preference and political support. Our results instead suggest that political context was of greater significance than the pandemic in determining the relationship between party preference and political support in Italian public opinion during COVID-19.

Anti-Liberal and Collectivist Orientations at the Onset of the COVID-19 Pandemic

The COVID-19 crisis was external, unanticipated, and severe, and as such generated substantial uncertainty for individuals regardless of economic position (Zola et al., 2024), likely leading many to look to authority for reassurance. This allowed governments to instate unprecedented forms of protection such as lockdown and temporary work policies with implicit approval from their electorates. Much previous research on individuals' values and orientations has found stability over the spring of 2020. While preferences across social groups may have become more polarised (Ares et al., 2021), with support for specific government spending domains like labour market protection increasing (Enggist et al., 2022), overall changes in support were found to be temporary (Ebbinghaus et al., 2022; Reeskens et al., 2021).

This presents something of a paradox. We argue that it is crucial to revisit and examine the extent of value stability during one of the most sudden and severe economic and epidemiological crises in generations. Is there evidence for a 'crisis moment' for anti-liberal and collectivist orientations at the start of the COVID-19 pandemic?

To explore this question, we use data collected on a weekly basis starting in the spring of 2020 among citizens of Germany, France, and Italy. This high-frequency approach to surveying (Blom et al., 2020) reveals short-run swings in orientations which are often overlooked by researchers, but which nonetheless may be crucial for interpreting the mechanisms that temporarily shift values in moments of crisis.

We suggest that the COVID-19 pandemic represented a unique crisis owing to the overwhelming uncertainty that it generated. Scholars have distinguished different types of crises based on which members of society are most impacted. While economic recessions often amplify risks for those in disadvantaged positions, others, such as wars or pandemics, can generate uncertainty for most of the population (Rehm, 2016). This distinction is particularly important for understanding individuals' orientations towards anti-liberal government reactions to crises. For example, a crisis that disproportionately affects the poor can provoke a counter-reaction to increased social protections, because high public spending outweighs the benefits for the middle and upper classes. This may help to explain why, for example, in the aftermath of the 2008 global financial crisis (GFC), austerity measures were widely accepted as a necessary response to perceived overspending before and during the crisis (Blyth, 2013; Stanley, 2014).

Our analyses of the mean support level for numerous anti-liberal and collectivist propositions at the onset of the pandemic suggest that the spring of 2020 was indeed a unique time in people's perspectives of their governments' roles in managing the crisis. In Germany, France, and Italy the first weeks of surveying right after the instatement of lockdown measures in each country represented the moment of highest support for anti-liberal and collectivist propositions. There was then a rapid decrease in support over a matter of weeks in all three countries. In Germany and Italy, where we have many repeated measures week over week in the spring of 2020, there is evidence that this decrease may not have been linear. Rather, there was a sharp drop in support in the first several weeks, followed by a flattening out around ten weeks into surveying. Although we do not have pre-pandemic measures of these attitudes to determine whether this was a return to a long-term baseline, the magnitude of change in support for some propositions appears to be impressive. For example, there was approximately a 15% drop on the response scales for whether the government should make unilateral decisions among Germans, and for whether the government should be allowed to take private goods for the public good among French respondents (Fig. 8.3).

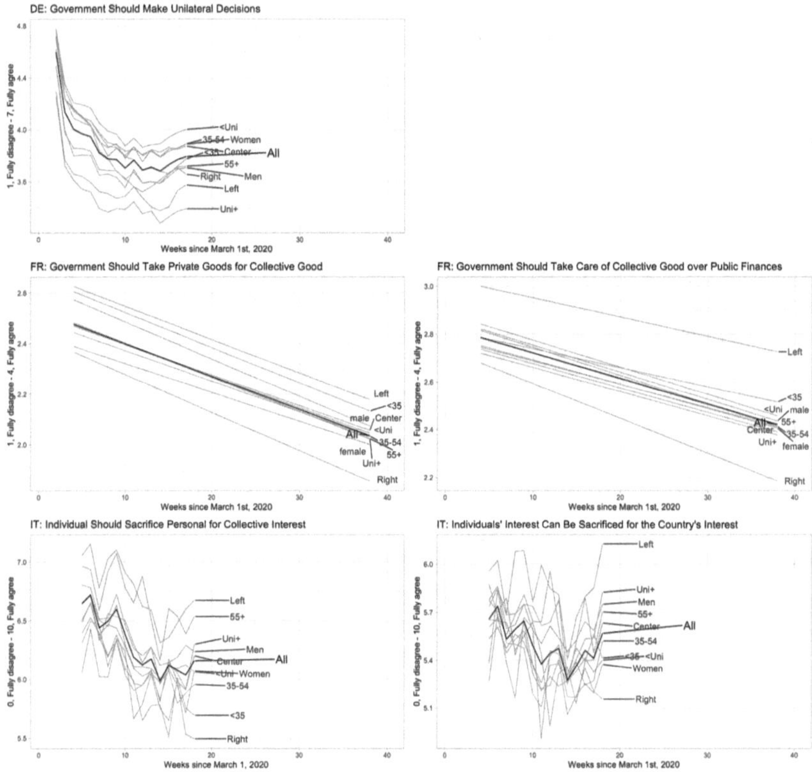

Fig. 8.3 Mean support level for anti-liberal and collectivist propositions in Germany, France, and Italy over the onset of the COVID-19 pandemic

We interpret this pattern as a reflection of the sudden uncertainty that impacted people throughout the socioeconomic spectrum, but which was swiftly managed as governments took a 'whatever it costs' approach to social protections (Macron, 2020). In the face of the steepest economic downturn since World War II, and lockdown measures that made work impossible for millions of people, the chances of catastrophic individual economic outcomes were significantly decreased. From the individual perspective, robust social protections shifted the nature of pandemic from one of widespread uncertainty to one in which risks were mitigated and stratified in a manner more consistent with life before COVID. While people initially appeared to largely support a firm reaction from the state, social protections may have responded effectively to their desire for greater state control.

Focusing on socio-political groups' mean support levels reveals that temporal trends align very closely across groups. This suggests that there was not a single instance of attitudinal unification across swaths of the public, but instead constant absolute differences across groups. We contend that this may provide further insight into the sort of 'rally round the flag' effect generated by the COVID-19 pandemic. While this may not have resulted in a moment of solidarity between groups, it may have instead provoked significant changes within groups.

We highlight the importance of high-frequency surveying in critical moments such as the onset of a crisis. Many scholars have found little evidence of attitudinal change throughout the pandemic's onset, as surveys that were administered even a few months after the pandemic's onset may have detected generalised stability. Instead, our findings reveal an underlying dynamic in which there was momentary, strong support for anti-liberal and authoritative policy reactions to the pandemic. This may be due to the benefits of emergency social protections outweighing the perceived costs for most citizens, thereby calming the uncertainty experience during the onset of the crisis.

As was clear in the years following the 2008 GFC, the political attitude consequences of a crisis can provide the democratic basis for subsequent policy decisions. If this is the case, the post-COVID policy landscape may be distinct from the 2010s: for example, electorates' compliance with austerity may be overturned (Ferragina & Zola, 2022). The first step in determining this will be situating short-run analyses of the pandemic's onset in the long term to provide researchers with a better understanding of how this crisis, through its unique social policy responses, disrupted life yet provided economic stability for many.

Conclusions

This chapter highlights and explores the complex and context-dependent dynamics of political support and societal attitudes during the COVID-19 pandemic. By examining cross-national trends alongside a case study of Italy, this analysis highlights crucial insights into how crises influence public opinion, trust in political institutions, and the relationship between individual and collective priorities. Three main findings dominate:

1. *The rallying effect and its limitations.* At the onset of the pandemic, a notable rallying effect was observed across all four countries. Government satisfaction and approval of crisis management peaked during the Shock phase, when uncertainty was at its highest. However, this surge was neither sustained nor consistent, revealing the significance of context. Polarisation emerged over time, particularly within social and political issues. This underscores the importance of contextual factors in determining the trajectory of political trust and satisfaction, and it invites further exploration into how varying political cultures and governance structures mediate such dynamics.
2. *The influence of party preferences.* The situation in Italy demonstrated that the pandemic did not fundamentally alter the relationship between political support and party preference. While the initial phase exhibited a 'rally round the flag' effect, this did not diminish existing divisions between political parties. Contextual factors, such as the development of the pandemic and milestones like the vaccination campaign, impacted overall political support, but did not disrupt the strong relationship between party preference and public opinion. The evidence suggests that the political context, particularly changes in government and coalition structures, was more significant than the pandemic in shaping public attitudes in Italy. This finding suggests the resilience of partisan dynamics, even during disruptive crises.
3. *Evolving attitudes towards anti-liberal and collectivist propositions.* The initial weeks of the pandemic saw momentary but robust support for anti-liberal and authoritative policy measures. This development coincided with the introduction of strict lockdowns and emergency measures aimed at curbing the crisis. This support quickly diminished as the immediate uncertainty decreased and the benefits of emergency social protections became apparent. The rapid decline in anti-liberal and collectivist orientations suggests a nuanced public response, where initial fears gave way to a recalibration of values as the situation stabilised. This finding emphasises the temporal dimensions of shifts in attitudes and values, and highlights the importance of timing in survey research on crisis responses.

While this chapter provides numerous insights, it also reveals several avenues for future research. Forthcoming work should prioritise longitudinal designs to capture the evolution of political trust and societal attitudes and values over extended periods, beyond the immediate crisis phases. Furthermore, expanding the comparative framework to include non-Western democracies and hybrid regimes could offer a wider understanding of how different political systems and cultures mediate the relationships between crises and public attitudes. Finally, investigating the influence of media narratives, misinformation, and communication strategies on public trust and attitudes during crises would provide a deeper understanding of such dynamics.

In addressing these issues, researchers can develop the findings presented in this chapter to advance a more comprehensive understanding of the interplay between crises, political trust, and societal values.

References

Ajzen, I. (2005). *Attitudes, personality and behavior* (2nd ed.). Open University Press.

Anderson, C. J. (1998). When in doubt, use proxies: Attitudes toward domestic politics and support for European integration. *Comparative Political Studies, 31*(5), 569–601.

Ares, M., Bürgisser, R., & Häusermann, S. (2021). Attitudinal polarization towards the redistributive role of the state in the wake of the COVID-19 crisis. *Journal of Elections, Public Opinion and Parties, 31*(supl), 41–55.

Baekgaard, M., Christensen, J., Madsen, J. K., & Mikkelsen, K. S. (2020). Rallying around the flag in times of COVID-19: Societal lockdown and trust in democratic institutions. *Journal of Behavioral Public Administration, 3*(2). https://doi.org/10.2139/ssrn.4318576

Beck, U., & Beck-Gernsheim, E. (2002). *Individualization: Institutionalised individualism and its social and political consequences*. Sage.

Bertero, A., & Seddone, A. (2021). Italy: Populist in the mirror, (De) politicizing the Covid-19 from government and opposition. In G. Bobba & N. Hubè (Eds.), *Populism and the politicization of the COVID-19 crisis in Europe* (pp. 45–58). Springer International Publishing.

Biolcati, F. (2021). Il ritorno del collettivismo. In N. Maggini & A. Pedrazzani (Eds.), *Come siamo cambiati* (pp. 53–64). Fondazione Giangiacomo Feltrinelli.

Blom, A. G., Cornesse, C., Friedel, S., Krieger, U., Fikel, M., Rettig, T., Wenz, A., Juhl, S., Lehrer, R., Möhring, K., Naumann, E., & Reifenscheid, M. (2020). High frequency and high quality survey data collection: The Mannheim Corona study. *Survey Research Methods, 14*(2), 171–178.

Blyth, M. (2013). *Austerity: The history of a dangerous idea*. Oxford University Press.

Bol, D., Giani, M., Blais, A., & Loewen, P. J. (2020). The effect of COVID-19 lockdowns on political support: Some good news for democracy? *European Journal of Political Research, 60*(2), 497–505.

Booth, J. A., & Seligson, M. A. (2009). *The legitimacy puzzle in Latin America: Political support and democracy in eight nations*. Cambridge University Press.

Cardenal, A. S., Castro, L., Schemer, C., Strömbäck, J., Ste, A., de Vreese, C., & Van Aelst, P. (2021). Divided we trust?: The role of polarization on rally-around-the-flag effects during the covid-19 crisis. In P. Van Aelst & J. G. Blumler (Eds.), *Political communication in the time of coronavirus* (pp. 157–173). Routledge.

Citrin, J., & Stoker, L. (2018). Political trust in a cynical age. *Annual Review of Political Science, 21*(1), 49–70.

Colloca, P., Roccato, M., & Russo, S. (2024). Rally 'round the flag effects are not for all: Trajectories of institutional trust among populist and non-populist voters. *Social Science Research, 119*, 102986.

Conti, N., & Memoli, V. (2015). Show the money first! Recent public attitudes towards the EU in Italy. *Italian Political Science Review/Rivista Italiana di Scienza Politica, 45*(2), 203–222.

Converse, P. E. (1964). The nature of belief systems in mass publics. In D. E. Apter (Ed.), *Ideology and discontent* (pp. 206–261). New York.

De Wilde, P. (2021). Rebound? The short-and long-term effects of crises on public support and trust in European governance. In M. Riddervold, J. Trondal, & A. Newsome (Eds.), *The Palgrave handbook of EU crises* (pp. 667–683). Palgrave Macmillan.

Devine, D., Gaskell, J., Jennings, W., & Stoker, G. (2021). Trust and the coronavirus pandemic: What are the consequences of and for trust? An early review of the literature. *Political Studies Review, 19*(2), 274–285.

Devine, D., Valgarðsson, V., Smith, J., Jennings, W., Scotto di Vettimo, M., Bunting, H., & McKay, L. (2024). Political trust in the first year of the COVID-19 pandemic: A meta-analysis of 67 studies. *Journal of European Public Policy, 31*(3), 657–679.

Dietz, M., Roßteutscher, S., Scherer, P., & Stövsand, L. C. (2023). Rally effect in the Covid-19 pandemic: The role of affectedness, fear, and partisanship. *German Politics, 32*(4), 643–663.

Easton, D. (1965). *A systems analysis of political life*. Wiley.

Easton, D. (1975). A re-assessment of the concept of political support. *British Journal of Political Science, 5*, 435–457.

Ebbinghaus, B., Lehner, L., & Naumann, E. (2022). Welfare state support during the COVID-19 pandemic: Change and continuity in public attitudes towards social policies in Germany. *European Policy Analysis, 8*(3), 297–311.

Enggist, M., Häusermann, S., & Pinggera, M. (2022). The COVID-crisis as an opportunity for welfare recalibration? Panel-data evidence on the effect of the

COVID-crisis on welfare preferences in Spain, Germany, and Sweden. *Journal of European Public Policy, 29*(12), 2007–2021.

Esaiasson, P., Sohlberg, J., Ghersetti, M., & Johansson, B. (2021). How the coronavirus crisis affects citizen trust in institutions and in unknown others: Evidence from 'the Swedish experiment'. *European Journal of Political Research, 60*(3), 748–760.

Ferragina, E., & Zola, A. (2022). The end of austerity as common sense? An experimental analysis of public opinion shifts and class dynamics during the Covid-19 crisis. *New Political Economy, 27*(2), 329–346.

Filsinger, M., & Freitag, M. (2022). Pandemic threat and authoritarian attitudes in Europe: An empirical analysis of the exposure to COVID-19. *European Union Politics, 23*(3), 417–436.

Goetz, K. H., & Martinsen, D. S. (2021). COVID-19: A dual challenge to European liberal democracy. *West European Politics, 44*(5–6), 1003–1024.

Gonthier, F. (2017). More state intervention, more equality. Changing economic attitudes in the European Union. In P. Bréchon & F. Gonthier (Eds.), *European values: Trends and divides over thirty years* (Vol. 17, pp. 137–152). Brill.

Guglielmi, S. (2021). Gli italiani e l'Unione Europea: dal disincanto alla messa alla prova. In N. Maggini & A. Pedrazzani (Eds.), *Come siamo cambiati? Opinioni, orientamenti politici, preferenze di voto alla prova della pandemia* (pp. 77–93). Fondazione Feltrinelli.

Guglielmi, S., Dotti Sani, G. M., Molteni, F., Biolcati, F., Chiesi, A. M., Ladini, R., Maraffi, M., Pedrazzani, A., & Vezzoni, C. (2020). Public acceptability of containment measures during the COVID-19 pandemic in Italy: How institutional confidence and specific political support matter. *International Journal of Sociology and Social Policy, 40*(9/10), 1069–1085. https://doi.org/10.1108/IJSSP-07-2020-0342

Hegewald, S., & Schraff, D. (2024). Who rallies around the flag? Evidence from panel data during the Covid-19 pandemic. *Journal of Elections, Public Opinion and Parties, 34*(1), 158–179.

Hooghe, L., & Marks, G. (2010). Types of multi-level governance. In M. Zürn, S. Wälti, & H. Enderlein (Eds.), *Handbook on multi-level governance* (pp. 17–31). Edward Elgar Publishing.

Hooghe, M., & Zmerli, S. (2011). Introduction: The context of political trust. In S. Zmerli & M. Hooghe (Eds.), *Political trust. Why context matters* (pp. 1–11). ECPR Press.

Inglehart, R. (1977). *The silent revolution: Changing values and political styles among Western publics*. Princeton University Press.

Inglehart, R. (1985). Aggregate stability and individual-level flux inmass belief systems: The level of analysis paradox. *American Political Science Review, 79*(1), 97–116.

Inglehart, R., & Welzel, C. (2005). *Modernization, cultural change, and the persistence of traditional values*. Cambridge University Press.
International IDEA. (2020, June 25). *A call to defend democracy*. Retrieved November 15, 2024, from https://www.idea.int/news-media/multimedia-reports/call-defend-democracy
Ioannou, A., & Tussyadiah, I. (2021). Privacy and surveillance attitudes during health crises: Acceptance of surveillance and privacy protection behaviours. *Technology in Society, 67*, 101774.
Jennings, W., Stoker, G., Valgarðsson, V., Devine, D., & Gaskell, J. (2021). How trust, mistrust and distrust shape the governance of the COVID-19 crisis. *Journal of European Public Policy, 28*(8), 1174–1196.
Jørgensen, F., Bor, A., Lindholt, M. F., & Petersen, M. B. (2021). Public support for government responses against COVID-19: Assessing levels and predictors in eight Western democracies during 2020. *West European Politics, 44*(5–6), 1129–1158.
Katz, G., & Levin, I. (2018). Varieties of political support in emerging democracies: A cross-national analysis. *Social Science Research, 70*, 55–70.
Kokkoris, M. D., & Kamleitner, B. (2020). Would you sacrifice your privacy to protect public health? Prosocial responsibility in a pandemic paves the way for digital surveillance. *Frontiers in Psychology, 11*, 578618.
Kritzinger, S., Foucault, M., Lachat, R., Partheymüller, J., Plescia, C., & Brouard, S. (2021). 'Rally round the flag': The COVID-19 crisis and trust in the national government. *West European Politics, 44*(5–6), 1205–1231. https://doi.org/10.1080/01402382.2021.1925017
Kudrnáč, A., & Klusáček, J. (2022). The temporary increase in trust in government and compliance with anti-pandemic measures at the start of the COVID-19 pandemic. *Sociologicky Casopis/Czech Sociological Review, 58*(2), 119–150.
Ladini, R. (2021a). Dopo la paura, cala la fiducia. E dopo la speranza…? In N. Maggini & A. Pedrazzani (Eds.), *Come siamo cambiati? Opinioni, orientamenti politici, preferenze di voto alla prova della pandemia* (pp. 19–33). Fondazione Feltrinelli.
Ladini, R. (2021b). Tra convergenza e divergenza: orientamento politico e fiducia degli italiani verso le istituzioni. *Quaderni di Sociologia, 87*, 65–88.
Ladini, R., & Maggini, N. (2023). The role of party preferences in explaining acceptance of freedom restrictions in a pandemic context: The Italian case. *Quality & Quantity, 57*(Suppl 1), 99–123.
Macron, E. (2020, mars 16). *Adresse aux Français*. Speech. https://www.elysee.fr/emmanuel-macron/2020/03/16/adresse-aux-francais-covid19
Merkley, E., Bridgman, A., Loewen, P. J., Owen, T., Ruths, D., & Zhilin, O. (2020). A rare moment of cross-partisan consensus: Elite and public

response to the COVID-19 pandemic in Canada. *Canadian Journal of Political Science/Revue canadienne de science politique, 53*(2), 311–318.

Mishler, W., & Rose, R. (2001). What are the origins of political trust? Testing institutional and cultural theories in post-communist societies. *Comparative Political Studies, 34*(1), 30–62.

Mueller, J. E. (1973). *War, presidents and public opinion.* Wiley.

Norris, P. (2017). The conceptual framework of political support. In S. Zmerli & T. W. Van der Meer (Eds.), *Handbook on political trust* (pp. 19–32). Edward Elgar Publishing.

Pedrazzani, A., Maraffi, M., Guglielmi, S., Biolcati, F., Chiesi, A. M., Dotti Sani, G. M., Ladini, R., Maggini, N., Molteni, F., Segatti, P., & Vezzoni, C. (2021). Is democracy effective against coronavirus? An analysis of citizens' opinions in Italy. *Partecipazione e Conflitto*, 176–201.

Reeskens, T., Muis, Q., Sieben, I., Vandecasteele, L., Luijkx, R., & Halman, L. (2021). Stability or change of public opinion and values during the coronavirus crisis? Exploring Dutch longitudinal panel data. *European Societies, 23*(supl), S153–S171.

Rehm, P. (2016). *Risk inequality and welfare states: Social policy preferences, development, and dynamics.* Cambridge University Press.

Roccato, M., Cavazza, N., & Colloca, P. (2024). This is not the end: How the appeal of populism changed due to the COVID-19 pandemic. In G. Sensales (Ed.), *Political psychology perspectives on populism* (pp. 235–262). Springer Nature Switzerland.

Roccato, M., Cavazza, N., Colloca, P., & Russo, S. (2020). A democratic emergency after a health emergency? Exposure to COVID-19, perceived economic threat and support for anti-democratic political systems. *Social Science Quarterly, 101*(6), 2193–2202.

Roccato, M., Colloca, P., Cavazza, N., & Russo, S. (2021). Coping with the COVID-19 pandemic through institutional trust: Rally effects, compensatory control, and emotions. *Social Science Quarterly, 102*(5), 2360–2367.

Rothstein, B., & Stolle, D. (2008). The state and social capital: An institutional theory of generalized trust. *Comparative Politics, 40*(4), 441–459.

Satherley, N., Zubielevitch, E., Greaves, L. M., Barlow, F. K., Osborne, D., & Sibley, C. G. (2022). Political attitude change over time following COVID-19 lockdown: Rallying effects and differences between left and right voters. *Frontiers in Psychology, 13*, 1041957.

Schwartz, S. H., & Bilsky, W. (1987). Toward a universal psychological structure of human values. *Journal of Personality and Social Psychology, 53*, 550–562.

Shi, T. (2015). *The cultural logic of politics in mainland China and Taiwan.* Cambridge University Press.

Sibley, C. G., Greaves, L. M., Satherley, N., Wilson, M. S., Overall, N. C., Lee, C. H. J., Milojev, P., Bulbulia, J., Osborne, D., Milfont, T. L., Houkamau,

C. A., Duck, I. M., Vickers-Jones, R., & Barlow, F. K. (2020). Effects of the COVID-19 pandemic and nationwide lockdown on trust, attitudes toward government, and well-being. *American Psychologist, 75*(5), 618–630. https://doi.org/10.1037/amp0000662

Siegrist, M., & Zingg, A. (2014). The role of public trust during pandemics. *European Psychologist, 19*(1), 23–32.

Stanley, L. (2014). 'We're reaping what we sowed': Everyday crisis narratives and acquiescence to the age of austerity. *New Political Economy, 19*(6), 895–917.

Uslaner, E. M. (2002). *The moral foundations of trust*. Cambridge University Press.

van der Meer, T. W. G. (2017). Political trust and the "crisis of democracy". In W. R. Thomson (Ed.), *Oxford research encyclopedia of politics*. Oxford University Press.

Wang, T. Y., & Cheng, S. F. (2021). COVID-19 and the anatomy of the rally effect in Taiwan. *Asian Survey, 61*(3), 388–410.

Welzel, C. (2013). *Freedom rising: Human empowerment and the quest for emancipation*. Cambridge University Press.

Yam, K. C., Jackson, J. C., Barnes, C. M., Lau, J., Qin, X., & Lee, H. Y. (2020). The rise of COVID-19 cases is associated with support for world leaders. *Proceedings of the National Academy of Sciences, 117*(41), 25429–25433. https://doi.org/10.1073/pnas.2009252117

Yang, W. Y., & Tsai, C. H. (2020). Democratic values, collective security, and privacy: Taiwan people's response to COVID-19. *Asian Journal of Public Opinion Research, 8*(3), 222–245.

Zhai, Y. (2018). Traditional values and political trust in China. *Journal of Asian African Studies, 53*(3), 350–365.

Zhai, Y. (2019). Popular democratic perception matters for political trust in authoritarian regimes. *Politics, 39*(4), 411–429.

Zola, A., Naumann, E., & Marzec, P. (2024). COVID-19 labor market protection and support for the welfare state: Job retention versus job loss in four European countries. *Social Policy & Administration*, Online first. https://doi.org/10.1111/spol.13090

CHAPTER 9

How COVID-19 Employment Protection Influenced Support for Unemployment Benefits and the Unemployed—Job Retention Versus Job Loss in Four European Countries

Andrew Zola, Elias Naumann, and Piotr Marzec

Supplementary Information The online version contains supplementary material available at https://doi.org/10.1007/978-3-031-99349-7_9.

This is a reprint of the article Zola, A., Naumann, E., & Marzec, P. (2025). COVID-19 Labor Market Protection and Support for the Welfare State: Job Retention Versus Job Loss in Four European Countries. Social Policy & Administration, 59: 889–911. Permission to reuse this article granted by Wiley and Sons is gratefully acknowledged. Reprinted with permission.

A. Zola (✉)
Centre for Research on Social Inequalities (CRIS), CNRS, Sciences Po, Paris, France
e-mail: andrew.zola@sciencespo.fr

E. Naumann et al. (eds.), *Social Life during COVID-19 in France, Germany, Italy and the UK*,
https://doi.org/10.1007/978-3-031-99349-7_9

The welfare state reduces risks, and research has shown that individuals' perceptions of risk influence their attitudes towards welfare (Cusack et al., 2006; Rehm, 2009). Nonetheless, few studies have examined how social policies influence these attitudes, partially because it is not feasible to implement an experimental design that allocates different benefits across eligible populations. However, because popular support has the potential to influence future policy directions (Cappelen et al., 2018; Chung et al., 2018), understanding the influence of social policies on individuals' welfare attitudes is crucial. This is especially true at a time when unstable employment (Kalleberg, 2011) and crises (Enggist et al., 2022) have exposed substantial portions of the workforce to heightened risks. Moreover, welfare retrenchment has rendered access to social protection increasingly conditional (Bleses & Seeleib-Kaiser, 2004; Ferragina, 2022; Jessop, 1993; Seeleib-Kaiser, 2008).

We argue that the COVID-19 pandemic provides a natural setting for addressing this research gap. Unlike previous contexts (Wehl, 2019), the pandemic's lockdown measures and economic recession unexpectedly posed a layoff risk for even those in stable employment. Simultaneously, unprecedented employment protection schemes shielded many Europeans from job loss (Ebbinghaus & Lehner, 2022). By late April 2020, up to 20% of the German labour force (IMF, 2020) and 30% of the French labour force (Lambert et al., 2020) had enrolled in job-retention schemes, with similar proportions of workers elsewhere in Europe relying on such policies (Drahokoupil & Müller, 2021). Given the pivotal role that the welfare state played in protecting workers against the labour market crisis, we have the opportunity to compare the consequences of job retention and job loss on welfare attitudes.

This context motivates us to address the following question: how do experiences of job retention and job loss, compared with continuous

---

E. Naumann
GESIS Leibniz Institute for the Social Sciences, Mannheim, Germany
e-mail: Elias.Naumann@gesis.org

P. Marzec
Institute for Social and Economic Research, University of Essex, Colchester, UK
e-mail: p.marzec@essex.ac.uk

employment during the first year of the epidemiological crisis, affect support for unemployment protection and attitudes towards the unemployed?

Our analysis draws on data gathered between January 2020 and January 2021, focusing on preferences among individuals active in the labour force. We adopt a two-step analytical approach. First, we employ two-way fixed-effects models to examine how changes in labour market status and perceived job-loss risks influenced support for the unemployed among German respondents during the onset of the pandemic. Second, we conduct cross-sectional analyses using data from all four countries to validate the longitudinal findings. These countries represent the largest European economies and differ in their welfare state arrangements (Esping-Andersen, 1990; Ferragina & Seeleib-Kaiser, 2011). While the German, French, and Italian welfare states have historically provided robust unemployment protection for labour market insiders (Emmenegger et al., 2012), unemployment benefits in the UK have been comparatively less generous and means-tested. Furthermore, narratives of welfare dependency and economic self-reliance are particularly prominent in the UK (Romano, 2015; Somers & Block, 2005). This enables us to offer comparative insights into the attitudinal impacts of the pandemic and Europe's unprecedented policy responses.

The results indicate a general, temporary rise in support among German workers for the state to ensure a decent standard of living for the unemployed during the early stages of the pandemic. This increase was particularly pronounced among those who experienced job loss, aligning with patterns found over the 2008 financial crisis (Margalit, 2013; Naumann et al., 2016). In contrast, individuals who benefited from job-retention schemes displayed attitudes similar to those who remained continuously employed. Comparative analyses reinforce these observations, revealing a positive correlation between unemployment and increased support for unemployment protection and the unemployed, and no statistically significant evidence of similar changes among those on job-retention schemes. In addition, we find that a heightened risk of job loss is positively linked to greater support for the unemployed in Germany; however, this does not account for the differences in preference changes between workers with different labour market trajectories.

These findings may challenge a core assumption in welfare attitudes research: that changes in preference as a result of job loss are primarily driven by shifts in individuals' immediate material circumstances. Job loss and retention are materially similar, as both involve a lack of work and reduced income. However, job loss carries greater risks, as returning to work is not guaranteed. By comparing attitudes among individuals with these two labour market experiences, our findings suggest that the increased support for unemployment benefits and the unemployed observed among those who lose their jobs may be predominantly shaped by non-material factors associated with the experience of unemployment. These factors may include a heightened risk of future financial hardship (Rehm, 2009), changing beliefs about the assistance the unemployed deserve, or interactions with other unemployed individuals.

This chapter builds on previous longitudinal studies of labour market protection preferences (Margalit, 2013; Naumann et al., 2016). By extending the analysis across multiple countries and focusing on a period when unemployment and risk of job loss were less predictable and not exclusively concentrated among people in precarious labour market positions, our findings achieve broader generalisability (Wehl, 2019). Additionally, we contribute to the growing body of literature addressing the welfare attitude implications of the pandemic (Ares et al., 2021; de Vries et al., 2023; Ebbinghaus et al., 2022; Enggist et al., 2022; Ferragina & Zola, 2022; Gandenberger et al., 2023; Reeskens et al., 2021a).

In the following sections, we examine how the pandemic and corresponding social policy measures in the four countries under study may have shaped attitudes towards unemployment benefits and the unemployed. We then outline our analytical approach and present the findings, concluding with a discussion of the political and policy implications of these results.

Theoretical Framework

Welfare attitudes are widely recognised as being shaped by enduring values and short-term changes in individuals' material circumstances (Jæger, 2006; Owens & Pedulla, 2014). The COVID-19 pandemic offers a valuable opportunity to study how rapid shifts in circumstances might affect support for unemployment protection and attitudes towards the unemployed. The labour market crisis was exogenous, unanticipated, and broad enough to threaten millions of jobs, including those held by workers in stable employment. At the same time, unprecedented employment protection measures helped many to avoid job loss across Europe. While we acknowledge the possibility that the pandemic may lead to long-term shifts in values, our focus is on how employment trajectories during this period may have shaped attitudes towards unemployment protection and the unemployed.

Welfare attitudes are inherently multifaceted (Roosma et al., 2014), encompassing views on various groups such as the unemployed, pensioners, and individuals with disabilities. They also include different dimensions, such as perceptions of policy effectiveness, willingness to pay taxes to welfare programmes, and concerns about the misuse of such programmes (Svallfors, 2011, 2012). Acknowledging this complexity, our analyses focus on attitudes towards unemployment benefits and the unemployed.

The COVID-19 Pandemic Labour Market Crisis and Attitudes

Research into the aggregate attitudinal impacts of the pandemic suggests that popular support may have moved in divergent directions (Ares et al., 2021; Ebbinghaus et al., 2022). The widespread threats to health and economic stability may have prompted individuals to prioritise their self-interest and to judge the benefits of labour market policies to outweigh the costs (Iversen & Soskice, 2001; Meltzer & Richard, 1981). This may have led to an increase in overall support for robust social protection (Bonoli et al., 2022). Accordingly, those who are unemployed (Margalit, 2013; Naumann et al., 2016) or who fear future unemployment (Rehm, 2009; Marx, 2014) are more likely to favour unemployment protection than those in stable employment. Increased unemployment and the risk of mass layoffs brought on by the pandemic and non-pharmaceutical interventions such as lockdown measures may have therefore boosted support for unemployment protection. Furthermore, the pandemic may have fostered a sense of solidarity towards those facing hardships (Gandenberger et al., 2023; Reeskens et al., 2021b). As job loss or the inability to work during lockdown was largely beyond individual control, the perceived deservingness of those relying on social policies during this time may have increased (van Oorschot, 2000, 2006).

Conversely, surges in state expenditure, public deficit, and debt may have raised concerns about the need to repay what was spent, potentially reducing public support for unemployment benefits (Ebbinghaus et al., 2022). Evidence suggests that a similar reaction occurred after the 2008 global financial crisis, as the public largely endorsed austerity measures in response to perceived overspending (Blyth, 2013; Stanley, 2014). However, empirical findings from the early stages of the pandemic indicate that this was not the case during this crisis. The unprecedented and unpredicted shock may have led many Europeans to increase their support for labour market protection policies (Enggist et al., 2022) and to reject austerity measures as inappropriate (Ferragina & Zola, 2022).

Attitudes towards unemployment benefits and the unemployed may have also varied across social groups at the outset of the COVID-19 pandemic, a period marked by heightened material inequalities (Witteveen, 2020). In many economic recessions, risks are predominantly borne by those in disadvantaged positions (Atkinson & Morelli, 2011), meaning that the costs of social protections tend to outweigh the potential benefits for high earners in secure employment. This can exacerbate a reaction against high public spending levels among these social groups (Rehm, 2016). However, the COVID-19 pandemic stands apart from other recent crises due to its abrupt amplification of employment and economic uncertainty across a broader segment of society, including those in previously stable positions. This may have contributed to a generalised increase in perceived risks (Ebbinghaus et al., 2022), a context that is associated with higher support for social insurance measures, such as robust labour market protection (Rehm, 2016). These considerations form the basis for our first hypothesis:

H1

On average, people active in the labour force will demonstrate higher favourability for unemployment protection throughout the first year of the COVID-19 pandemic than before its onset.

Individuals' Labour Market Experiences and Attitudes

Germany, France, and Italy have historically provided generous unemployment protection, particularly for workers with permanent contracts and high wages (Emmenegger et al., 2012). By contrast, the UK has offered unemployment benefits that are less generous and more heavily means-tested. At the onset of the pandemic, all four countries supplemented their unemployment protection policies by expanding or introducing (as in the UK) robust job-retention schemes (Müller et al., 2022; OECD, 2020a; see also Sacchi et al., 2011).[1] These policies enabled firms

[1] Job retention includes temporary work, furlough, and wage subsidy schemes. While these programmes differ in several respects (Drahokoupil & Müller, 2021), the schemes imple-

to retain employees on their payroll by reducing hours—often entirely—and receiving state subsidies to cover wages lost during unworked hours (Müller et al., 2022). These measured were implemented to help European governments reach the key objective of reducing skill dispersion during a period that would have otherwise seen mass layoffs (Ebbinghaus & Lehner, 2022).

While job-retention policies were overall effective in reducing unemployment, the pandemic did cause significant job losses. The pattern was consistent across all four countries, with the key risk factors being the sector, industry, and occupation in which individuals worked. Industries such as food services, tourism and accommodation, leisure, and entertainment were particularly affected by the crisis, as most jobs in these sectors could not be performed remotely and were deemed non-essential. Although these industries had the highest uptake of job-retention measures, they also experienced the highest proportion of job losses, suggesting that the protections implemented were insufficient to fully offset the effects of the pandemic (Adams-Prassl et al., 2020; Fana et al., 2020; OECD, 2020b, 2021a, 2021b; Pope & Shearer, 2021). A key difference between those who successfully utilised job-retention schemes and those who lost their jobs was the type of contract. Job losses were less common among salaried employees on permanent contracts and more likely for employees working on part-time, fixed-term, and temporary contracts. As non-permanent roles are concentrated in these sectors, this further exacerbated the situation (Adams-Prassl et al., 2020; Insee, 2020; OECD, 2021a).

These disparities resulted in the pandemic having a disproportionate impact across various demographic groups, with women, young people, and those with low educational attainment particularly affected (Adams-Prassl et al., 2020; Cribb & Salisbury, 2021; OECD, 2021a, 2021b). The overrepresentation of these groups in the most affected sectors, coupled with their higher prevalence in part-time and temporary roles, contributed to their elevated unemployment rates.

The benefits provided by unemployment protection and the job-retention schemes in Germany, France, and Italy were broadly similar.

mented by the four countries in this study align with the technical definition of short-time work. This is partly because compensation for lost working hours was channelled through employers and not paid directly to workers, as is typical of furlough schemes. The UK programme is widely referred to as furlough, although it is classified as a short-time work scheme (Müller et al., 2022).

Eligibility for both was typically extended to all employees with a work contract, with unemployment protection requiring prior contributions to the social security system and job retention dependent on reduced working hours due to pandemic restrictions. Replacement rates generally reached 60% to 80% of lost wages, with exceptions for very high earners and some Italian workers. The duration of benefit eligibility was extended to a year or more. The UK, however, differed somewhat. While the financial support provided by the Coronavirus Job Retention Scheme was comparable to the other three countries—covering most employees on reduced hours and replacing 80% of gross wages—access to unemployment benefits was subject to means testing and required social security contributions for the previous two to three years. Unemployment benefits amounted to £84.80 per week. Further details on workers' experiences of job retention and unemployment benefits are outlined in Table 9.1.

Unlike the material similarities that unemployment and job retention benefits afforded, we argue that the experiences of job loss and job retention involve substantially different risks. Individuals assess their risks based on the information they possess about their circumstances, including their labour market status, macroeconomic conditions (Ahrens, 2023), and the social protections for which they qualify. In the context of the pandemic, the unemployed may have been likely to perceive a heightened risk of long-term unemployment, influenced in part by weak hiring trends (Cusack et al., 2006), and of economic hardship, informed by the individual's anticipated capacity to maintain a decent standard of living without employment. By contrast, perceived risks among those on job retention may have been lower because there was a guarantee of return to work and the preservation of future income.

This difference in perceived risks between those who lose their jobs and those who experience job retention may influence their attitudes, as support for social protection tends to rise with increased risk exposure (Rehm, 2009). People tend to be risk averse, and therefore favourable to changes in the present that will diminish the possibility of undesirable future outcomes. Researchers have demonstrated that the distribution of risks can help explain differences in support for social protection across social groups. In countries whose welfare states maintain a high degree of universalism like Sweden, people have historically been more supportive of redistribution than in countries with more conditional welfare states like the United States (Larsen, 2008, 2016; see also Korpi, 1980; Svallfors,

Table 9.1 Summary of the experiences of job retention and unemployment benefits from the worker's perspective in Germany, France, Italy, and the UK

Job Retention	*DE*	*FR*	*IT*	*UK*
Eligibility	Effectively all employed people with reduced hours except those in "mini-jobs"; Compensation paid once 10% of the firm's workforce had substantial loss in working hours	Effectively all employed people with reduced hours	Effectively all employed people with reduced hours	March to June, 2020: Effectively all employed people whose working hours had been reduced to zero for three weeks; July 2020 onwards: Effectively all employed people with reduced hours
Payout	60% of wages on lost hours (67% for workers with children); 70% (77% with children) after 4 months on the scheme; 80% (87% with children) after 6 months on the scheme; Caps calculated based on many factors including initial gross wage, tax bracket, number of working hours lost, and region of residence (Müller, 2021)	84% of wages on lost hours (70% after social security contributions); Floor set at the minimum wage; Cap on income over 4.5 times the minimum wage (equivalent to 6927€ gross per month in 2020)	80% gross wage cap; Income up to 2160€/month: 940€Income above 2160€/ month: 1129€ (Faioli and Bologna 2021)	80% gross wage; Cap equal to 2500 GBP

(*continued*)

Table 9.1 (continued)

Job Retention	*DE*	*FR*	*IT*	*UK*
Duration[a]	24 months	12 months	Extended multiple times	Extended multiple times for an effective maximum duration of 19 months
Adjustments to the pandemic	Increase of payout for those on the scheme for more than four months; Lowered firm and employee eligibility criteria	Lowered eligibility criteria: inclusion of temporary and part-time workers, workers at public companies, etc. (Vincent, 2021); Extension of the maximum duration	Creation of a STW scheme for people not eligible for the pre-existing job retention schemes; Lowered firm and employee eligibility criteria: inclusion of employees outside the industrial sector and in firms with fewer than 15 workers (Faioli & Bologna, 2021); Simplified application procedure	Creation of the scheme

(*continued*)

Table 9.1 (continued)

Job Retention	*DE*	*FR*	*IT*	*UK*
Adjustments during the first year of the pandemic	Extension of the maximum duration from 12 to 24 months in September 2020	Co-payment from companies starting in June 2020	Co-payment from companies from August to December 2020	Possibility to retain part-time working hours introduced in July 2020; Co-payment from companies from September to October 2020 (Fulton, 2021)
Unemployment	*DE*	*FR*	*IT*	*UK*
Eligibility	Contribution to unemployment insurance for 12 of the 30 months prior to application; Requirement to actively seek employment	Proof of work for six months in the two years prior to application; Requirement to actively seek employment	Contribution to unemployment insurance for 13 weeks in the four years prior to application (lowered for people in the entertainment sector and atypical employment)	Regular contribution to the national insurance scheme for two to three years prior to application; Means-testing on savings for access to Universal Credit

(*continued*)

Table 9.1 (continued)

Job Retention	*DE*	*FR*	*IT*	*UK*
Payout	60% of average wages (67% for workers with children) from the 12 months leading up to job loss (*Arbeitslosengeld I*); Long-term unemployed were subjected to means-testing and a low, social assistance payout was applied, usually amounting to no more than several hundred euros per month (*Arbeitslosengeld II*)	Determined by average daily wage; 75% wage cap	1470€/month gross cap[b]; Income up to 1352€/month: 75% of the monthly reference income Income above 1352€/month: 1014€ (75% of 1352€) + 25% of the reference income exceeding the ceiling	84.80 GBP/ week[b]
Duration	The initial period was dependent on length of contribution to the insurance scheme	2 years		182 days[b]
Adjustments to the pandemic	Extension of payout by 3 months for those already unemployed at the start of the pandemic			

Source: Authors' elaboration

[a]Initial duration periods were extended several times in 2020 in many countries so that job retention was available continuously from March 2020 to January 2021 in all four countries (Drahokoupil & Müller, 2021)

[b]As of 2024

1997). This may be in part due to a more even distribution of risks across the socioeconomic spectrum (Rehm et al., 2012).

We propose that this perspective can also explain differences in support for unemployment benefits and attitudes towards the unemployed across labour market statuses during the pandemic. For those whose employment remained uninterrupted, any increased job insecurity in a context of generalised uncertainty may contribute to a rise in support at the onset of the pandemic. For those who lost their jobs, both the poor present circumstances including diminished income, as well as the risks of financial insecurity and prolonged unemployment in a recession environment may influence their preferences. Experience with job retention may stand in between. While workers in this position experienced a decrease in income and working hours similar to those who lost their jobs, they maintained a work contract and a guarantee of return to work and stable future income. We use these variations in risks across labour market statuses to frame our second and third hypotheses:

H2
Experiencing unemployment in the first year of the COVID-19 pandemic will be associated with higher support for unemployment protection and the unemployed compared to those who worked continuously.

H3
Experiencing job retention in the first year of the COVID-19 pandemic will be associated with no significant difference in support for unemployment protection and the unemployed compared to those who worked continuously.

Data and Methods

We first examine attitudes towards unemployment protection among people active in the German labour force from January 2020 to January 2021 and who experienced different work status trajectories between employment, job loss, and job retention. We take advantage of the longitudinal nature of the German data to control for all unobserved time-invariant factors that may influence individual attitudes, allowing us to get closer to an experimental design for testing the role that work status changes have on attitude changes. We then validate these findings with cross-sectional analyses of individuals who were employed, unemployed, or on job retention across Germany, France, Italy, and Great Britain in 2020.

Four Data Sources

Our data collection focused on individuals eligible for job retention and unemployment benefits.[2] This includes those who were employed (including individuals on parental or sick leave), unemployed, or on job-retention schemes during the surveying period. It excludes those who were inactive in the labour force or self-employed. The timing of data collection across the four countries is detailed in Chap. 3.[3]

Outcome Variables

Each survey was conducted independently, meaning that welfare preference questions varied across countries and addressed different aspects of support for unemployment benefits and the unemployed. In the *GIP* and *MCS*, the outcome variable of interest asks if 'the state [should] be responsible for ensuring a decent standard of living for the unemployed', highlighting the preferred role of government and an element of perceived deservingness (van Oorschot, 2000). Responses to this question range from '0, Should not be at all responsible' to '10, Should be fully responsible'.

The *CoCo* project included two questions. The first focused on policy preferences, asking whether 'compared to the situation before the pandemic…we need more, the same, or less spending on unemployment

[2] Eligibility for job retention and eligibility for unemployment benefits do not completely overlap. For example, access to job-retention benefits in Germany required that at least 10% of a firm's employees experience reduced working hours, whereas eligibility for unemployment benefits in 2020 required individuals to have contributed to social security for at least 12 months within the 30 months preceding application. While our data do not allow us to filter respondents on every eligibility criterion, we recognise that there may be some cases of individuals in our samples who were not eligible for either of the two forms of labour market protection at the onset of the pandemic. Nevertheless, we expect these to be rare.

[3] *ResPOnsE* employs weights calculated based on age, gender, highest level of education, and area of residence. Among the other surveys, the *MCS* contains response propensity and raking weights that project the characteristics of the *MCS* to the *GIP* sample and to the German population, respectively. They are calculated using data from the employment and occupational sector, combined with information taken from the *Mikrozensus* on age, gender, highest level of education, federal state of residence, marital status, household size. The *ELIPSS* contains post-stratification weights calculated using information taken from the census on age, gender, highest level of education, area of residence (ZEAT), and nationality. The *BSA* contains weights calculated based on age, gender, highest level of education, area of residence, ethnicity, and housing tenure.

insurance', with responses categorised into five options from 'Much less' to 'Much more'. The second question probed attitudes towards welfare scrounging and perceived laziness of the unemployed (Somers & Block, 2005), asking whether 'the unemployed could find a job if they really wanted', with respondents grouped into those who totally disagree and those who totally agree.

ResPOnsE examined the extent to which benefits in cases of unemployment are 'an essential characteristic of democracy', with responses ranging from '1, Not at all essential' to '10, Definitely essential'. Finally, the *BSA*—similarly to *CoCo*—asks whether respondents believe that the unemployed could find a job if they really wanted one. Responses were on a five-point scale from 'Disagree strongly' to 'Agree strongly'.

While these variables provide a multidimensional perspective on attitudes towards unemployment protection and its beneficiaries, they also prevent direct comparisons across the four countries. Consequently, we focus on identifying common preference patterns among individuals with varying employment statuses across countries. This may provide a more robust indication of how reliance on job-retention schemes influenced attitudes, compared to analysing a single country context.

Cross-Sectional and Longitudinal Analyses

Research on welfare attitudes frequently uses cross-sectional data to explore the relationship between individuals' circumstances and their preferences. We begin with this approach by presenting weighted descriptive analyses that investigate cross-nationally the sociodemographic characteristics of individuals who experienced continuous employment, job loss, and job retention, alongside their attitudes towards unemployment and the unemployed. We then estimate regression models to analyse the correlations between work status and attitudes, while accounting for a broad range of sociodemographic factors. These models are specified as:

$$y_i = \beta_{0i} + \beta_i \mathbf{X}_i + \varepsilon_i$$

The preferences y of each individual i are modelled as a function of predictor variables contained in the vector $\mathbf{X}$ with associated coefficients β and respondent residual ε. For each attitude, a separate model is estimated using Ordinary Least Squares (OLS) or logistic regression (logit) for binary outcome variables.

Achieving accurate estimations of the correlations between work status and the outcome variables can be difficult due to omitted variable bias, where the estimate of direct effects includes the sum of the true effects and any unobserved indirect effects. In addition, cross-sectional analyses are inherently limited in their capacity to establish causal claims, as they cannot determine the sequence of an event and subsequent changes in attitudes. To investigate the impact of experiences with job loss and job retention on attitudes towards unemployment benefits and the unemployed, we implement a two-way fixed-effects model on the longitudinal German data. This method focuses solely on changes within individuals and eliminates bias caused by unobserved time-invariant confounders, which often influence both labour market status and preferences. In addition, we introduce a time-fixed effect to account for the social and economic transformations experienced by all respondents across survey waves. This consideration is particularly crucial during the pandemic's early stages, when deep economic recession and shifts in the labour market likely influenced attitudes. The two-way fixed-effects model is specified as:

$$y_{it} = \beta \mathbf{X}_{it} + c_i + f_t + \varepsilon_{it}$$

In this context, **X** represents time-varying predictor variables, c_i denotes individual-specific effects, and f_t refers to time-specific effects. However, two-way fixed-effects models have limitations (Naumann, 2023; Vaisey & Miles, 2017). These include the potential for bias from omitted time-varying variables, the assumption that time trends are parallel between those who experienced job loss or job retention and those who remained continuously employed, and the risk of inferential bias arising from non-random panel attrition.

We expect omitted variables not to challenge the validity of our longitudinal analyses due to the inclusion of time-fixed effects. Weekly response rates in the *MCS* were over 60% (Blom et al., 2020). To examine patterns of attrition within our data, Appendix Table 1 presents the sociodemographic characteristics of respondents based on their frequency of participation in the survey waves where the outcome variable was administered and for whom we have data on labour market trajectories. The majority of respondents participated in all three waves, while women, the young, and those with lower educational attainment were slightly overrepresented among respondents who participated in only one wave. To address potential bias arising from panel attrition, we apply a response propensity weight.

Predictor Variables

Our primary predictor variable of interest is labour market status. In our cross-sectional analyses, this is defined as the individual's status at the time they responded to the outcome variable. Labour market status is categorised into three groups: (1) people who are in work or on temporary parental or sick leave, (2) on job retention, and (3) unemployed. To minimise the risk of omitted variable bias and model overfitting, we prioritise controlling for key factors that may influence attitudes towards unemployment and the unemployed.[4] These include gender (men and women), age (in five-year brackets in Germany and France, and continuous in Italy and Great Britain), age-squared (in Italy and Great Britain), and educational attainment.[5] We also include monthly household income (continuous in €

[4] Our data sources do not allow us to control for sector or type of contract, as this information, when available, was not systematically gathered from the unemployed. Instead, we control for diverse sociodemographic differences and recognise that they may absorb unobserved effects related to the quality of the respondent's work. We also make the decision not to harmonise controls across countries as our objective is to determine whether there are common attitudinal patterns between work statuses, and not to make direct comparisons.

[5] The levels are country-specific, although they range from no/elementary qualifications to a university degree or higher in all four cases. The German classification includes (1) Noch in beruflicher Ausbildung, (2) Schüler/-in und besuche eine berufsorientierte Aufbau-, Fachschule o. ä., (3) Keinen beruflichen Abschluss, (4) Beruflich-betriebliche Berufsausbildung, (5) Beruflich-schulische Ausbildung (Berufsfachschule, Handelsschule, Vorbereitungsdienst für den mittleren Dienst in der öffentlichen Verwaltung), (6) Ausbildung an einer Fachschule der DDR, (7) Ausbildung an einer Fach-, Meister-, Technikerschule, Berufs- oder Fachakademie, (8) Bachelor an (Fach-)Hochschule, (9) Fachhochschulabschluss (z. B. Diplom, Master), (10) Universitätsabschluss (z. B. Diplom, Magister, Staatsexamen, Master), (11) Promotion, (12) Ein anderer beruflicher Abschluss. The French classification includes (1) Aucun diplôme, (2) CEP (certificat d'études primaires), (3) BEPC, brevet élementaire, brevet des collèges, (4) CAP, brevet de compagnon, (5) BEP, (6) Baccalauréat général, brevet supérieur, (7) Baccalauréat technologique ou professionnel, brevet professionnel ou de technicien, BEA, BEC, BEI, BEH, capacité en droit, (8) Diplôme de 1er cycle universitaire, BTS, DUT, diplôme des professions sociales ou de la santé, d'infirmier(ère), (9) Diplôme de 2e ou 3e cycle universitaire (y compris médecine, pharmacie, dentaire), diplôme d'ingénieur, d'une grande école, doctorat, etc. The Italian classification includes (1) Elementare/privo di titolo, (2) Media inferiore, (3) Superiori in corso, (4) Diploma di istituto professionale (3 anni), (5) Diploma di maturità (5 anni), (6) Università in corso/nes-

in Germany and France, four groups in Great Britain including £0–£1410; £1411–£2560; £2561–£4350; £4351+), monthly household income-squared (in Germany and France), and socio-professional class (the PCS-6 in France and the NS-SEC in Great Britain).[6]

Our longitudinal analysis examines changes to individuals' labour market statuses between January 2020 and January 2021. The *MCS* collected data during the first months of the COVID-19 pandemic at high frequency (Blom et al., 2020), so respondents' labour market statuses are available on a weekly basis. In contrast, longitudinal surveys of welfare attitudes typically collect this information only a few times per year, making our analysis comparatively sensitive to brief periods of job loss. This is advantageous for the time frame studied, when rapid changes to labour market statuses were likely more common. However, this also means that we are unable to distinguish between individuals who were long-term unemployed and those who experienced a very short period without a job.

To address the diverse trajectories between employment, job retention, and unemployment, we classify respondents into five groups: (1) worked continuously or were on temporary parental or sick leave, (2) lost their job and returned to work, (3) lost their job and remained out of work, (4) relied on job retention and returned to work, and (5) relied and remained on job retention. To empirically assess whether shifts in perceived risks influence attitudinal shifts, we incorporate an additional analysis that accounts for respondents' self-reported likelihood of job loss in the 12 months following the survey (categorised as 'not at all likely', 'unlikely', 'moderately likely', 'quite likely', 'very likely').[7] This question was included

suna laurea conseguita, (7) Diploma universitario/laurea breve, (8) Laurea triennale di I livello, (9) Laurea specialistica di II livello o laurea 4–5 anni, (10) Master/scuola di specializzazione post laurea, (11) Dottorato di ricerca. The British classification includes (1) No qualifications, (2) Other qualifications, (3) Qualifications below A-levels, (4) A-levels/SCE highers, (5) Other higher education, (6) Degree or equivalent, and above.

[6]The French PCS-6 includes the groups (1) Agriculteurs exploitants, (2) Artisans, commerçants et chefs d'entreprise, (3) Cadres et professions intellectuelles supérieures, (4) Professions intermédiaires, (5) Employés, (6) Ouvriers. The British NS-SEC includes the groups 1. Managerial and professional occupations, (2) Intermediate occupations, (3) Lower supervisory and technical occupations, (4) Semi-routine and routine occupations, as well as Small employers and own account workers, which we exclude because they are self-employed.

[7]We treat this variable as continuous in the model. Using a dichotomised version of the variable between no risk ('not at all likely') and some risk (all other response categories) produces very similar results (analyses not shown).

in the same three waves as the outcome variable of interest, enabling us to treat it as a time-varying predictor variable. However, since it was not administered to unemployed individuals, we are unable to include those experiencing ongoing unemployment in this analysis, which consequently restricts the scope of our conclusions.

Results

Overall, our longitudinal results indicate an increase in support at the onset of the pandemic (*H1*). The cross-sectional and longitudinal analyses reveal that, compared to those who remained continuously employed, respondents who experienced job loss exhibit a higher level of or increase in support for unemployment benefits and attitudes towards the unemployed (*H2*). Although we anticipated a comparable level of support among respondents who relied on job-retention schemes and those who worked continuously (*H3*), our findings do not entirely align with this expectation of a null effect. Reliance on job-retention schemes is associated with changes in support for unemployment benefits, though the impact is less pronounced than that observed following unemployment. These findings are further explored below.

Descriptive Results

Before testing our hypotheses, we aim to examine the proportions of individuals in various labour market statuses and their characteristics across different sociodemographic groups. Table 9.2 displays the weighted proportions of German respondents with different trajectories, based on data collected 19 times from January 2020 to January 2021. Additionally, it presents the weighted proportions of French, Italian, and British respondents with different statuses, gathered through cross-sectional data collection.

Across all four countries, the majority of respondents were employed at the time of surveying, indicating that despite strict non-pharmaceutical interventions like lockdowns and curfews, labour forces were able to adapt and continue working. Nonetheless, a significant portion of respondents experienced job loss or relied on job-retention schemes, with notable variations in magnitude across countries. These differences probably reflect structural differences in national labour markets, as well as variations in the timing of data collection. For instance, unemployment was higher in the

Table 9.2 Weighted proportions table of German respondents with each labour market status trajectory and French, Italian, and British respondents with each labour market status by sociodemographic groups, based on data collected between January 2020 and January 2021

DE (trajectories) Jan 2021	*Continuously employed/on leave*	*Job reten., returned to work*	*Job reten., ongoing*	*Job loss, returned to work*	*Job loss, ongoing*	*FR (Cross-sectional) April–May 2020*	*Employed/ On leave*	*Job retention*	*Unemployed*
Sex						Sex			
Men	69.9%	17.1%	6.7%	3.6%	2.7%	Men	71.6%	22%	6.4%
Women	80.4%	9.7%	4.0%	4.4%	1.5%	Women	67.3%	14.4%	18.3%
Age						Age			
18–34	74.8%	11.7%	5.7%	6.4%	1.4%	18–34	45.5%	23.2%	31.3%
35–44	71.8%	15.3%	8.0%	3.4%	1.4%	35–44	70.3%	21.8%	7.9%
45–54	73.3%	16.0%	5.3%	3.3%	2.2%	45–54	74.7%	17.1%	8.2%
55+	79.1%	11.7%	2.9%	2.6%	3.7%	55+	83.8%	6.7%	9.5%
Education						Education			
Less than uni	69.7%	16.5%	6.9%	4.6%	2.4%	Less than uni	68.7%	19.8%	11.4%
Some uni and more	81.6%	9.9%	3.5%	3.0%	1.9%	Some uni and more	69.8%	15.1%	15.1%

IT (Cross-sectional) May–July 2020	*Employed/On leave*	*Job retention*	*Unemployed*	*GB (Cross-sectional) Oct–Dec 2020*	*Employed/On leave*	*Job retention*	*Unemployed*
Sex				Sex			
Men	80.3%	6.9%	12.8%	Men	88.3%	5.1%	6.6%
Women	67.6%	10.1%	22.3%	Women	87.6%	5.5%	6.8%

Age				Age			
18–34	69.6%	6.4%	24.0%	18–34	87.4%	4.5%	8.1%
35–44	74.1%	10.5%	15.5%	35–44	89.8%	4.6%	5.6%
45–54	75.9%	7.2%	16.9%	45–54	89.2%	6%	4.8%
55+	78.3%	9.1%	12.6%	55+	85.5%	7%	7.6%
Education				Education			
Less than uni	70.9%	9.4%	19.7%	Less than uni	83.2%	7.9%	9%
Some uni and more	84.7%	5.5%	9.8%	Some uni and more	91.8%	3.4%	4.9%

Italian than the British sample, likely due to inflexible labour market policies that contribute to higher unemployment rates in non-crisis times, and to the fact that *ResPOnsE* data were collected in the spring of 2020 and the *BSA* in autumn of 2020 when lockdown restrictions were lower.

Furthermore, experiences of job loss and job retention were not evenly distributed across sociodemographic groups. Higher rates of unemployment were generally observed among women, younger individuals, and those with lower levels of education. Similarly, job retention was more common among the young or middle-aged and the less educated. However, no consistent gender pattern emerges across all four countries; German and French men, and Italian women, experienced higher rates of job retention. These trends suggest that social groups traditionally disadvantaged in the labour market may have been more vulnerable to job loss and job-retention schemes,[8] aligning with findings from previous research (Adams-Prassl et al., 2020; Cribb & Salisbury, 2021; OECD, 2021a, 2021b).

Turning to attitudes, Fig. 9.1 illustrates the weighted mean response to each outcome variable of interest among individuals who were employed or on temporary leave, unemployed, or relying on job-retention schemes. Across all cases, unemployed respondents were more supportive of unemployment policies and the unemployed compared to those who were employed. Respondents on job-retention schemes display similarly or slightly greater support for unemployment protection than those working, although in Great Britain they express more agreement with the notion that the unemployed could find a job if they really wanted to. From a longitudinal perspective, Germany posed the same question twice following the onset of the pandemic. These responses reveal that all groups of respondents were slightly more supportive of the state providing the unemployed with a decent standard of living in July 2020 than in January 2021.

[8] The unequal distribution of job loss and retention across social groups does not compromise the generalisability of our fixed-effects analyses, as these are resilient to time-invariant factors. However, this disparity highlights the importance of including diverse socio-demographic controls when estimating our cross-sectional models. The associated limitations are further explored in the conclusion.

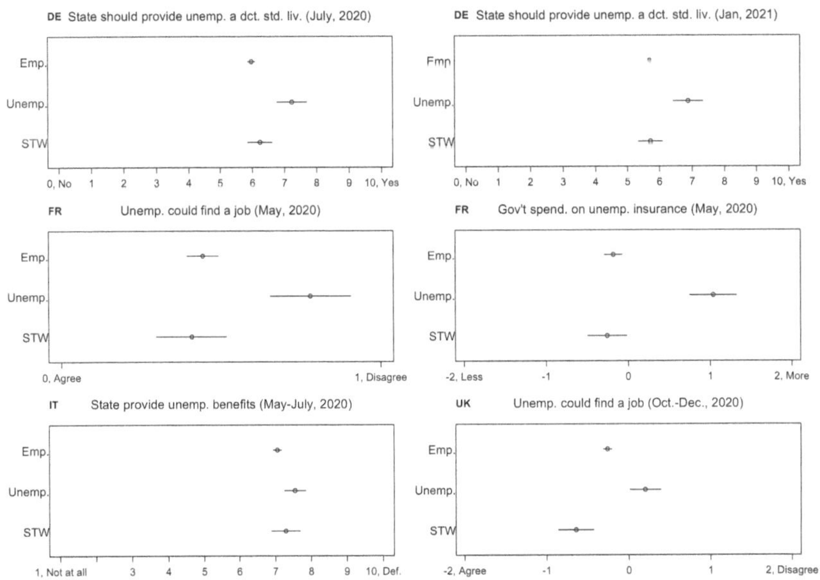

Fig. 9.1 Weighted mean levels of support for unemployment protection and the unemployed and 95% confidence intervals among people working or on leave, unemployed, and job retention (single predictor, weighted OLS regressions)

Longitudinal and Cross-sectional Results

We begin with the two-way fixed-effects analysis of German workers (Table 9.3). The time-fixed effects at the bottom of the table show how support among the continuously employed (the reference group) evolved over time. Respondents who remained continuously employed were estimated to increase their support for providing the unemployed with a decent standard of living by 0.46 points on the 0 (no state responsibility) to 10 (full state responsibility) scale from January to July 2020. This suggests that the pandemic heightened favourability towards state assistance.

Factors such as the economic recession, disruptions to normal routines such as work from home, and the epidemiological risks for in-person workers may have contributed to a greater perception of job insecurity for many people, despite the robust social protections. Between January 2020 and January 2021, the change in support among workers was 0.17 points,

Table 9.3 Two-way fixed-effects regression results among respondents active in the German labour market from January 2020 to January 2021

	State should provide unemp. a dct. std. liv. (0, No – 10, Yes)
Outcome variable:	
Job retention, returned (ref: Continuously working)	0.097
	(0.147)
Job retention, ongoing (ref: Continuously working)	0.395*
	(0.167)
Job loss, returned (ref: Continuously working)	0.407
	(0.281)
Job loss, ongoing (ref: Continuously working)	0.955***
	(0.284)
July 2020 (ref: January 2020)	0.459***
	(0.061)
January 2021 (ref: January 2020)	0.172**
	(0.062)
Observations	4113
R^2	0.036
Adjusted R^2	−0.449
F Statistic	16.946*** ($df = 6; 2736$)

Note: * $p < 0.05$; ** $p < 0.01$; *** $p < 0.001$

indicating that as uncertainties surrounding the economic and employment impacts of the crisis eased, perceived risks likely diminished.

If risk perceptions are the key driver of these temporal differences, support may have been greater at the pandemic's onset, specifically between March and July 2020, than these observations suggest. Nonetheless, the temporal trends provide evidence in favour of hypothesis 1 that workers increased their support for unemployment protection during the pandemic, especially in its early stages. However, it is important to note though that this trend is based on individuals eligible for job-retention schemes and unemployment benefits, including those employed (such as those on parental or sick leave), but excludes those who were inactive in the labour force or self-employed.

Considering how different labour market trajectories influence in changing attitudes, individuals who lost their jobs increased their support for the state to provide the unemployed with a decent standard of living more than those who were continuously employed. Those who lost their jobs and returned to work and those who lost their jobs but remained out of work increased their support by 0.41 and 0.96 points, respectively, more than those who sustained employment. Meanwhile, those who experienced job retention and returned to work and those who were continuous using job-retention schemes increased their support by 0.10 and 0.40 points, respectively, more than those who remained working.

Three conclusions can be drawn from these findings. First, the experience of job loss heightens individuals' support for the unemployed, and it may leave a reduced, but lasting effect even after the individual returns to work (Naumann et al., 2016). Job loss simultaneously results in a decrease to income and an increased risk, such that it is unclear which of these two mechanisms accounts for the attitude change. Unlike job loss, job retention is expected to influence risk perceptions, but has similar effects on an individual's income. As such, our second finding opposes initial expectations: job retention temporarily boosts support for the unemployed. However, the effect is weaker than job loss and almost vanishes among those who returned to regular work. So, while *H3* is rejected, these results follow our overall theoretical argument, that the experience of job retention may be less impactful than the experience of job loss during the pandemic. The third remark confirms this reading, as the impact of job retention on boosting support is less pronounced than for those who lost their jobs. Through comparing the magnitudes of the coefficients associated with these trajectories, it is clear that the experience of job loss and returning to work has a similar effect to the experience of job retention.

To further compare the effects of job loss and job retention, Appendix Table 2 presents the same model with the reference group changed to individuals in ongoing unemployment. The results indicate that respondents who relied on job retention and returned to work demonstrated a significantly smaller increase in support than those who were in ongoing unemployment. Moreover, Appendix Table 3 provides a weighted two-way fixed-effects analysis, confirming several findings from the main analysis. Respondents who lost their jobs are estimated to exhibit a larger increase in support, whereas those relying on job-retention schemes do not show a statistically significant increase in support compared to individuals who worked continuously. However, differences emerge between the unweighted and weighted analyses. For example, in the unweighted model, individuals who lost their jobs and returned to work were estimated to increase their support by 0.41 points compared with those in continuous work, whereas the corresponding estimate in the weighted model is just 0.08 points. In this instance, we place greater confidence in the unweighted analysis, as the weighting approach employed was not designed for subsample analyses like ours, where the sample is confined to individuals active in the labour force at a specific time.

In summary, these analyses demonstrate that experiencing unemployment in the first year of the COVID-19 pandemic is linked with increased support for the unemployed, in comparison to those who remained continuously employed. In addition, the findings indicate a smaller difference in shifting levels of support between those individuals who relied on job-retention schemes and those who worked continuously.

To explore whether these attitudinal patterns can be attributed to shifts in perceived risks when individuals experience a disruption in their labour market status, we assess the impact of perceived risk of job loss on changes in support for the unemployed. Using a two-way fixed-effects model, we include a time-varying control that demonstrates a significantly positive relationship between an increase in perceived risk of job loss and support for the unemployed (Table 9.4). As risk perceptions were not collected from unemployed individuals, this analysis excludes those experiencing ongoing unemployment. Instead, we adopt a stepwise modelling approach to evaluate the impact of controlling for risk. Comparing the estimates in models 1 and 2 in Table 9.4 reveals that adding risk perceptions as a control reduces the effect size of job retention on attitudes by less than 0.1 points on the outcome scale, with the overall results remaining consistent. Contrary to our expectation, we find no clear evidence that job retention is more comparable to continuous employment after accounting for the perceived risk of job loss. However, we lack the data needed to examine the influence of other types of risks, such as financial precarity, on changing attitudes over time. This limitation is addressed in more detail in the discussion and conclusion.

To further investigate this unexpected finding, we examine how the different employment trajectories influence perceptions of unemployment risk (Table 9.4, model 3). The time-fixed effects reveal a general increase in perceived unemployment risk among the continuously employed, rising by 0.13 points on the five-point measurement scale between January and July 2020. Although this increased risk perception diminishes slightly by January 2021, it clearly remains above the pre-pandemic level (0.11 in January 2021). We initially assumed that job-retention schemes would provide job security and mitigate increases in perceived unemployment risk. However, this assumption is not supported by our data. Individuals relying on job-retention schemes experience a larger increase in perceived

Table 9.4 Additional two-way fixed-effects regression results among respondents working or on job retention in the German labour market from January 2020 to January 2021

	State should provide unemp. a dct. std. liv. (0, No – 10, Yes)		*Reported unemp. risk (1, Not at all – 5, Very likely)*
	(1)	*(2)*	*(3)*
Outcome variable:			
Job retention, returned (ref: Continuously working)	0.104 (0.144)	0.068 (0.145)	0.287*** (0.048)
Job retention, ongoing (ref: Continuously working)	0.390* (0.165)	0.332* (0.167)	0.451** (0.054)
Job loss, returned (ref: Continuously working)	0.294 (0.341)	0.364 (0.342)	−0.548*** (0.112)
July 2020 (ref: January 2020)	0.430*** (0.061)	0.413*** (0.061)	0.132*** (0.020)
January 2021 (ref: January 2020)	0.166** (0.062)	0.153* (0.062)	0.108*** (0.020)
Perceived risk of unemployment (ref: None)		0.128* (0.059)	
Observations	3963	3963	3978
R^2	0.029	0.030	0.079
Adjusted R^2	−0.460	−0.458	−0.384
F Statistic	15.504*** (df = 5; 2637)	13.721*** (df = 6; 2636)	45.246*** (df = 5; 2647)

Note: *$p < 0.05$; ** $p < 0.01$; *** $p < 0.001$

unemployment risks compared to those continuously employed. The change is weaker among those who returned to work (0.29) compared with those who experience ongoing job retention (0.45), suggesting that returning to one's previous job helps to slightly reduce risk perceptions. In addition, unemployment risk perceptions among those who lost their job after January 2020 but secured new employment by January 2021 show a significant decrease (−0.55 compared with the continuously employed). While we cannot pinpoint whether this change occurred before, during, or after unemployment, we interpret these results as evidence that finding a new job has a potentially strong impact on risk perceptions. Overall, this exploratory analysis of the trends of unemployment risk perceptions does not support the assumption that those in job-retention schemes have similar unemployment risk perceptions than those continuously employed. This discrepancy may help to explain why the inclusion of perceived risk in our main empirical analysis does not alter the overall results.

Our comparative cross-sectional analyses (Table 9.5) support the patterns identified in the main longitudinal analyses. Across all four countries, people who were unemployed at the time of questioning show higher support for unemployment protection and the unemployed compared to those who were employed. In contrast, support levels are only slightly higher among individuals who were on job-retention schemes than those who were working. None of these differences are statistically significant. These results have their limitations. First, they cannot establish the temporal sequence of attitudinal versus labour market status changes, nor the risk of omitted variable bias. And second, the magnitudes of the coefficients are not comparable across countries due to differences in the model specifications. Nevertheless, the patterns that emerge when comparing the estimates of different labour market statuses within countries provide evidence of a comparable trend to the longitudinal analyses. Consequently, they confirm hypothesis 2: experience with unemployment is associated with higher support for unemployment benefits and the unemployed than being in regular work or on temporary leave. Although hypothesis 3 is not clearly supported by our results, the consistently weaker relationship between job-retention schemes and increased support for the unemployed (compared to being unemployed or having lost a job) supports the argument that risk perceptions and other non-material mechanisms are the key factors of support for unemployment benefits and the unemployed. Furthermore, the cross-sectional analyses suggest that attitudinal patterns observed across different labour market statuses during the first year of the COVID-19 pandemic were less likely similar across European countries that implemented robust job-retention policies to protect against mass layoffs.

Finally, we offer provisional observations regarding support patterns across sociodemographic groups (Appendix Table 4). Among the various attitudes analysed, being unemployed appears to be the strongest predictors of greater support for unemployment benefits and the unemployed. In relation to attitudes on whether the unemployed could find a job if they wanted, findings in France and Great Britain suggest that younger individuals, workers in intermediate and managerial professions, and Britons

Table 9.5 Cross-sectional regression results among respondents active in the German, French, Italian, and British labour markets

Country:	*DE:*		*FR:*		*IT:*	*GE:*
Question:	*State should provide unemp. std. liv. (0, Not at all - 10, Completely)*		*Unemp. could find job (0, Agree - 1, Disagree)*	*Gov't should spend (-2, Much less – 2, Much more) on unemp. insurance*	*State should provide unemp. bens. (1, No - 10, Yes)*	*Unemp. could find job (-2, Agree strongly - 2, Disagree strongly)*
Administered:	*June–July, 2020*	*Jan., 2021*	*May, 2020*	*May, 2020*	*May–July, 2020*	*Oct.-Dec., 2020*
Outcome variable:						
Work Stat: Unemployed (ref: Working/On leave)	1.176*** (0.301)	1.062*** (0.225)	0.800 (0.442)	0.454* (0.180)	0.500** (0.169)	0.581*** (0.123)
Work Stat: Job retention (ref: Working/On leave)	0.281 (0.220)	0.083 (0.169)	0.248 (0.301)	0.173 (0.129)	0.245 (0.210)	−0.191 (0.122)
Full table with all country-specific control variables can be found in Appendix Table 4						
Constant	6.420*** (1.164)	5.209*** (0.595)	−1.742 (1.290)	−0.301 (0.548)	7.393*** (1.248)	−0.131 (0.331)
Observations	1613	2666	427	408	1723	1911
R^2	0.046	0.039		0.124	0.027	0.070
Adjusted R^2	0.031	0.031		0.069	0.019	0.062
Log Likelihood			−265.988			
Akaike Inf. Crit.			581.977			
Residual Std. Error	2.281 (*df* = 1587)	2.168 (*df* = 2642)		0.895 (*df* = 383)	2.167 (*df* = 1707)	1.109 (*df* = 1894)

(*continued*)

Table 9.5 (continued)

Country:	*DE:*		*FR:*		*IT:*	*GB:*
Question:	*State should provide unemp. std. liv. (0, Not at all - 10, Completely)*		*Unemp. could find job (0, Agree - 1, Disagree)*	*Gov't should spend (-2, Much less – 2, Much more) on unemp. insurance*	*State should provide unemp. bens. (1, No - 10, Yes)*	*Unemp. could find job (-2, Agree strongly - 2, Disagree strongly)*
Administered:	*June–July, 2020*	*Jan., 2021*	*May, 2020*	*May, 2020*	*May–July, 2020*	*Oct.-Dec., 2020*
F Statistic	3.031*** ($df = 25; 1587$)	4.682*** ($df = 23; 2642$)		2.249*** ($df = 24; 383$)	3.198*** ($df = 15; 1707$)	8.904*** ($df = 16; 1894$)

NB: Country-specific control variables can be found in the full table in Appendix Table 4

Note: * $p < 0.05$; ** $p < 0.01$; *** $p < 0.001$

with higher education are less likely to perceive the unemployed as capable of finding a job. These patterns do not seem to apply to other attitudes, suggesting that perceptions of the unemployed as lazy or as welfare scroungers (Somers & Block, 2005) may be contentious compared with policy-related questions. Nonetheless, it is important to approach these comparisons with caution, given that the models across countries differ.

Discussion and Conclusion

The COVID-19 pandemic marked an extraordinary period for European labour markets, as non-pharmaceutical interventions led to the temporary shutdown of entire sectors, a severe economic recession, and the implementation of robust employment protection policies. This study sought to explore this context from an individual perspective, focusing on how labour market protection influences attitudes towards unemployment benefits and the unemployed. Analyses of the German labour force revealed a general rise in support for providing the unemployed with a decent standard of living following the onset of the pandemic. The abrupt closure of entire economic sectors heightened job insecurity even for those in stable positions, which may have temporarily increased support levels. Furthermore, the exogenous nature of the economic crisis—where individuals' needs were beyond their own control—may have enhanced perceptions of deservingness for the unemployed during this period. A reaction against overspending or a transformative change in attitudes did not occur. Instead, the increase in support appeared modest and temporary.

When comparing attitudinal differences among individuals with various labour market trajectories, those who experienced job loss exhibit the greatest increase in support, whereas the increase is less pronounced among those who relied on job-retention schemes. Similar trends appear between those who were employed, unemployed, and on job-retention schemes in our cross-sectional analyses in Germany, France, Italy, and Great Britain, offering a comparative perspective on attitudes during the pandemic within Europe's largest economies.

Although our analysis of job loss risk does not fully align with the expectation that risk perceptions are comparable between individuals on job-retention schemes and those who worked uninterrupted, the findings support the view that attitudinal changes following job loss are not predominantly driven by changes in immediate material situation. This is evidenced by the fact that individuals on job-retention schemes often faced conditions resembling job loss, such as a lack of working hours and lower income. Instead, our analyses highlight the importance of other theoretical, non-material mechanisms in shaping preferences, which are closely tied to the experience of unemployment. These may include perceptions of potential future financial hardship, shifts in beliefs about the unemployed and the support they deserve, or even interactions with other unemployed individuals.

We recognise, however, that testing these mechanisms lies beyond the scope of our data. Future research could address this limitation by examining the role that risks, such as reductions in expected future income (Rehm, 2009), in shaping attitudinal differences across individuals with different labour market statuses. A second limitation of our study is that, while the pandemic increased the risk of layoffs even for those in stable employment, the distribution of job loss and job retention was not equal across the socioeconomic spectrum. Selection bias into different labour market statuses complicates the analysis of labour market protection preferences from a self-interest perspective (Wehl, 2019). Although our within-individual research design for German respondents accounts for this by mitigating biases from unobserved time-invariant factors, the results of our cross-sectional analyses should be considered with caution, as they are not entirely free from the risk of omitted variable bias.

From a social policy perspective, our findings highlight how the emergency labour market protection measures taken by European governments over the COVID-19 pandemic impacted attitudes towards unemployment benefits and the unemployed. Specifically, job-retention schemes may have fostered a perception of a 'soft landing', preventing what might otherwise have been an economic disaster. By reducing the risk of adverse outcomes such as financial hardship, these social policies likely contributed to the relative stability of attitudes towards unemployment benefits and the unemployed during the pandemic. For millions of workers across Europe who benefitted from job-retention schemes, the pandemic may have been a unique but financially manageable crisis, rather than a catastrophic moment in their labour market trajectories. This provides a possible explanation for the observed gap in many studies between the resurgence of the welfare state in public discourse and relative stability in welfare attitudes in 2020 (Ares et al., 2021; Ebbinghaus et al., 2022; Reeskens et al., 2021a).

Our study suggests that emergency employment protection policies contributed to substantial attitudinal stability over the first year of the pandemic. However, we encourage future research to investigate the longer-term attitudinal effects of the unprecedented social spending. The 'whatever it costs' approach to funding labour market protection (Macron, 2020) could potentially challenge the acceptance of austerity measures that followed the 2008 global financial crisis (Ferragina & Zola, 2022), creating a post-COVID era marked by a distinct attitudinal shift in Europe compared with the 2010s. A crucial step in this direction would involve situating short-run analyses of the pandemic's onset within a longer-term analysis. This would enable researchers to better understand how this crisis, and the exceptional social policy responses it prompted, disrupted lives while also providing economic stability for many.

References

Adams-Prassl, A., Boneva, T., Golin, M., & Rauh, C. (2020). *Inequality in the impact of the coronavirus shock: Evidence from real time surveys.* IZA Discussion Papers, No. 13183, IZA – Institute of Labor Economics.

Ahrens, L. (2023). Labor market risks and welfare preferences: A bounded rationality approach. *Socio-Economic Review.*

Ares, M., Bürgisser, R., & Häusermann, S. (2021). Attitudinal polarization towards the redistributive role of the state in the wake of the COVID-19 crisis. *Journal of Elections, Public Opinion and Parties, 31*(1), 41–55.

Atkinson, A., & Morelli, S. (2011). *Economic crises and inequality.* SSRN Scholarly Paper ID 2351471. Social Science Research Network.

Bleses, P., & Seeleib-Kaiser, M. (2004). *The dual transformation of the German welfare state.* Palgrave Macmillan.

Blom, A., Cornesse, C., Friedel, S., Krieger, U., Fikel, M., Rettig, T., Wenz, A., Juhl, S., Lehrer, R., Möhring, K., Naumann, E., & Reifenscheid, M. (2020). High frequency and high quality survey data collection: The Mannheim Corona study. *Survey Research Methods, 14*(2).

Blyth, M. (2013). *Austerity: The history of a dangerous idea.* Oxford University Press.

Bonoli, G., Fossati, F., Gandenberger, M., & Knotz, C. (2022). Sometimes needs change minds: Interests and values as determinants of attitudes towards state support for the self-employed during the COVID-19 crisis. *Journal of European Social Policy, 32*(4), 407–421.

Cappelen, A., Cappelen, C., Kuhnle, S., & Tungodden, B. (2018). How to retrench the welfare state: Attitudes in the general population. *Social Policy & Administration, 52*(4), 862–879.

Chung, H., Taylor-Gooby, P., & Leruth, B. (2018). Political legitimacy and welfare state futures: Introduction. *Social Policy & Administration, 52*(4), 835–846.

Cribb, J., & Salisbury, A. (2021). *Employment and the end of the furlough scheme.* IFS Green Budget 2021. Institute for Fiscal Studies.

Cusack, T., Iversen, T., & Rehm, P. (2006). Risks at work: The demand and supply sides of government redistribution. *Oxford Review of Economic Policy, 22*(3), 365–389.

de Vries, R., Geiger, B., Scullion, L., Summers, K., Edmiston, D., Ingold, J., Robertshaw, D., & Young, D. (2023). Welfare attitudes in a crisis: How COVID exceptionalism undermined greater solidarity. *Journal of Social Policy*, 1–20.

Drahokoupil, J., & Müller, T. (2021). *Job retention schemes in Europe: A lifeline during the Covid-19 pandemic*. SSRN Scholarly Paper 3931230.

Ebbinghaus, B., & Lehner, L. (2022). Cui bono – Business or labour? Job retention policies during the COVID-19 pandemic in Europe. *Transfer: European Review of Labour and Research, 28*(1), 47–64.

Ebbinghaus, B., Lehner, L., & Naumann, E. (2022). Welfare state support during the COVID-19 pandemic: Change and continuity in public attitudes towards social policies in Germany. *European Policy Analysis, 8*(3), 297–311.

Emmenegger, P., Hausermann, S., Palier, B., & Seeleib-Kaiser, M. (2012). *The age of Dualization: The changing face of inequality in deindustrializing societies*. Oxford University Press.

Enggist, M., Häusermann, S., & Pinggera, M. (2022). The COVID-crisis as an opportunity for welfare recalibration? Panel-data evidence on the effect of the COVID-crisis on welfare preferences in Spain, Germany, and Sweden. *Journal of European Public Policy, 29*(12), 2007–2021.

Esping-Andersen, G. (1990). *The three worlds of welfare capitalism*. Princeton University Press.

Faioli, M., & Bologna, S. (2021). Job Retention Schemes in Europe: Italy (ETUI Working Paper). ETUI.

Fana, M., Pérez, S. T., & Fernández-Macías, E. (2020). Employment impact of COVID-19 crisis: From short term effects to long term prospects. *Journal of Industrial and Business Economics, 47*(3), 391–410.

Ferragina, E. (2022). Welfare state change as a double movement: Four decades of retrenchment and expansion in compensatory and employment-oriented policies across 21 high-income countries. *Social Policy & Administration*.

Ferragina, E., & Seeleib-Kaiser, M. (2011). Thematic review: Welfare regime debate: Past, present, futures? *Policy & Politics, 39*(4), 583–603.

Ferragina, E., & Zola, A. (2022). The end of austerity as common sense? An experimental analysis of public opinion shifts and class dynamics during the Covid-19 crisis. *New Political Economy, 27*(2), 329–346.

Fulton, L. (2021). Job retention schemes in Europe: United Kingdom (ETUI Working Paper). ETUI.

Gandenberger, M., Knotz, C., Fossati, F., & Bonoli, G. (2023). Conditional solidarity—Attitudes towards support for others during the 2020 COVID-19 pandemic. *Journal of Social Policy, 52*(4), 943–961.

IMF. (2020). *Kurzarbeit: Germany's short-time work benefit*. IMF. https://www.imf.org/en/News/Articles/2020/06/11/na061120-kurzarbeit-germanys-short-time-work-benefit

Insee. (2020). *France, social portrait – 2020 edition, "Insee Références" collection*. National Institute of Statistics and Economic Studies (Insee).

Iversen, T., & Soskice, D. (2001). An asset theory of social policy preferences. *American Political Science Review, 95*(4), 875–893.

Jæger, M. (2006). What makes people support public responsibility for welfare provision: Self-interest or political ideology?: A longitudinal approach. *Acta Sociologica, 49*(3), 321–338.

Jessop, B. (1993). Towards a Schumpeterian workfare state? Preliminary remarks on post-Fordist political economy. *Studies in Political Economy, 40*(1), 7–39.

Kalleberg, A. (2011). *Good jobs, bad jobs: The rise of polarized and precarious employment Systems in the United States, 1970s–2000s*. Russell Sage Foundation.

Korpi, W. (1980). Social policy and distributional conflict in the capitalist democracies. A preliminary comparative framework. *West European Politics, 3*(3), 296–316.

Lambert, A., Cayouette-Remblière, J., Guéraut, É., Le Roux, G., Bonvalet, C., Girard, V., & Langlois, L. (2020). Le travail et ses aménagements: Ce que la pandémie de covid-19 a changé pour les Français. *Population & Sociétés, 579*(7), 1–4.

Larsen, C. (2008). The institutional logic of welfare attitudes: How welfare regimes influence public support. *Comparative Political Studies, 41*(2), 145–168.

Larsen, C. (2016). *The institutional logic of welfare attitudes: How welfare regimes influence public support*. Routledge.

Macron, E. (2020). Adresse aux Français, 16 mars 2020 [Speech]. https://www.elysee.fr/emmanuel-macron/2020/03/16/adresse-aux-francais-covid19

Margalit, Y. (2013). Explaining social policy preferences: Evidence from the great recession. *American Political Science Review, 107*(1), 80–103.

Marx, P. (2014). Labour market risks and political preferences: The case of temporary employment. *European Journal of Political Research, 53*(1), 136–159.

Meltzer, A. H., & Richard, S. F. (1981). A rational theory of the size of government. *Journal of Political Economy, 89*(5), 914–927.

Müller, T. (2021). Job retention schemes in Europe: Germany (ETUI Working Paper). ETUI.

Müller, T., Schulten, T., & Drahokoupil, J. (2022). Job retention schemes in Europe during the COVID-19 pandemic – Different shapes and sizes and the role of collective bargaining. *Transfer: European Review of Labour and Research, 28*(2), 247–265.

Naumann, E. (2023). Support for the welfare state over the life course: Analysing individual attitude change with multiwave panel data. In F. In Roosma &

T. Laenen (Eds.), *A research agenda for public attitudes to welfare* (pp. 161–180). Edward Elgar Publishing.

Naumann, E., Buss, C., & Bähr, J. (2016). How unemployment experience affects support for the welfare state: A real panel approach. *European Sociological Review, 32*(1), 81–92.

OECD. (2020a). *Job retention schemes during the COVID-19 lockdown and beyond.* https://www.oecd.org/coronavirus/policy-responses/job-retention-schemes-during-the-covid-19-lockdown-and-beyond-0853ba1d/

OECD. (2020b). *OECD economic surveys: Germany 2020.* OECD Publishing. https://doi.org/10.1787/91973c69-en

OECD. (2021a). *OECD economic surveys: Italy 2021.* OECD Publishing. https://doi.org/10.1787/07d8b9cd-en

OECD. (2021b). *OECD economic surveys: France 2021.* OECD Publishing. https://doi.org/10.1787/289a0a17-en

Owens, L., & Pedulla, D. (2014). Material welfare and changing political preferences: The case of support for redistributive social policies. *Social Forces, 92*(3), 1087–1113.

Pope, T., & Shearer, E. (2021). *The coronavirus job retention scheme: How successful has the furlough scheme been and what should happen next?* Institute for Government.

Reeskens, T., Muis, Q., Sieben, I., Vandecasteele, L., Luijkx, R., & Halman, L. (2021a). Stability or change of public opinion and values during the coronavirus crisis? Exploring Dutch longitudinal panel data. *European Societies, 23*(sup1), S153–S171.

Reeskens, T., Roosma, F., & Wanders, E. (2021b). The perceived deservingness of COVID-19 healthcare in The Netherlands: A conjoint experiment on priority access to intensive care and vaccination. *BMC Public Health, 21*, 447.

Rehm, P. (2009). Risks and redistribution: An individual-level analysis. *Comparative Political Studies, 42*(7), 855–881.

Rehm, P. (2016). *Risk inequality and welfare states: Social policy preferences, development, and dynamics.* Cambridge University Press.

Rehm, P., Hacker, J., & Schlesinger, M. (2012). Insecure alliances: Risk, inequality, and support for the welfare state. *American Political Science Review, 106*(2), 386–406.

Romano, S. (2015). Idle paupers, scroungers and shirkers: Past and new social stereotypes of the undeserving welfare claimant in the UK. In L. Foster & A. Brunton (Eds.), *In defence of welfare 2.* Policy Press.

Roosma, F., van Oorschot, W., & Gelissen, J. (2014). The preferred role and perceived performance of the welfare state: European welfare attitudes from a multidimensional perspective. *Social Science Research, 44*, 200–210.

Sacchi, S., Pancaldi, F., & Arisi, C. (2011). The economic crisis as a trigger of convergence? Short-time work in Italy, Germany and Austria. *Social Policy & Administration, 45*(4), 465–487.

Seeleib-Kaiser, M. (2008). *Welfare state transformations: Comparative perspectives*. Palgrave Macmillan.

Somers, M., & Block, F. (2005). From poverty to perversity: Ideas, markets, and institutions over 200 years of welfare debate. *American Sociological Review, 70*(2), 260–287.

Stanley, L. (2014). 'We're reaping what we sowed': Everyday crisis narratives and acquiescence to the age of austerity. *New Political Economy, 19*(6), 895–917.

Svallfors, S. (1997). Worlds of welfare and attitudes to redistribution: A comparison of eight Western nations. *European Sociological Review, 13*(3), 283–304.

Svallfors, S. (2011). A bedrock of support? Trends in welfare state attitudes in Sweden, 1981–2010. *Social Policy & Administration, 45*(7), 806–825.

Svallfors, S. (Ed.). (2012). *Contested welfare states: Welfare attitudes in Europe and beyond*. Stanford University Press.

Vaisey, S., & Miles, A. (2017). What you can—And can't—Do with three-wave panel data. *Sociological Methods & Research, 46*(1), 44–67.

van Oorschot, W. (2000). Who should get what, and why? On deservingness criteria and the conditionality of solidarity among the public. *Policy & Politics, 28*(1), 33–48.

van Oorschot, W. (2006). Making the difference in social Europe: Deservingness perceptions among citizens of European welfare states. *Journal of European Social Policy, 16*(1), 23–42.

Vincent, C. (2021). Job retention schemes in Europe: France (ETUI Working Paper). ETUI.

Wehl, N. (2019). The (ir)relevance of unemployment for labour market policy attitudes and welfare state attitudes. *European Journal of Political Research, 58*(1), 141–162.

Witteveen, D. (2020). Sociodemographic inequality in exposure to COVID-19-induced economic hardship in the United Kingdom. *Research in Social Stratification and Mobility, 69*, 100551.

CHAPTER 10

The Odd One Out—Life and Death in Sweden During the COVID-19 Pandemic

Olof M. Östergren

Introduction

Sweden emerged as an early hotspot for COVID-19. At the time, there was no established system for detecting infections, but several independent indicators suggested that the virus would spread widely in early March 2020. Surges were observed in calls to the healthcare hotlines, reporting headaches, cough, and sniffles, sick leave spells with undefined respiratory infections, and, later, COVID-related hospitalisations and deaths (Coronakommissionen, 2021a; Dyrdak et al., 2024). The impact was particularly severe in Stockholm, the capital, which had recently concluded a school break with many residents returning from skiing holidays in the Alps (Björk et al., 2021; Coronakommissionen, 2021a).

Sweden offers an intriguing and distinctive case study compared with the four broadly similar countries analysed in this book: France, Germany, Italy, and the UK. While these nations imposed strict lockdowns (see

O. M. Östergren (✉)
Department of Public Health Sciences, Stockholm University,
Stockholm, Sweden
e-mail: olof.ostergren@su.se

E. Naumann et al. (eds.), *Social Life during COVID-19 in France, Germany, Italy and the UK*,
https://doi.org/10.1007/978-3-031-99349-7_10

Chap. 2), the Swedish government chose instead to issue guidance and place significant emphasis on individual responsibility to control the spread of the virus. Despite the initially severe toll in terms of deaths, Sweden maintained this general strategy throughout the pandemic, although stricter measures were progressively introduced as the crisis evolved (Björkman, 2023; Kamerlin & Kasson, 2020; Winblad et al., 2022). Figure 10.1 provides an overview of the pandemic's progression in Sweden, focusing on two epidemiological indicators: laboratory-confirmed infections (cases) and COVID-19-related deaths.

The pandemic can be characterised by three distinct waves, which unfolded in a manner similar to many other Western European countries (see Chaps. 2 and 3). The first wave, referred to as the *shock wave*, saw a rapid increase in deaths but few confirmed infections, reflecting the limited availability of testing at the time. The second wave, termed the *winter*

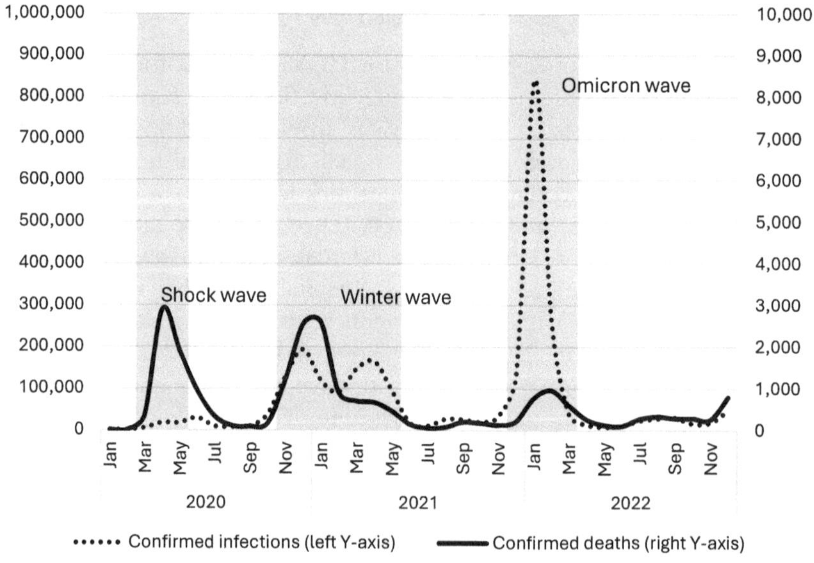

Fig. 10.1 Confirmed infections of SARS-CoV and deaths from COVID-19 in Sweden, 2020–2022. (Note: Confirmed infections are defined as laboratory-confirmed infections with SARS-CoV-2 reported to the national SmiNet database. Deaths are defined as deaths where COVID-19 was reported as either the underlying or contributing cause of death to the national cause of death register)

wave, was bimodal in terms of cases but not in terms of deaths, largely owing to the vaccine rollout, which progressively protected vulnerable groups during this period (Myndigheten för vård- och omsorgsanalys, 2022). The third major wave was driven by the emergence of the Omicron variant, which was highly contagious but less severe (Alimohamadi et al., 2021; Araf et al., 2022). The *Omicron wave* led to an unprecedented number of cases in a short period of time but comparatively fewer deaths.

The chapter is structured as follows. First, I outline the institutional and legal context that underpins crisis management in Sweden. This is followed by a summary of the measures implemented in Sweden, focusing on measures that shaped the everyday life of the population. Second, I present findings from empirical analysis using linked administrative register data on social inequalities in physical and mental health, gender inequalities in unpaid work, and remote work and unemployment risks. These findings are contextualised with reference to relevant literature. Lastly, I offer some concluding remarks.

Materials and Methods

The Swedish response to COVID-19 was controversial both internationally and within Sweden. In 2020, the Swedish parliament launched an independent inquiry into the nation's pandemic management (Ludvigsson, 2023). The Corona commission (*Coronakomissionen*), an autonomous government agency inside the Swedish Government Offices, conducted its work from June 2020 to February 2022. Their findings were published across five volumes, totalling 2800 pages encompassing all aspects of the crisis management. The commission determined that although the overall strategy of relying on advice and personal responsibility was robust, the response to the first wave of the COVID-19 was late and not sufficiently strict: this is likely to have resulted in unnecessary deaths, particularly among vulnerable groups and in nursing homes (Coronakommissionen, 2021c). The outline of institutional framework and summary of interventions concerning daily life are predominantly based on the work of the commission.[1]

[1] As part of their work, the commission initiated a research project, SWECOV, which collected a substantial number of administrative registers, allowing the commission to administer independent empirical evaluations. Since the end of the commission, the research programme has continued and grown. The data used for the original empirical analyses presented here were accessed through participation in this project.

The empirical analyses were based on administrative register data on the Swedish population from 2019 to 2022. Information on basic demographic characteristics and socioeconomic position was gathered by Statistics Sweden; data on mortality and psychiatric care were collected from the National Board of Health and Welfare; data on temporary parental leave were collected from the Swedish Social Insurance fund; and data on unemployment were provided by The Swedish Unemployment Insurance Funds. These sources were linked using an anonymised identifier that allows researchers to connect records which belong to the same individual in different registers without revealing the identity of that individual. While administrative data do not contain information on several factors relevant to this study—for example, the gender division of unpaid labour within household, or individual perceptions of health or political beliefs—they do provide information on the whole population regarding several aspects of demographic characteristics and socioeconomic conditions, as well as work, health, and use of social insurance. Furthermore, administrative data is also not subject to low response rates, selection bias, nor are participants lost in follow-up collections.

The period is divided into the *pre-pandemic phase* (January 2019–February 2020), the *shock wave* (March 2020–May 2020), *summer 2020* (June 2020–October 2020), the *winter wave* (November 2020–May 2021), *summer 2021* (June 2021–November 2021), the *Omicron wave* (December 2021–March 2022), and, finally, the *post-pandemic phase* (April 2022–December 2022). In each of these periods, I estimate incidence rates and ratios for several indicators, thus attempting to capture some of the processes examined in the other chapters of this volume (Table 10.1).

Inequalities in physical and mental health are approximated using differences in all-cause mortality and visits to specialised psychiatric clinics by educational achievement. Gender differences relating to unpaid care work are estimated using temporary parental leave by sex and cohabitation status of the parents. The role of remote work is examined through the distribution of individuals working in occupations that facilitate remote work, distinguished by sex, migrant status, and income, as well as unemployment risks in remote and non-remote occupations. The incidence rates and rate ratios are estimated using event-history analysis that allows an estimation of seasonally adjusted incidence rates for specific groups and measures of inequalities within the different periods from the same model.

Table 10.1 Definitions of populations, events, and groups used in the chapter

Dimension	*Population*	*Event*	*Groups*
Physical health	All individuals aged 30 years or older Individuals: 7,156,882 Person years: 26,633,586	Death from any cause Events: 368,918	College No college
Mental health	All individuals aged 30 years or older Individuals: 7,156,882 Person years: 26,633,586	Visit to a specialised psychiatric clinic in outpatient care Events: 2,781,442	College No college
Unpaid care work	All parents with at least one child under 19 years living in the household Individuals: 2,279,567 Person years: 7,643,634	Use of temporary parental leave Events:16,403,253	Men Women Cohabiting parents Single parents
Unemployment	All individuals between 30 and 64 years old that are active in the labour market Individuals: 4,328,219 Person years: 15,192,151	Unemployment spells Events: 688,760	Occupation allows remote work Occupation does not allow remote work

Why Was Sweden So Different?

The Institutional Framework of Sweden Shaped the Pandemic Response

As in other nations, the policy response to the pandemic in Sweden was governed by politicians and other decision makers. Regardless, decisions are made within the context of institutional characteristics, traditions of governance, and social norms, which can more easily facilitate some courses of action. Accordingly, Sweden favoured a less invasive approach to non-pharmaceutical interventions for both institutional and cultural motives (Brusselaers et al., 2022; Yan et al., 2020).

The principles of crisis management in Sweden dictate that governmental bodies should operate as normal as far as possible. Sweden has a comparatively small central government and instead comprises several relatively independent national agencies with clearly defined responsibilities. They maintain such responsibilities in a crisis and there are no regulations permit increased executive authority to the central government in a non-military crisis (Coronakommissionen, 2021c). Parliament may alter the responsibilities of government agencies and award additional authority to the central government, but only by introducing new laws or changing existing laws. Such procedure can be accelerated in crises. In April 2020, a temporary change was implemented to the Communicable Diseases Act, which allowed the national government to restrict public gatherings, shut down commercial areas, restaurants, and gyms, and limit domestic and international travel. These changes resembled a lockdown, but these hypothetical measures were never activated and the temporary change expired in July 2020 (Coronakommissionen, 2021a). Two other temporary laws were also introduced. These further limited interactions in public, private, and commercial settings, and made it possible for local authorities to intervene and shut down or fine businesses that did not comply. The first law, *lag (2020:526) om tillfälliga smittskyddsåtgärder på serveringsställen*, was introduced in July 2020 and placed further restriction on restaurants, cafés, and bars to limit close interpersonal contacts. The second, *lag (2021:4) om särskilda begränsningar för att förhindra spridning av sjukdomen covid-19,* was introduced in January 2021 and extended these regulations to include shops, sporting and cultural events, gyms, public transport, and private gatherings. Both laws were deactivated in April 2022.

Sweden is nationally decentralised into independent areas of responsibility, which are upheld during a crisis and can be altered only through legislation. The distinct levels of Swedish government also reflect such decentralisation. Aside from the national parliament, Sweden has 21 county councils and 290 municipal parliaments, which are appointed through independent elections, collect their own taxes, and function autonomously from both each other and the national government (Pierre, 2015). Local agencies are responsible for crisis management, not the national government (Garcia et al., 2024; Nordgren, 2015). The county councils are responsible for healthcare, which includes the management of infectious diseases. While the Public Health Agency of Sweden is responsible for tracking the epidemiological development of a pandemic and for coordinating a subsequent response, it may not implement any course of action. Instead, the focus was on coming to a consensus between local authorities that would then enable a coherent national strategy (Coronakommissionen, 2021a).

The Communicable Diseases Act emphasises preventive measures and voluntary measures observed by individuals, both those who are infected and those at risk of infection. In some circumstances, individuals can be forced to undergo a medical investigation, resulting in a restriction of their freedom of movement, quarantine, or isolation, but only if the individual has refused voluntary measures and, typically, a court decision is required (Coronakommissionen, 2021a; Winblad et al., 2022). The law was implemented during the AIDS crisis and the law was written with the forcible detainment of intravenous drug users, often preparing for psychiatric comorbidities (Coronakommissionen, 2021a). The law places several legal responsibilities on the individual. If an individual believes that they may be infected by a disease that is classified as a threat to society—for example, COVID-19 at the time of the pandemic—they are legally required to notify the authorities and to take the necessary precautions to protect others from infection. There are, however, no legal consequences for those that do not adhere to these rules (Coronakommissionen, 2021a).

Freedom and Responsibility: The Swedish Pandemic Response

The Swedish response to COVID-19 relied on the general public following advice given by government agencies. Individuals were asked to work from home where possible, maintain distance from others in public settings, wash hands, avoid shaking hands, avoid crowds, not unnecessarily travel, and stay at home in case of infection or suspected infection (Andersen et al., 2022; Coronakommissionen, 2021a). When testing became available, individuals were asked to take tests if they exhibited even very mild symptoms. As vaccines became available, the population was asked to get vaccinated. Face masks were not part of the general advice to the public, aside from a period between January and June 2021, when individuals born before 2004 were requested to wear a face mask on public transport (Coronakommissionen, 2021a). This advice was intended to provide individuals with practical ways to fulfil their legal obligation to prevent the spread of COVID-19. Such an approach relies on individuals being aware of the development of the pandemic and outbreaks in their close personal networks. However, at times, the communication from the government to the public was unclear, conflicting, or overly technical (Coronakommissionen, 2021c). In addition, there were substantial delays and difficulties in establishing an operational programme for testing and contact tracing, and several counties in Sweden never reached this goal (Almgren & Björk, 2021). Both factors probably made it more challenging for individuals to effectively limit the spread of the virus.

To prevent an economic crisis and to protect incomes and standards of living, and to allow individuals to more easily follow advice without fear of economic consequences, Sweden introduced substantial support to the social protection system (Coronakommissionen, 2021b). These included updating existing schemes, such as increasing the maximum for the replacement rate of unemployment insurance and increasing the replacement rate for sick pay. New schemes were also introduced: for example, reimbursements were made available for those infected, such that they were not required to work in-person, and reimbursement schemes were implemented for individuals in medical risk groups. The social protection system substantially buffered the decrease in income during the pandemic (Adermon et al., 2024; Coronakommissionen, 2021b) and limited the increase in income inequality (Angelov & Waldenström, 2023).

Although there was no general order for individuals to stay at home, public gatherings were limited to 500 on 12 March 2020, and to 50 on 29 March 2020. This limit was maintained throughout the remainder of 2020, but was reduced to eight participants in November (Coronakommissionen, 2022). In the winter of 2020/21, restaurants and bars serving alcohol were forced to close by 10 pm in November and December, at 8 pm in January and February, which was subsequently extended to 10 pm. Such temporary restrictions ended in April 2021

(Coronakommissionen, 2021a). With few exceptions—such as some religious ceremonies—the limitation of public gatherings to eight participants was maintained until October 2021. Beyond this period followed regulations concerning the safety precautions of a gathering, rather than only numbers. For example, gatherings could be held if there was distance between participants, it was held outside, and, later, vaccine certificates were registered. Most of the restrictions on public gatherings were removed in February 2022 (Coronakommissionen, 2022).

On 17 March 2020, the Swedish government announced that upper secondary schools, universities, and educational institutions for adults must adopt remote teaching. Preschools and compulsory schools remained open. This decision was based on assessments from the National Public Health Agency of Sweden, which suggested that children did not substantially contribute to the spread of SARS-CoV-2 and that closing schools would indirectly negatively affect the health and wellbeing of children, especially vulnerable children from socially disadvantaged homes and children with functional disabilities (Coronakommissionen, 2022).

A national restriction that prevented family from visiting relatives in nursing homes was imposed between April and September 2020. The restriction was lifted when the rate of COVID-19 had decreased and the negative consequences on the mental health of the residents and next of kin were considered to outweigh the benefits of a general ban: prior to this, in many cases, family members were unable to be with their partners or relatives in their final moments. Even after the ban, individuals who managed nursing homes were responsible for ensuring that visits were safe and could deny visitors if necessary (Coronakommissionen, 2020).

Sweden deploys very different measures to the other four countries studied in this book. However, the intention was similar: to limit the spread of SARS-CoV-2 by mitigating interpersonal contacts. Although no strict lockdown was enforced, mobility patterns in Sweden demonstrate that the population largely stayed home (Östh et al., 2023; Shuttleworth et al., 2024). Sweden is a society with a high level of trust (Grönlund & Setälä, 2007), which contributes to the success of such a strategy in which individuals are expected to follow the advice given by the authorities and take responsibility for protecting themselves and others. The decline in mobility occurred prior to government recommendations to stay at home, and was correlated with the local rate of infections (Akerman et al., 2022; Coronakommissionen, 2021a). Individual behavioural changes predating government interventions have also been documented in the United

States (Chetty et al., 2024). These findings suggest that individuals may act to protect themselves and others independently from government interventions.

Figure 10.2 presents data on time spent in residential areas from Google mobility reports for the countries included in this volume. The Swedish population stayed home much less during the onset of the pandemic, during which time other countries imposed lockdowns. During the remainder of the pandemic, however, Swedes stayed at home as much as people in other countries, indicated by the grey fields. The increase in time spent in residential areas was consistent in Sweden throughout the summer periods, suggesting that behavioural changes were maintained, even when transmission rates were low. Although Sweden imposed fewer restrictions on daily life than other European nations, life did not continue as usual.

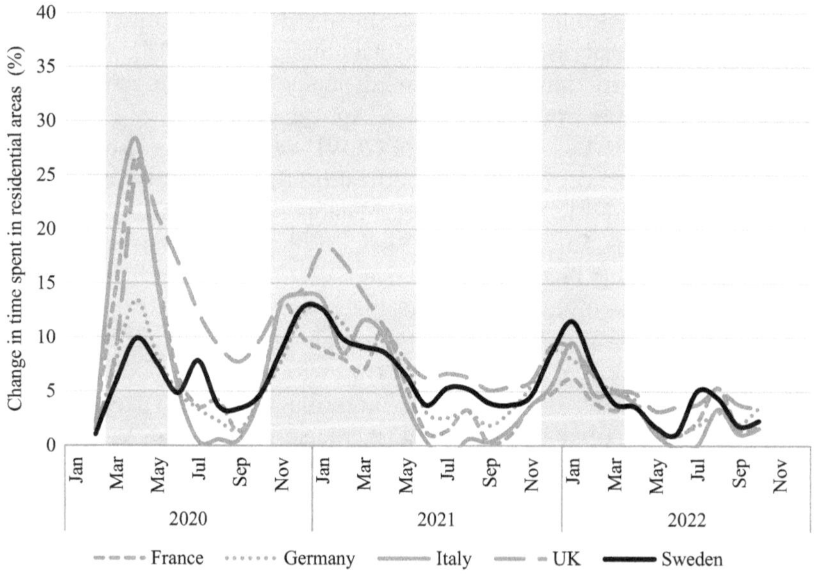

Fig. 10.2 Changes in time spent in residential areas in France, Germany, Italy, The United Kingdom, and Sweden, February 2020–October 2022. (Note: Data from Google COVID-19 Community Mobility Reports. The changes denote changes in time that google users spent in residential areas compared to the baseline period, 3 January to 6 February 2020. The data have been aggregated to monthly averages)

Social Inequalities in Health

Inequalities in Physical Health

COVID-19 caused more than 21,000 deaths in Sweden between 2020 and 2022. Men, socioeconomically disadvantaged groups, migrants, and older individuals were disproportionately affected (Altmejd et al., 2023; Andersson et al., 2021; Aradhya et al., 2021). However, the health consequences of the pandemic are not limited to only death and illness caused directly by the disease. Reduced access to health care, unemployment and income loss, behavioural changes, social isolation, and stress and uncertainty of the future are likely to have influenced both the mental and physical health of the population. Furthermore, health, social, and economic resources in Sweden are unequally distributed, resulting in discrepancies as to how individuals were able to cope with the different types of strain caused by the pandemic. Figure 10.3 presents incidence rates of all-cause mortality, a summary measure of physical health, by educational attainment.

Mortality increased for both groups during the shock wave. This surge was more pronounced in individuals without college education, but proportionally less intense. Therefore, relative inequalities, indicated by incidence rate ratios in the figure, were during the shock wave compared to the pre-pandemic period. After this phase, mortality rates and inequalities returned to levels closer to those observed before the pandemic. In both groups, there was a far less pronounced elevation of mortality during the winter wave, and inequalities remained stable. However, during the Omicron wave, mortality increased among individuals without a college education, but not among those with college education, which resulted in widening inequalities. During the post-pandemic period, mortality levels and inequalities were comparable to those observed prior to the pandemic. Altmejd et al. (2023) compared annual estimates of inequalities in nine different negative life events—including all-cause mortality—by education, income, sex, and country of birth, before and during the pandemic. They found generally similar patterns of larger absolute inequalities during the pandemic but stable relative inequalities (Altmejd et al., 2023). By comparing the waves of the pandemic, as opposed to years, the estimates presented here show that inequalities temporarily shifted during the most intense phases of the pandemic, but returned to pre-pandemic levels afterwards.

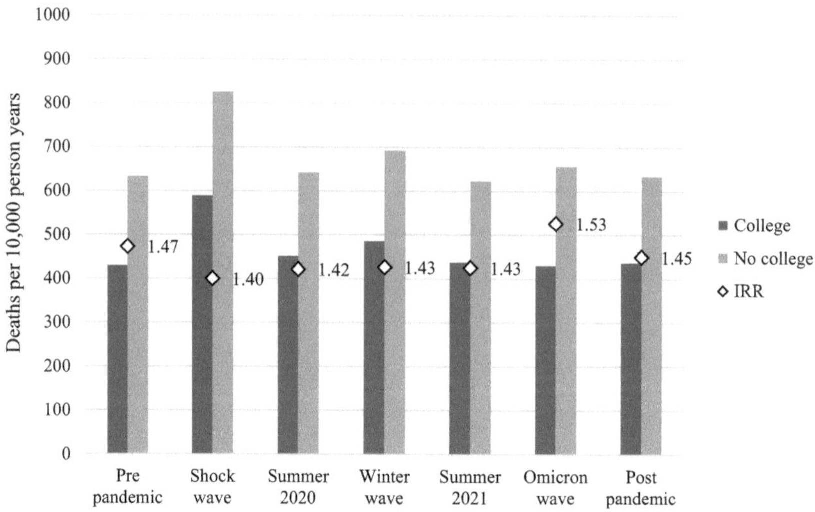

Fig. 10.3 Incidence rates and incidence rate ratios for all-cause mortality by education and period among all individuals aged 30 or older in Sweden, 2019–2022. (Note: Estimated using Poisson regression where death from any cause was defined as the event and time at risk was the offset. The association between education and death risk was allowed to vary by period. Adjusted for sex, age, and calendar month to account for seasonality in death risks)

In a study comparing income inequalities in risk of receiving intensive care due to COVID-19 over the course of the pandemic, Gauffin et al. (2023) find that inequalities were small during the first wave, but increased progressively over following waves, while the rate of intensive care declined (Gauffin et al., 2023). These patterns are almost identical to the all-cause mortality observed. The authors' observation, that this is in line with the fundamental cause theory, which suggests that as the overall burden of disease decreases, inequalities tend to grow as more becomes known about treatment and prevention (Gauffin et al., 2023; Link & Phelan, 1995), also applies here. Health inequalities in preventable and treatable diseases tend to be larger than those observed for diseases that are unpreventable and untreatable (Mackenbach et al., 2015). This observation has been interpreted to suggest that as the causes and cures of a disease are found, resources can be activated to protect individuals. As these resources are not equally distributed, treatable diseases tend to cluster in groups with fewer resources (Link & Phelan, 1995; Mackenbach et al., 2015). Figure 10.3 supports this finding and demonstrates that the burden of COVID-19 fell increasingly on socially disadvantaged groups as it became more preventable —first through remote work and then via vaccines.

Inequalities in Mental Health

There are several reasons to think that the pandemic resulted in a general decline of mental health: for example, concerns about the health of loved ones, economic instability, and social isolation may all impact wellbeing. There are also numerous reasons to think that it may have led to have facilitated better mental health, such as spending less time at work, more time with family, and a feeling of social cohesion in working to overcome a common threat. The pandemic influenced nearly all aspects of social and economic life, making it challenging to predict how mental health may have changed.

Figure 10.4 displays the incidence of visits to specialised psychiatric clinics in outpatient care by education. The most common disorders that are treated in specialised outpatient care in the adult population are depression, anxiety, and ADHD. Substance abuse, schizophrenia, and personality disorders comprise a much smaller proportion (Socialstyrelsen, 2024). Throughout the period, there were marginal variations in the incidence rates and inequalities between groups did not change. There was a tendency for lower rates during the waves—particularly during the shock wave—and higher rates in the intermediate periods, likely indicative of challenges in accessing mental health services or apprehension surrounding seeking care due to perceived risk of infection. The previously mentioned study by Altmejd et al. (2023) suggests similar patterns and further compares inequalities in visits to psychiatric clinics to initiated treatments with antidepressants and suicides (Altmejd et al., 2023). Taken together, this suggests that there were no clear trends in mental health, nor in inequalities in mental health, as demonstrated by register-based measures of mental health.

Register-based measures only reveal severe mental health problems and only in individuals actively engaged with mental health care services. They do not capture less severe issues or cases in which individuals do not seek care. Although it is possible that longer-term consequences on mental health and wellbeing will emerge in the future, longitudinal survey data do not indicate that the pandemic had substantial negative effects on the

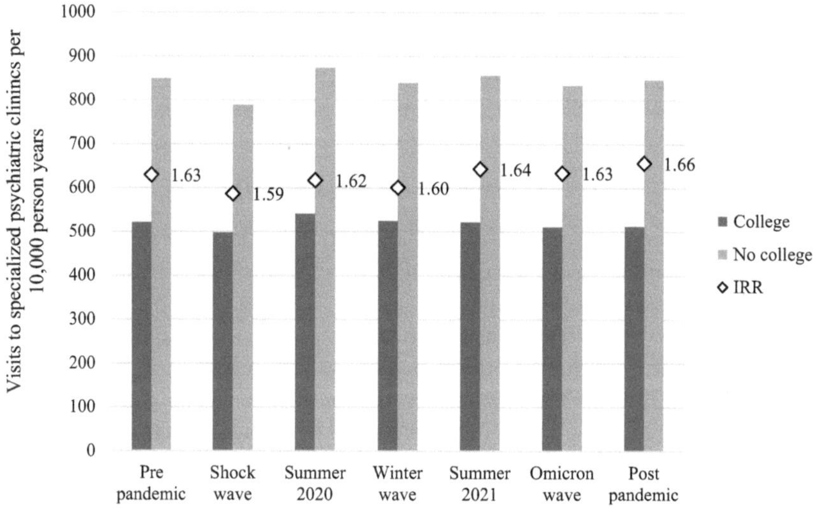

Fig. 10.4 Incidence rates and incidence rate ratios for visits to specialised psychiatric clinics by education and period among all individuals aged 30 or older in Sweden, 2019–2022. (Note: Estimated using Poisson regression where a visit to a psychiatric outpatient clinic was defined as the event and time at risk was the offset. The association between education and psychiatric care was allowed to vary by period. Adjusted for sex, age, and calendar month to account for seasonality)

mental health of Swedish residents. Comparable to other countries that participate in the *Survey of Health, Ageing, and Retirement* (SHARE) study, Swedish respondents reported overall lower levels of feelings of sadness and sleeping problems, particularly among older adults (Van Winkle et al., 2021; Wester et al., 2022), but increased levels of loneliness (Wester et al., 2022) during the pandemic. Although the mental health of the general population did not appear to deteriorate—and may even have improved—several studies have found that individuals who were affected by the pandemic, either directly or indirectly, report poorer mental health. For example, former patients report high rates of depressive symptoms one year after receiving intensive care for COVID-19 (Hussain et al., 2024). Infections and hospitalisation in partners and family members was associated with higher rates of depressive and anxiety symptoms (Lovik et al., 2023). Individuals who lost their job during the pandemic had an increased risk of reporting depressive symptoms, compared to those in continuous employment (Blomqvist et al., 2023). Both severe COVID-19 morbidity and job loss disproportionately impacted vulnerable groups (Altmejd et al., 2023), which indicates that the mental health of vulnerable groups may also have been disproportionately affected, albeit indirectly.

Gender Inequality in Unpaid Care Work

Compared to other countries, gender equality is high in Sweden, though women still perform most unpaid care work (Evertsson, 2014; Lane & Jordansson, 2020; Nyberg, 2002). Equality of unpaid care work is one of the six policy goals of the gender equality legislature. As part of the evaluation of the progress of this goal, Statistic Sweden estimate the time spent on unpaid work every ten years. There was a survey administered in the autumn of 2021 which found that, on average, women spend more time cooking, cleaning, and doing laundry, while men spend more time in paid work and managing household finances. While women and men spend the same amount of time playing with their children and helping with homework, women spend more time on feeding, clothing, managing hygiene, and putting the children to bed (Statistiska Centralbyrån, 2021). Owing to the extended interval between surveys, it is not possible to examine whether these patterns were shifted by the pandemic. Similar issues apply to other surveys on unpaid work that are better suited to detect changes that occur over several years, as opposed to the sudden changes in daily life that characterised the pandemic.

Administrative data on the use of temporary parental benefits for the care of a sick child, in Swedish abbreviated to VAB (*vård av barn*), provide an alternative source of information. The scheme provides social insurance that compensates parents who must stay home from work to care for ill children (Försäkringskassan, 2021). Use of the scheme reached record levels during the pandemic (Försäkringskassan, 2023). While making use of VAB allows parents to care for their children with reduced financial consequences, it also results in missing career opportunities. Here, this is interpreted as a proxy for the main care giver in the household (cf. Duvander & Johansson, 2015; Eriksson & Nermo, 2010). The Swedish Social Insurance Agency keeps register information on each use of VAB, allowing the tracing of the development of this indicator over short periods of time. Figure 10.5 presents the incidence of VAB by sex in Sweden throughout the pandemic.

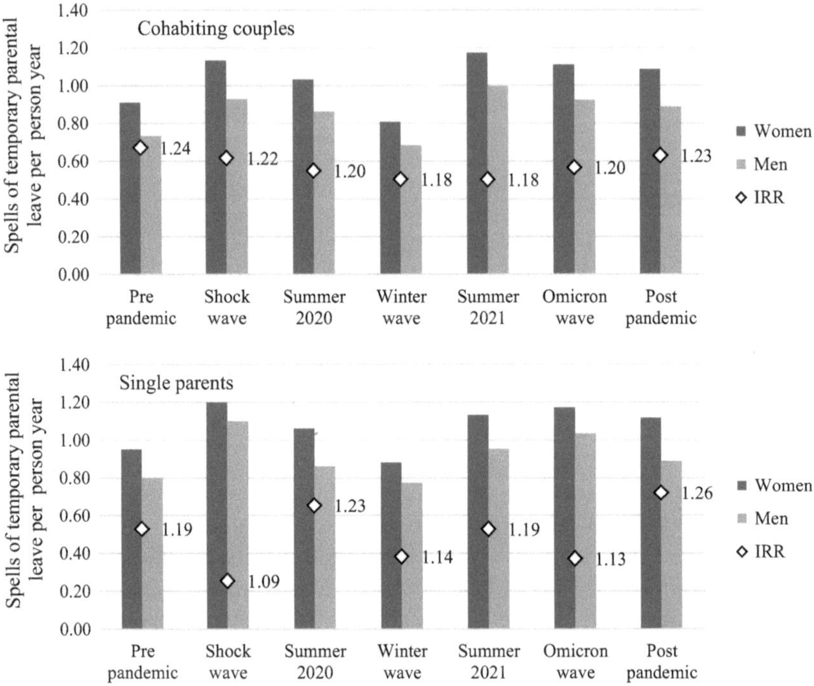

Fig. 10.5 Incidence rates and incidence rate ratios for spells of temporary parental leave (VAB) by gender among parents with at least one child under 18 living in the household, Sweden, 2019–2022. (Note: Estimated using Poisson regression where a spell of temporary parental leave was defined as the event and time at risk was the offset. The association between gender and temporary parental leave was allowed to vary by period. Adjusted for age and calendar month to account for seasonality)

The rate of use of VAB varied throughout the pandemic. It increased during the shock wave and remained high during the summer of 2020. The estimates presented in the figure are adjusted for seasonality and the absolute number of uses was far less in the summer compared to the winter. The use of VAB was comparatively low during the winter wave, likely due to the widespread adoption of remote work. The rate was high in the summer of 2021 and remained high during the Omicron wave and in 2022. During the pandemic, the norms for when children were sent home by preschools and schools changed. Children displaying mild symptoms were advised to be sent home and kept home for an extended period to help minimise transmission (Försäkringskassan, 2023). This likely contributed to the high rates of VAB in the final stages of the pandemic and in the post-pandemic phase, when parents returned to work but COVID and other infections were still common.

For cohabiting couples, women were about 20–25% more likely to use VAB than men. There was a tendency of smaller gender differences during the pandemic, though these changes were only marginal. However, there was a clear tendency of smaller gender differences during the three waves among single parents, particularly during the shock wave. During periods of high transmission rates, it is feasible that resources outside of the home were less available to support sick children. This applies also to grandparents or other relatives who are sensitive to infections. If single fathers tended to more heavily rely on such resources than single mothers, this can in part explain the temporary reduction in gender equality for this group. During periods of low transmission and after the pandemic, the gender difference was comparable or slightly greater than prior to the pandemic. These patterns indicate small and temporary shifts to greater gender equality in taking time off work to care for children during the pandemic. However, it is challenging to come to conclusions concerning gender equality in unpaid work without more detailed information on responsibilities and time use within cohabiting couples.

Remote Work and Unemployment Risks

The COVID-19 pandemic caused a dual shock to the Swedish economy, affecting both exports and domestic consumption. The Swedish economy relies on exports and the global economic crisis in 2020 affected companies in Sweden, particularly those that principally traded with countries that were severely hit during the first wave (Akerman et al., 2022; Coronakommissionen, 2021b). Swedish residents were asked to stay at home as much as possible, which was reflected in the decline of domestic consumption, an effect that was particularly concentrated in parts of Sweden with high transmission rates and in sectors providing services that require interpersonal contact (Akerman et al., 2022; Coronakommissionen, 2021b). During the initial stages of the pandemic, both employment and income levels decreased (Adermon et al., 2024) and the number of residents receiving social welfare increased (Socialstyrelsen, 2021).

The economic crisis was quickly combatted with generous support to individuals and companies. By the end of 2020, unemployment rates were comparable to pre-pandemic levels. However, not all individuals were equally impacted. Those with a lower socioeconomic position and migrants were more likely to lose wages, employment, and disposable income in comparison to other groups (Akerman et al., 2022; Altmejd et al., 2023), and income inequalities increased (Angelov & Waldenström, 2023). Additionally, there was a tendency for individuals working in occupations that allowed for remote working to be more likely to retain employment (Coronakommissionen, 2021b).

To avoid infections, Swedish residents were asked to work from home as much as possible. Survey data indicate a dramatic increase in remote work during the pandemic (Medlingsinstitutet, 2024), and, moreover, that the majority of the workforce adopted such measures during the pandemic (Samuelsson et al., 2022). Individuals with higher levels of education (Samuelsson et al., 2022) and occupational class (Medlingsinstitutet, 2024) reported higher rates of remote work. The top panel in Fig. 10.6 presents the proportion of individuals who were able to work remotely and unemployment risk by gender, migrant status, education, and income. The estimated proportion that could work remotely is calculated through applying an index of remote work to the specific occupation held by the individual. The index was developed by the Centre for Epidemiology and Social Medicine at the Stockholm County Council and denotes occupations that require in-person work at least 50% of the time for 430 unique occupations (Centrum för epidemiologi och samhällsmedicin, 2020). The opportunity to work from home is not evenly distributed throughout the population and the groups that were the least able to work from home were more likely to experience unemployment. While there were no large gender differences, immigrants, those without a college education, and low-income earners had fewer opportunities for remote work and consequentially higher unemployment risks. Individuals with at least one foreign-born parent had a higher risk of unemployment, despite having similar opportunities for remote work. Mutually adjusting for the included factors and the ability to work remotely only marginally account for the differences in unemployment risks between the groups.

The bottom panel in Fig. 10.6 displays how unemployment risks by the opportunity to work remotely developed over the pandemic. These risks are adjusted for sex, migrant status, education, income, and calendar month to account for seasonality. Unemployment risks grew dramatically

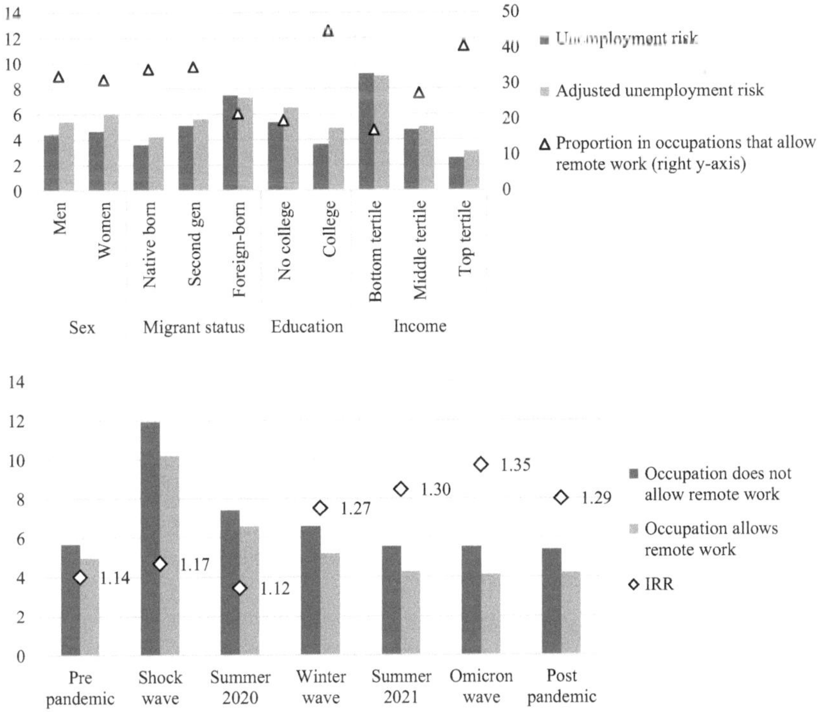

Fig. 10.6 The proportion working in occupations that allows for remote work and the average one-year unemployment risk in 2019–2022 by sex, migrant status, education, and income among individuals aged 30–64 that were active in the work force (top panel) and unemployment risk and incidence rate ratios by the ability to work remotely by period. (Note: The adjusted unemployment risks were adjusted by the sex, migrant status, education, income, and ability to work from home in the occupation. The adjusted unemployment risks in the bottom panel were additionally adjusted for calendar month and the association between the ability to work remotely and unemployment was allowed to vary by period)

during the shock wave and remained somewhat higher during the summer of 2020, but then returned to pre-pandemic levels. The ability to work remotely became a stronger predictor of unemployment risk as the pandemic evolved. It was associated with an unemployment risk 14% higher before the pandemic, which increased to 27% during the winter wave, before peaking at 35% during the Omicron wave, and finally settled at 29%

after the pandemic. This trend indicates that the ability to work remotely may have become a more important predictor of job stability after the pandemic.

Concluding Remarks

Although the Swedish policy response to the COVID pandemic was distinct from that of other European countries, it was perhaps more of a difference in tactics than in strategy. Using the resources available within the context and principles of crisis management, Swedish authorities attempted to limit the spread of the virus through reducing the intensity of interpersonal contacts while also protecting vulnerable groups. Rather than implementing lockdowns, Sweden relied on voluntary behavioural changes, simultaneously boosting economic and social insurance schemes to mitigate negative consequences for individuals who chose to stay home. Issues with vague or conflicting information from government agencies and difficulties with testing and tracing likely resulted in greater challenges for individuals to come to appropriate decisions. Regardless, many Swedes did change their behaviour, spending more time at home, even at times of low transmission. The majority of employees who were able to work from home chose to do so. More restrictive interventions were also implemented in Sweden. Higher education switched to remote teaching, relatives were prevented from visiting nursing homes, public gatherings were limited to eight individuals, and restaurants had restricted opening hours. Overall, daily life did not go on undisturbed.

The early stage of the pandemic affected Sweden unexpectedly severely, having an impact on both the health of the population and the economy. Subsequent waves differed from this. The economic crisis was largely restricted to spring of 2020 and by autumn of that same year—when transmission rates increased—individuals had established routines for remote work. At this point, large-scale testing had been established (Almgren & Björk, 2021) and vaccinations became available midway through the winter (Warren & Lofstedt, 2022). The initial pandemic shock in 2020 also stands out in the analyses presented here. Social inequalities in all-cause mortality, and to a lesser degree psychiatric care, decreased and temporary parental leave was more evenly distributed by gender (though mainly among single parents). These tendencies continued, but were far less pronounced during the winter wave. During this period, the inability to work remotely emerged as a stronger predictor of unemployment and it remained important throughout the post-pandemic phase. During the short-lived but intense Omicron wave, social inequalities in mortality increased. This aligns with fundamental cause theory (Link & Phelan, 1995), which suggests that social gradients are more pronounced for health problems that can be prevented or treated.

Although the pandemic shifted patterns of incidence and inequalities in the measures under consideration here, it is important to emphasise that these shifts were generally short-lived. Aside from the association between remote work and unemployment risk, and higher levels of temporary parental leave, both incidence rates and inequalities were comparable before and after the pandemic. Similar patterns have previously been reported for several additional indicators of health, health care access, and economic strain by several additional dimensions of inequality (Altmejd et al., 2023). Such conclusions are comparable to what this study finds. Although the pandemic was a dramatic, ubiquitous, and multidimensional event, affecting health and most aspects of social and economic life, existing structures of inequality remained intact.

Acknowledgements I am thankful to Mats Melin and Adam Altmejd for their generous support and insightful comments on the text.

References

Adermon, A., Laun, L., Lind, P., Olsson, M., Sauermann, J., & Sjögren, A. (2024). Earnings losses and the role of the welfare state during the COVID-19 pandemic: Evidence from Sweden. *Review of Income and Wealth, 70*(4), 981–1010. https://doi.org/10.1111/roiw.12670

Akerman, A., Ekholm, K., Persson, T., & Nordström Skans, O. (2022). Sweden's COVID-19 recession: How foreign and domestic infections struck against firms and workers. *SSRN Electronic Journal.* https://doi.org/10.2139/ssrn.4154051

Alimohamadi, Y., Tola, H. H., Abbasi-Ghahramanloo, A., Janani, M., & Sepandi, M. (2021). Case fatality rate of COVID-19: A systematic review and meta-analysis. *Journal of Preventive Medicine and Hygiene, 62*(2), E311–E320. https://doi.org/10.15167/2421-4248/jpmh2021.62.2.1627

Almgren, M., & Björk, J. (2021). *Kartläggning av skillnader i regionernas insatser för provtagning och smittspårning under coronapandemin.*

Altmejd, A., Östergren, O., Björkegren, E., & Persson, T. (2023). Inequality and COVID-19 in Sweden: Relative risks of nine bad life events, by four social gradients, in pandemic vs. prepandemic years. *Proceedings of the National*

Academy of Sciences, 120(46), e2303640120. https://doi.org/10.1073/pnas.2303640120

Andersen, P. T., Loncarevic, N., Damgaard, M. B., Jacobsen, M. W., Bassioni-Stamenic, F., & Eklund Karlsson, L. (2022). Public health, surveillance policies and actions to prevent community spread of COVID-19 in Denmark, Serbia and Sweden. *Scandinavian Journal of Public Health, 50*(6), 711–729. https://doi.org/10.1177/14034948211056215

Andersson, G., Drefahl, S., Mussino, E., Modig, K., & Meyer, A. C. (2021). *Patterns in COVID-19 mortality and morbidity in Sweden during the pandemic year March 2020–February 2021.* Stockholm Research Reports in Demography. https://doi.org/10.17045/sthlmuni.16953607.v1

Angelov, N., & Waldenström, D. (2023). COVID-19 and income inequality: Evidence from monthly population registers. *The Journal of Economic Inequality, 21*(2), 351–379. https://doi.org/10.1007/s10888-022-09560-8

Aradhya, S., Brandén, M., Drefahl, S., Obućina, O., Andersson, G., Rostila, M., Mussino, E., & Juárez, S. P. (2021). Intermarriage and COVID-19 mortality among immigrants. A population-based cohort study from Sweden. *BMJ Open, 11*(9), e048952. https://doi.org/10.1136/bmjopen-2021-048952

Araf, Y., Akter, F., Tang, Y., Fatemi, R., Parvez, M. S. A., Zheng, C., & Hossain, M. G. (2022). Omicron variant of SARS-CoV-2: Genomics, transmissibility, and responses to current COVID-19 vaccines. *Journal of Medical Virology, 94*(5), 1825–1832. https://doi.org/10.1002/jmv.27588

Björk, J., Mattisson, K., & Ahlbom, A. (2021). Impact of winter holiday and government responses on mortality in Europe during the first wave of the COVID-19 pandemic. *European Journal of Public Health, 31*(2), 272–277. https://doi.org/10.1093/eurpub/ckab017

Björkman, A. (2023). The Swedish COVID-19 control measures and the national commission report. *Acta Paediatrica (Oslo, Norway: 1992), 112*(1), 8–10. https://doi.org/10.1111/apa.16582

Blomqvist, S., Högnäs, R. S., Virtanen, M., LaMontagne, A. D., & Magnusson Hanson, L. L. (2023). Job loss and job instability during the COVID-19 pandemic and the risk of depression and anxiety among Swedish employees. *SSM - Population Health, 22*, 101424. https://doi.org/10.1016/j.ssmph.2023.101424

Brusselaers, N., Steadson, D., Bjorklund, K., Breland, S., Stilhoff Sörensen, J., Ewing, A., Bergmann, S., & Steineck, G. (2022). Evaluation of science advice during the COVID-19 pandemic in Sweden. *Humanities and Social Sciences Communications, 9*(1), 1–17. https://doi.org/10.1057/s41599-022-01097-5

Centrum för epidemiologi och samhällsmedicin. (2020). *Socioekonomiska faktorer och covid-19 i Stockholms län* (2020:10). Region Stockholm. https://www.ces.regionstockholm.se/globalassets/verksamheter/forskning-och-utveckling/centrum-for-epidemiologi-och-samhallsmedicin/folkhalsoguiden/rapporteroch-faktablad/rapport-2020.10-socioekonomiska-faktorer-och-covid-19-i-stockholms-lan_november-2020_.pdf

Chetty, R., Friedman, J. N., Stepner, M., & Opportunity Insights Team. (2024). The economic impacts of COVID-19: Evidence from a new public database built using private sector data*. *The Quarterly Journal of Economics, 139*(2), 829–889. https://doi.org/10.1093/qje/qjad048

Coronakommissionen. (2020). *Delbetänkande 1: Äldreomsorgen under pandemin SOU 2020:80.* Statens Offentliga Utredningar. Government report. The Swedish Government Offices.

Coronakommissionen. (2021a). *Delbetänkande 2: Sverige under pandemin vol 1: Smittspridning och smittskydd SOU 2021:89.* Statens Offentliga Utredningar. Government report. The Swedish Government Offices.

Coronakommissionen. (2021b). *Slutbetänkande: Sverige under pandemin vol 1: Samhällets, företagens och enskildas ekonomi SOU 2022:10.* Statens Offentliga Utredningar. Government report. The Swedish Government Offices.

Coronakommissionen. (2021c). *Slutbetänkande: Sverige under pandemin vol 2: Förutsättningar, vägval och utvärdering SOU 2022:10.* Statens Offentliga Utredningar. Government report. The Swedish Government Offices.

Coronakommissionen. (2022). *Sverige under pandemin—Volym 2—Förutsättningar, vägval och utvärdering.*

Duvander, A.-Z., & Johansson, M. (2015). *Reforms in the Swedish parental leave system and their effects on gender equality.* Stockholm Research Reports in Demography. Stockholm University.

Dyrdak, R., Hodcroft, E. B., Broddesson, S., Grabbe, M., Franklin, H., Gisslén, M., Holm, M. E., Lindh, M., Nederby-Öhd, J., Ringlander, J., Sundqvist, M., Neher, R. A., & Albert, J. (2024). Early unrecognised SARS-CoV-2 introductions shaped the first pandemic wave, Sweden, 2020. *Eurosurveillance, 29*(41), 2400021. https://doi.org/10.2807/1560-7917.ES.2024.29.41.2400021

Eriksson, R., & Nermo, M. (2010). Care for Sick Children as a proxy for gender equality in the family. *Social Indicators Research, 97*(3), 341–356. https://doi.org/10.1007/s11205-009-9505-y

Evertsson, M. (2014). Gender ideology and the sharing of housework and child Care in Sweden. *Journal of Family Issues, 35*(7), 927–949. https://doi.org/10.1177/0192513X14522239

Försäkringskassan. (2021). *Tillfällig föräldrapenning vid vård av barn—Varför ökade totalt antal nettodagar 2009–2018?* Socialförsäkringsrapport 2021:2.

Försäkringskassan. (2023). *Promemoria – Uppföljning av nyttjandet av tillfällig föräldrapenning.* FK 2023/017942. https://www.forsakringskassan.se/download/18.79fa09981888fc8f7f414b/1696946489671/uppfoljning-av-nyttjandet-av-tillfallig-foraldrapenning-svar-pa-regeringsuppdrag-dnr-fk-2023-017942.pdf

Garcia, F., Järnland, E., Nordensvärd, J., Sommar, C.-J., & Wihlborg, E. (2024). *Chapter 6: Sweden: Relaxed crisis management*. https://www.elgaronline.com/edcollchap-oa/book/9781035336531/book-part-9781035336531-17.xml

Gauffin, K., Östergren, O., & Cederström, A. (2023). Waves of inequality: Income differences in intensive care due to Covid-19 in Sweden. *European Journal of Public Health*, ckad094. https://doi.org/10.1093/eurpub/ckad094

Grönlund, K., & Setälä, M. (2007). Political trust, satisfaction and voter turnout. *Comparative European Politics, 5*(4), 400–422. https://doi.org/10.1057/palgrave.cep.6110113

Hussain, N., Samuelsson, C. M., Drummond, A., & Persson, C. U. (2024). Prevalence of symptoms of anxiety and depression one year after intensive care unit admission for COVID-19. *BMC Psychiatry, 24*(1), 170. https://doi.org/10.1186/s12888-024-05603-8

Kamerlin, S. C. L., & Kasson, P. M. (2020). Managing coronavirus disease 2019 spread with voluntary public health measures: Sweden as a case study for pandemic control. *Clinical Infectious Diseases, 71*(12), 3174–3181. https://doi.org/10.1093/cid/ciaa864

Lane, L., & Jordansson, B. (2020). How gender equal is Sweden? An analysis of the shift in focus under neoliberalism. *Social Change, 50*(1), 28–43. https://doi.org/10.1177/0049085719901067

Link, B. G., & Phelan, J. (1995). Social conditions as fundamental causes of disease. *Journal of Health and Social Behavior*, 80–94.

Lovik, A., González-Hijón, J., Hoffart, A., Fawns-Ritchie, C., Magnúsdóttir, I., Lu, L., Unnarsdóttir, A. B., Kähler, A. K., Campbell, A., Hauksdóttir, A., Chourpiliadis, C., McCartney, D. L., Thordardóttir, E. B., Joyce, E. E., Frans, E. M., Jakobsdóttir, J., Trogstad, L., Andreassen, O. A., Magnus, P., et al. (2023). Elevated symptoms of depression and anxiety among family members and friends of critically ill COVID-19 patients – An observational study of five cohorts across four countries. *The Lancet Regional Health – Europe, 33*. https://doi.org/10.1016/j.lanepe.2023.100733

Ludvigsson, J. F. (2023). How Sweden approached the COVID-19 pandemic: Summary and commentary on the National Commission Inquiry. *Acta Paediatrica, 112*(1), 19–33. https://doi.org/10.1111/apa.16535

Mackenbach, J. P., Kulhánová, I., Bopp, M., Deboosere, P., Eikemo, T. A., Hoffmann, R., Kulik, M. C., Leinsalu, M., Martikainen, P., Menvielle, G., Regidor, E., Wojtyniak, B., Östergren, O., & Lundberg, O. (2015). Variations in the relation between education and cause-specific mortality in 19 European populations: A test of the "fundamental causes" theory of social inequalities in health. *Social Science & Medicine, 127*, 51–62.

Medlingsinstitutet. (2024). *Löneskillnaden mellan kvinnor och män 2023*. Medlingsinstitutet.

Myndigheten för vård- och omsorgsanalys. (2022). *Riktade vaccinationsinsatser—Lärdomar från regionernas arbete för en hög och jämlik vaccinationstäckning mot covid-19* (2022:5). Myndigheten för vård- och omsorgsanalys. https://www.vardanalys.se/digital-publikation/riktade-vaccinationsinsatser/

Nordgren, A. (2015). Crisis management and public health: Ethical principles for priority setting at a regional level in Sweden. *Public Health Ethics, 8*(1), 72–84. https://doi.org/10.1093/phe/phu028

Nyberg, A. (2002). Gender, (de)commodification, economic (in)dependence and autonomous households: The case of Sweden. *Critical Social Policy, 22*(1), 72–95. https://doi.org/10.1177/02610183020220010701

Östh, J., Toger, M., Türk, U., Kourtit, K., & Nijkamp, P. (2023). Leisure mobility changes during the COVID-19 pandemic – An analysis of survey and mobile phone data in Sweden. *Research in Transportation Business & Management, 48*, 100952. https://doi.org/10.1016/j.rtbm.2023.100952

Pierre, J. (2015). *The Oxford handbook of Swedish politics.* Oxford University Press.

Samuelsson, J., Johansson, G., Forsell, Y., & Möller, J. (2022). How the shift toward working from home has impacted people's work and private life. *Journal of Occupational and Environmental Medicine, 64*(11), 970. https://doi.org/10.1097/JOM.0000000000002623

Shuttleworth, I., Toger, M., Türk, U., & Östh, J. (2024). Did Liberal lockdown policies change spatial behaviour in Sweden? Mapping daily Mobilities in Stockholm using Mobile phone data during COVID-19. *Applied Spatial Analysis and Policy, 17*(1), 345–369. https://doi.org/10.1007/s12061-023-09543-w

Socialstyrelsen. (2021). *Utvecklingen av ekonomiskt bistånd i spåren av covid-19 – faktablad 3.* Dnr 5.7-24430/2020.

Socialstyrelsen. (2024). *Statistik om specialiserad psykiatrisk vård 2023.* 2024-12–9377.

Statistiska Centralbyrån. (2021). *En fråga om tid (TID2021)—En studie av tidsanvändning bland kvinnor och män 2021.* https://www.scb.se/contentassets/4e98132b0b784a01b6e4762e909a6fa2/le0103_2021a01_br_lebr2202.pdf

Van Winkle, Z., Ferragina, E., & Recchi, E. (2021). The unexpected decline in feelings of depression among adults ages 50 and older in 11 European countries amid the COVID-19 pandemic. *Socius, 7*, 23780231211032741. https://doi.org/10.1177/23780231211032741

Warren, G. W., & Lofstedt, R. (2022). COVID-19 vaccine rollout management and communication in Europe: One year on. *Journal of Risk Research, 25*(9), 1098–1117. https://doi.org/10.1080/13669877.2021.2001674

Wester, C. T., Bovil, T., Scheel-Hincke, L. L., Ahrenfeldt, L. J., Möller, S., & Andersen-Ranberg, K. (2022). Longitudinal changes in mental health following the COVID-19 lockdown: Results from the survey of health, ageing, and retirement in Europe. *Annals of Epidemiology, 74*, 21–30. https://doi.org/10.1016/j.annepidem.2022.05.010

Winblad, U., Swenning, A.-K., & Spangler, D. (2022). Soft law and individual responsibility: A review of the Swedish policy response to COVID-19. *Health Economics, Policy and Law, 17*(1), 48–61. https://doi.org/10.1017/S1744133121000256

Yan, B., Zhang, X., Wu, L., Zhu, H., & Chen, B. (2020). Why do countries respond differently to COVID-19? A comparative study of Sweden, China, France, and Japan. *The American Review of Public Administration, 50*(6–7), 762–769. https://doi.org/10.1177/0275074020942445